# St Helena

**Ascension • Tristan da Cunha**

the Bradt Travel Guide

**Susan Britt-Gallagher**
**Tricia Hayne**

www.bradtguides.com

Bradt Travel Guides Ltd, UK
The Globe Pequot Press Inc, USA

edition

D1057229

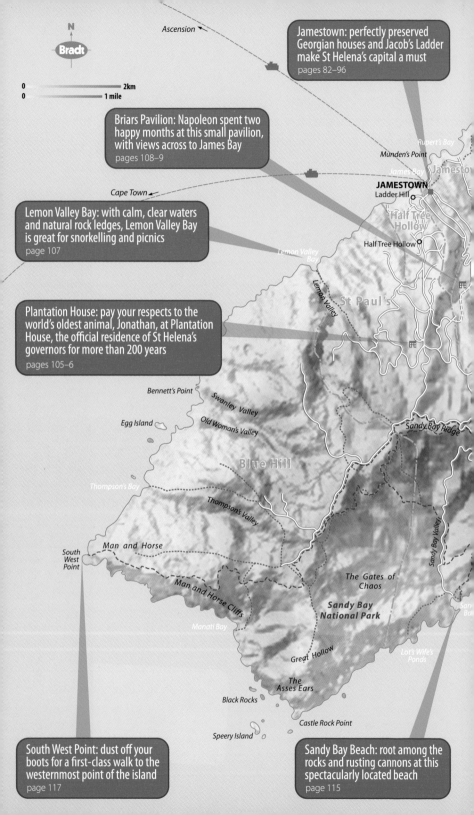

N

**Bradt**

0 — 2km
0 — 1 mile

Ascension ←

Cape Town ←

**Jamestown:** perfectly preserved Georgian houses and Jacob's Ladder make St Helena's capital a must
pages 82–96

**Briars Pavilion:** Napoleon spent two happy months at this small pavilion, with views across to James Bay
pages 108–9

**Lemon Valley Bay:** with calm, clear waters and natural rock ledges, Lemon Valley Bay is great for snorkelling and picnics
page 107

**Plantation House:** pay your respects to the world's oldest animal, Jonathan, at Plantation House, the official residence of St Helena's governors for more than 200 years
pages 105–6

Rupert's Bay
Munden's Point
James Bay    **Jamesto**
**JAMESTOWN**
Ladder Hill
Half Tree Hollow
Half Tree Hollow

St Paul's

Lemon Valley Bay
Lemon Valley

Bennett's Point
Swanley Valley
Old Woman's Valley
Egg Island

Blue Hill

Sandy Bay Ridge

Thompson's Bay
Thompson's Valley

Man and Horse
South West Point
Man and Horse Cliffs
Manati Bay

The Gates of Chaos

**Sandy Bay National Park**

Sandy Bay Valley

Great Hollow

Lot's Wife's Ponds

Sandy Bay

Black Rocks
The Asses Ears
Castle Rock Point
Speery Island

**South West Point:** dust off your boots for a first-class walk to the westernmost point of the island
page 117

**Sandy Bay Beach:** root among the rocks and rusting cannons at this spectacularly located beach
page 115

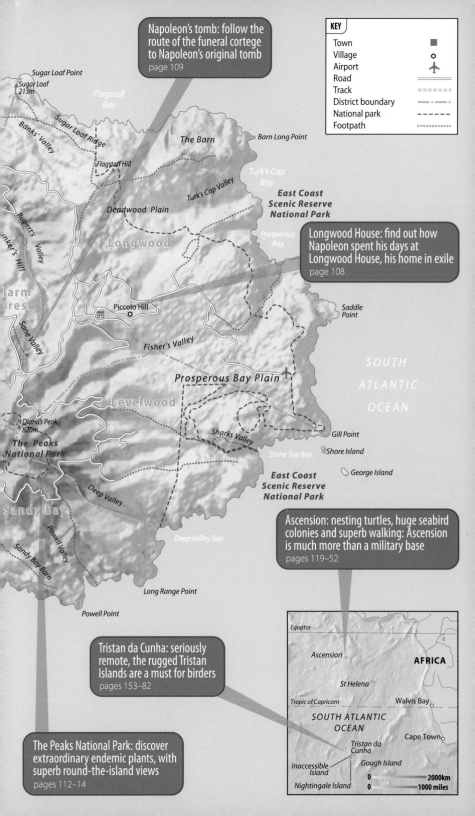

**KEY**

| | |
|---|---|
| Town | ■ |
| Village | ○ |
| Airport | ✈ |
| Road | —— |
| Track | ====== |
| District boundary | —·—·— |
| National park | – – – |
| Footpath | ······· |

Napoleon's tomb: follow the route of the funeral cortege to Napoleon's original tomb
page 109

Longwood House: find out how Napoleon spent his days at Longwood House, his home in exile
page 108

Ascension: nesting turtles, huge seabird colonies and superb walking: Ascension is much more than a military base
pages 119–52

Tristan da Cunha: seriously remote, the rugged Tristan Islands are a must for birders
pages 153–82

The Peaks National Park: discover extraordinary endemic plants, with superb round-the-island views
pages 112–14

Sugar Loaf Point
Sugar Loaf 213m
Sugar Loaf Ridge
Banks' Valley
Flagstaff Bay
Flagstaff Hill
The Barn
Barn Long Point
Turk's Cap Bay
Turk's Cap Valley
Deadwood Plain
East Coast Scenic Reserve National Park
Rupert's Valley
Longwood
Prosperous Bay
anker's Hill
Piccolo Hill
Saddle Point
Sane Valley
Farm Forest
Fisher's Valley
Prosperous Bay Plain
SOUTH ATLANTIC OCEAN
Levelwood
Diana's Peak 820m
Sharks Valley
Gill Point
Shore Island
The Peaks National Park
Stone Top Bay
George Island
Deep Valley
East Coast Scenic Reserve National Park
Sandy Bay
Powell Valley
Deep Valley Bay
Sandy Bay Barn
Long Range Point
Powell Point

Equator
Ascension
AFRICA
St Helena
Tropic of Capricorn
Walvis Bay
SOUTH ATLANTIC OCEAN
Cape Town
Tristan da Cunha
Gough Island
Inaccessible Island
Nightingale Island
0 — 2000km
0 — 1000 miles

# St Helena Don't miss...

### Jamestown
A castle in name only, the Castle in Jamestown certainly has an imposing entrance
(pages 91–2) (t/A)

### Napoleonic sites
Napoleon's residence on St Helena, Longwood House looks at its best when the agapanthus are in flower
(page 108) (AT)

## Unique wildlife

*right* St Helena's wirebird (*Charadrius sanctaehelenae*) is readily spotted on Deadwood Plain (page 42) (BB)

*left* Endemic to St Helena and Ascension, cunningfish (*Chaetodon sanctahelenae*) may form a fishy 'snowdome' around snorkellers and divers (page 46) (MS/EMD)

## Dramatic landscapes

Lot's Wife stands guard over the dramatic scenery of Sandy Bay (page 116) (TH)

## Superb walks

South West Point is one of the best and most accessible of the postbox walks (page 117) (TH)

# St Helena in colour

*above left* — Descending Jacob's Ladder in traditional style is not for the faint-hearted (pages 94–5) (BH)

*above right* — The Saints are good at festivals, including the annual Gravity Rush go-kart race through Jamestown (page 52) (DP)

*below* — Seen from Briars Village, Jamestown winds up the valley from James Bay (pages 82–96) (TH)

*above left* The romantic Heart-shaped Waterfall flows only after the winter rains (pages 95–6) (JPG)

*above right* Tungi, the local spirit, is produced from the fruit of the prickly pear (page 69) (TH)

*right* Seabirds flock to the rocky outcrop of Speery Island, which can be easily viewed from land or sea (page 117) (TH)

*below* Lot's Wife's Ponds make a great reward at the end of a strenuous trek (page 116) (TH)

*above*    Plantation House has been home to St Helena governors for more than 200 years, as well as to several giant tortoises such as Jonathan (pictured here), who may be the oldest animal in the world (pages 105–6) (TH)

*left*    Military artefacts are rarely far away on St Helena (TH)

*below*    High Knoll Fort commands superb views over the interior of the island (pages 104–5) (SHT)

# AUTHORS

**Susan Britt-Gallagher** grew up in the northeast of the USA. After completing her education, she travelled across North America, Europe and northern Africa. Thousands of bus, train and cargo-ship miles later, she settled down in Switzerland. From November 1997 to January 1998, Sue, her husband and their young daughters spent three amazing months 'living' on St Helena. That's when Sue fell in love with the people and the island of St Helena,

and the first edition of the Bradt guide was born. A lot has changed since then, but the memories of this fascinating island and its wonderful people still remain in her heart.

**Tricia Hayne** stumbled upon St Helena in 2000, when as editorial director of Bradt Travel Guides she commissioned a guide to the remote trio of islands that made up what were then known as St Helena and Dependencies. With a lifelong fascination for islands, she was sufficiently enticed by these mid-Atlantic outposts to come on board for this third edition. She counts walking, diving and natural history among her interests, has written Bradt guides

to the Cayman Islands and – as co-author – to the Turks and Caicos Islands, and has updated several more to a number of African destinations.

## AUTHORS' STORY

In 1985, Sue's husband made a ship's journey from Avonmouth in the UK to St Helena, stopping briefly at Tristan da Cunha before continuing on to Cape Town. Finally, in 1997, along with their two young children, they were able to make the trip as a family.

It wasn't until the manuscript of Sue's guide landed on my desk in 2001 that I, too, became intrigued by St Helena. What was so special about this place that she was prepared to make the long journey *en famille*? That the tiny population – barely enough to make up an English village – could leave such a deep impression? That you could leave after months wanting to go back?

Sue realised there was something unique about St Helena the moment her ship anchored in James Bay and she saw how many people had gathered to welcome its passengers. Now, I and my husband have experienced that welcome: the natural greetings, the friendly chat in the street, the invitations into family homes. With St Helenian guides we have explored the island, from the volcanic grandeur of the coastal scenery and the verdant central ridge to the mist-covered hills where Napoleon must have vented his frustration. We've stood on the top of Diana's Peak, marvelled at plants that we'll see nowhere else in the world, and explored beneath the surface of James Bay. And we, like Sue, are hooked.

**PUBLISHER'S FOREWORD**    *Adrian Phillips, Managing Director*

Remote islands have an enduring fascination, and nothing comes much more remote than the three specks in the Atlantic Ocean that are St Helena, Tristan da Cunha and Ascension Island. The fact that they are also among the last vestiges of the British Empire adds to the attraction. Susan Britt-Gallagher and Tricia Hayne do more than describe the places of interest in these three islands; they convey to the reader the welcome to outsiders and hospitality that is part of isolation. With an airport opening in 2016, St Helena is destined for change. See it now, before the tourist floodgates open.

**Third edition October 2015**
First published 2002
Bradt Travel Guides Ltd, IDC House, The Vale, Chalfont St Peter, Bucks SL9 9RZ, England
www.bradtguides.com
Print edition published in the USA by The Globe Pequot Press Inc, PO Box 480, Guilford, Connecticut 06437-0480

Text copyright © 2015 Susan Britt-Gallagher, Tricia Hayne
Maps copyright © 2015 Bradt Travel Guides Ltd
Photographs copyright © 2015 Individual photographers (see below)
Illustrations copyright © 2015 Hedvika Fraser
Project manager: Laura Pidgley
Cover research: Pepi Bluck, Perfect Picture

The authors and publisher have made every effort to ensure the accuracy of the information in this book at the time of going to press. However, they cannot accept any responsibility for any loss, injury or inconvenience resulting from the use of information contained in this guide. All rights reserved. No part of this publication may be reproduced, stored in a retrieval system, or transmitted in any form or by any means, electronic, mechanical, photocopying, recording or otherwise without the prior consent of the publisher. Requests for permission should be addressed to Bradt Travel Guides Ltd in the UK (print and digital editions), or to The Globe Pequot Press Inc in North and South America (print edition only).

**British Library Cataloguing in Publication Data**
A catalogue record for this book is available from the British Library

ISBN: 978 1 84162 939 1 (print)
ISBN: 978 1 78477 137 9 (e-pub)
ISBN: 978 1 78477 237 6 (mobi)

**Photographs**
Alamy: travelbild.com (t/A); Adrian Turner (AT); Ascension Island Government (AIG); Bob Hayne (BH); Chantal Steyn (CS); David Pryce (DP); John and Pauline Grimshaw (JPG); Marc Lavaud (ML); Marine section, Environmental Marine Division (MS/EMD); St Helena Tourism (STH); SuperStock (SS); Tricia Hayne (TH)
*Front cover* St Paul's Cathedral, St Helena (ML)
*Title page* White fairy tern (*Gygis alba*) (DP); Napoleon's tomb (TH); Land crab road sign (TH)
*Back cover* Jacob's Ladder (STH); Tristan thrush (MT)

**Illustrations** Hedvika Fraser

**Maps** David McCutcheon FBCart S; colour map relief base by Nick Rowland FRGS; Gough map reproduced by kind permission of the Royal Geographical Society; some town plan maps include data © OpenStreetMaps contributors (under Open Database License)

Typeset from the authors' disk by Ian Spick, Bradt Travel Guides
Production managed by Jellyfish Print Solutions; printed in India
Digital conversion by www.dataworks.in

# Acknowledgements

It is with huge gratitude that I thank Libby Weir-Breen of Island Holidays, whose belief in the book kick-started this third edition, and St Helena Tourism – particularly Cathy Alberts, Chanelle Marais, Melissa Fowler and Matt Joshua – who turned it into reality. Thank you, too, to AW Ship Management and the crew of the RMS *St Helena*, who not only brought us safely from Ascension to Cape Town, but did so in style.

I am also indebted to Sam Kirton and Simon Quarendon of Keene Communications, Janet Shankland of St Helena Tourism in the UK, Jonathan Hall of the RSPB, Sue Farrington, for her inside information on St Helena, Ascension and Tristan, and Ian Mathieson of Miles Apart, for his very helpful comments on the text.

**On St Helena**, this and previous editions have been considerably enhanced by the specialist contributions of historian Dr Alexander Schulenburg, botanist David Sayers and geologist Tim Ireland. Thank you to Basil and Barbara George, who – along with Patsy Flagg, Valerie Joshua, Linda and Derek Richards, and Craig and Keith Yon – contributed so much to our understanding of the island. To David Pryce (aka the Bug Man) of the St Helena National Trust, for sharing his infectious enthusiasm for the natural world, and for his input on geology. To Dr Niall O'Keeffe of Enterprise St Helena and Governor Mark Capes and his wife, Tamara, for their help and support. To Hazel Wilmot for her kind hospitality. To Sam Cherrett, Elizabeth Clingham, Mickey Hemmings, Paula McLeod and many others, for answering endless apparently trivial questions. And to readers Peter Johnston, Rich Perkins, Jennifer Turnbull and Sir Brian Unwin for their valuable feedback on the previous edition.

**On Ascension**, thank you to Johnny Hobson and Andy McKay, who made our whistle-stop tour of the island possible and – along with conservation officer Dr Nicola Weber and Drew Avery of Ascension Heritage Society – kindly checked through the text and made valuable suggestions and corrections.

**On Tristan da Cunha**, I owe a considerable debt to Richard Grundy, editor of the *Tristan da Cunha Newsletter* and manager of the Tristan website, and Mike Hentley, the islands' administrator from 2004 to 2007, both of whom made a major contribution to the second edition of this guide. Thanks, too, to naturalist and conservationist Julian Fitter (*www.julianfitter.co.nz*), for his considerable input on the outer islands. For this edition, tourism co-ordinator Dawn Repetto has been tireless in her response to my many questions, aided by Trevor Glass in the Conservation Department, Andy Repetto, Conrad Glass and James Glass. Wildlife specialist and lecturer Will Wagstaff provided some valuable suggestions, particularly on the birdlife, and others came from reader Robert Kipp, while Sue Farrington and John Price shared their knowledge and enthusiasm. Thank you all.

At Bradt Travel Guides, I'd particularly like to thank Laura Pidgley for her calm and efficient project management, and cartographer David McCutcheon for waving his usual magic wand over our maps.

And finally, a big thank you to my husband, Bob, for sorting out the maps, walking the walks, diving the deeps, and quite literally keeping the show on the road.

## DEDICATION

To the people of St Helena

# Contents

## A NOTE ON MAPS

It must be stressed that while these maps can indicate the location of roads and places, they cannot even hint at the road infrastructure. On St Helena, rugged, mountainous terrain, narrow roads and hairpin bends make it difficult to judge distances, so it's important to use these maps with caution, and allow far longer for an apparently short journey than you would in, say, the UK or USA – despite the lack of traffic.

**KEYS AND SYMBOLS** Town maps include alphabetical keys covering the locations of those places to stay, eat or drink that are featured in the book.

**GRIDS AND GRID REFERENCES** Several maps use gridlines to allow easy location of sites. Map grid references are listed in square brackets after the name of the place or sight of interest in the text, with page number followed by grid number, eg: [103 C3].

## FOLLOW BRADT

For the latest news, special offers and competitions, subscribe to the Bradt newsletter via the website www.bradtguides.com and follow Bradt on:

- f www.facebook.com/BradtTravelGuides
- ▶ @BradtGuides
- @bradtguides
- ⓟ www.pinterest.com/bradtguides

## FEEDBACK REQUEST AND UPDATES WEBSITE

At Bradt Travel Guides we're aware that guidebooks start to go out of date on the day they're published – and that you, our readers, are out there in the field doing research of your own. You'll find out before us when a fine new family-run hotel opens or a favourite restaurant changes hands and goes downhill. So why not write and tell us about your experiences? Contact us on ✆ 01753 893444 or e info@bradtguides.com. We will forward emails to the author who may post updates on the Bradt website at www.bradtupdates.com/sthelena. Alternatively you can add a review of the book to www.bradtguides.com or Amazon.

# Introduction

Prospero would have felt at home on St Helena. So, too, would Macbeth's witches three, for this tiny vestige of the British Empire has all the feel of an enchanted isle. But what enchantment! Step onto the wharf in Jamestown, and you'll find yourself on an ancient volcano, its roots firmly on the sea bed some three miles below, its verdant head 820m up in the clouds. In between, as the narrow roads twist and turn through a landscape formed millions of years ago, you'll move almost seamlessly from one world to another. From rolling hills grazed by sheep to dauntingly high cliffs that drop straight down to the ocean; from multi-coloured volcanic rocks worn smooth over millennia to forests of eucalyptus that plunge down the hillside; from balmy pinewoods beloved of fairy terns to the pinnacle of the island: a rolling series of deep-green valleys and ridges that stretch out to the sea, endless sea.

So much for the setting, but like all good plays, it needs characters: enter the Saints. The people of St Helena may have their roots in many countries, but one thing they share is an innate friendliness. Walk through Jamestown at any time of day and you will be greeted on all sides with a friendly nod, a quick 'good morning', a genuine smile that is of itself immensely welcoming. The shops may not have the latest goods, you may struggle to find apples, or cereal, or decent Wi-Fi, but somehow it doesn't matter on an island where people live in the here and now.

These are the people who now find themselves on the cusp of change. By the end of 2016, their island lifeline, the RMS *St Helena*, will be no more, swapped for a Boeing 737 that will whisk visitors to them in five hours, not five days. For the first time, it will be possible to spend a week's holiday exploring St Helena, rather than the three weeks that is currently a necessity. The island will at last be open to those for whom downtime is finite.

So why would you go to St Helena? Would it be for the scenery, the walking or the endemic plantlife? The diving or the fishing? Napoleon, or the Saints? Arguably it's all of these, and none, for St Helena is a bit like a mosaic: each piece forms an important part of the whole, but not until the last piece is in place does the picture come to life. So if you've always thought that the island was only worth visiting by sea, then think again. St Helena will still be remote; you'll just get there a little faster. And if you're taking the first steps towards considering the island for a week's holiday – why not make it a fortnight? The very things that make St Helena special are not going to change overnight – and, airport or no, it's not a place to be hurried.

## ST HELENA, ASCENSION AND TRISTAN DA CUNHA AT A GLANCE

**Location** South Atlantic Ocean
**Status** British Overseas Territory
**Population** 5,698 (2015 estimate)
**Language** English
**Religion** Predominantly Christian
**Currency** Pound sterling or St Helenian pound (= £1 sterling)
**Time** GMT
**Electricity** 240v, 50Hz
**Weights and measures** Metric, with some imperial remnants
**National anthem** 'God Save the Queen'

# St Helena, Ascension and Tristan da Cunha: An Overview

Three small volcanic rocks, widely spaced in the South Atlantic Ocean. Over the centuries, maritime history has conspired to throw them and their attendant islands together to form a single British Overseas Territory, united under the British Crown and overseen by a single British governor. Yet despite their common status, each island has its own strongly individual character, its own attractions, its own challenges.

Beneath the surface, however, there is a strong unifying thread: the volcanic forces that created them.

## GEOLOGY  *Tim Ireland*

Perhaps surprisingly, the islands of the South Atlantic Ocean are not randomly located. They are all of volcanic origin, and relate directly to locations of highly anomalous heat-flow from the Earth. Some 120 million years ago, extreme heat-flow in the same locations caused an ancient supercontinent to rift apart, separating the modern African and South American continental blocks. Yes, the continents move.

St Helena, Ascension and Tristan da Cunha are isolated, broadly conical volcanic edifices that each rise more than 3,000m above the ocean floor, and actually cause the oceanic crust to subside beneath their weight. They are located on the flanks of the Mid-Atlantic Ridge (MAR), a continuous volcanic ridge that runs the entire length of the Atlantic Ocean, but rather than being a result of the ridge, they are part of its cause. There are hundreds of similar volcanoes, but the vast majority are concealed beneath the water. The islands themselves are the tip of the proverbial iceberg; only 1% of the total volume of Ascension, for example, is exposed above water.

**FORMATION**  The islands are geologically very young; volcanism on St Helena ceased only eight million years ago, and on Ascension only a few thousand years ago (by comparison the Earth formed over 3.6 billion years ago). Tristan da Cunha remains active, erupting twice in the last 50 years above a deep mantle plume known as a hotspot: in 1961, the entire population was evacuated to the UK, and in 2004, when a submarine event produced lava blocks, which were found floating in the sea. It is likely to erupt again.

Volcanism in the South Atlantic has been exciting compared to that in other famous volcanic archipelagos such as Hawaii. In addition to lava flows indicative of effusive eruption, these South Atlantic islands are also composed of a roughly equal proportion of fire-fragment (pyroclastic) rocks. Deep underground, molten rock contains significant amounts of dissolved gases. Eruption at the surface causes dramatic release of the confining pressure, and the contained gases expand and explode inside the lava, tearing it into tiny fragments that are propelled into the air as a cloud of scalding ash. Lava is erupted at temperatures around 1,000°C, and because there is abundant water in the oceanic environment, eruptions on volcanic islands are often augmented by steam explosions caused by instantaneous boiling of seawater upon contact with lava or ash.

Each island consists of many – possibly several hundred – overlapping volcanic cones and fissures from which lava and/or ash has erupted. On Tristan da Cunha there is a clear distinction between a main, repeatedly active central crater zone, and a peripheral zone of multiple, small-scale, single-event explosive cones. Volcanism began on the sea floor, and each eruption has built on to the edifice, so that today the formation breaches sea level.

The rocks generated by volcanism on the South Atlantic islands have a distinctive and diverse chemistry that tells us about the interior of our planet. At any one time, there are up to 20 spots around the world where heat is channelled from the Earth's interior toward the surface. High heat-flow causes dramatically increased melting of the Earth's mantle, and a plume of ascending molten material causes volcanoes at the surface. The lavas of Ascension, St Helena and Tristan da Cunha are indisputably of mantle origin; they tend to contain no quartz, unusually high concentrations of sodium and potassium, and have characteristic patterns of radioactive and trace element abundance. The chemistry of these lavas suggests that they are the result of selective partial melting of the most easily mobilised components of the original mantle.

**SEAMOUNTS** Undersea volcanoes (called 'seamounts') occur along parallel linear ridges in the South Atlantic that lead northeast to mainland Africa – from Tristan da Cunha to Namibia along the distinct Walvis Ridge, and from St Helena to Cameroon/Nigeria – becoming progressively older as they approach the continent. The rocks of each seamount chain share a subtle geochemical 'fingerprint' that is characteristic of a particular mantle plume. Ascension is not part of a seamount chain, and is considered to be caused by a weak and intermittent plume.

The upwelling plumes of molten material are evidence of convection in the upper part of the mantle. The Earth's crust consists of numerous discrete plates, which are pushed around by convective currents in the mantle like buoyant rafts. When the dinosaurs were at their prime, Africa and South America were part of the same continent, Gondwanaland. At that time, several new plumes, including those under St Helena and Tristan da Cunha, emerged under Gondwanaland, and split the supercontinent along a zigzag line connecting the plumes. As the continents have continued to rift apart along the MAR, the African plate has slid over the stationary plume sites, which continue to cause volcanism. Broadly, as a volcano forms on the sea floor, the continent drifts slowly past the plume, and the molten rock finds a new conduit to the surface, thus forming a new volcano. In this way, seamount chains are formed.

There are other, less well-defined seamount chains in the western Atlantic, that trace back to volcanic rocks in Brazil. Realisation of continuous sequential age progression, from continental volcanic rocks out along the seamount chains to the volcanic islands near the MAR, is one of a handful of strong arguments for the widely accepted 'Continental Drift' theory.

For more on the geology of the individual islands, see pages 3–4 and 121–4.

# Part One

ST HELENA

## ST HELENA AT A GLANCE

**Location** South Atlantic Ocean, 1,200 miles (1,950km) west of Angola, 1,800 miles (2,900km) east of Brazil

**Size** 47 square miles (122km²)

**Highest point** 2,690ft (820m)

**Climate** Tropical, kept mild by southeast trade winds

**Status** British Overseas Territory

**Population** 4,236 (2012)

**Population growth rate** 3% (2015 estimate)

**Birth rate** per 1,000 population 7.8 (2012)

**Death rate** per 1,000 population 11.3 (2012)

**Capital** Jamestown

**Economy** Fishing, tourism, philately, but largely dependent on UK subsidy

**Average per capita income** £6,670 (2013/14)

**Language** English

**Religion** Predominantly Christian

**Currency** St Helena pound (= £1 sterling) and pound sterling

**Time** GMT

**Electricity** 240V, 50Hz. Standard electrical socket is 13-amp flat pin, as in UK.

**Weights and measures** Metric, with some imperial remnants

**International dialling code** +290

**Emergency telephone** 999 (police/fire), 911 (hospital)

**Flag** Blue with flag of UK in upper quadrant and St Helena shield centred on outer half of flag. The shield features a rocky coastline and a three-masted sailing ship, with the wirebird at the top.

**National anthem** 'God Save the Queen'

**National bird** Wirebird (St Helena plover)

**National flower** Ebony (*Trochetiopsis ebenus*), but formerly the arum lily

**National tree** Gumwood (*Commidendrum robustum*)

**Public holidays** 1 January, Good Friday, Easter Monday, 21 May, Whit Monday (day after Whitsuntide), second Saturday in June, last Monday in August, 25–26 December

**Website** www.sthelenatourism.com

# 1

# Background Information

## GEOGRAPHY

It feels apt to describe the location of St Helena in maritime terms: at ⊕15°55.615'S, 05°43.006'W it is little more than a dot in the Atlantic Ocean, some 1,200 miles (1,950km) east of the Angolan coast. The nearest land, however, is Ascension Island, a mere 703 miles (1,131km) to the northwest, while sailing west for about 1,800 miles (2,900km) would bring you to the east coast of Brazil.

St Helena itself is just 47 square miles (122km²), measuring six miles (10km) by ten (17km), barely a third of the size of the Isle of Wight, or half that of Martha's Vineyard in Massachusetts. A tiny island of volcanic origin, it rises dramatically from the ocean, culminating at 2,690ft (820m) in Diana's Peak. All around, sheer barren cliffs are intersected with deep valleys, or 'guts', which slope steeply from the central ridges. The terrain is steep and rocky, with small, scattered plateaux and plains; there is very little flat land. Despite this, there are only a very few small mountain streams, and even these occasionally dry up in the summer months.

On the higher central ground, bush and semi-tropical vegetation is plentiful. This changes to grassland and pastures before the terrain becomes drier and semi-barren below 1,640ft (500m) and down to the sea.

### GEOLOGY  *with thanks to David Pryce*

St Helena was formed from not just one but two separate volcanoes. Unlike the spectacular Plinian volcano witnessed at Pompeii, where gas-powered explosions blasted rock and ash fragments into a column as high as the stratosphere before collapsing to form superheated pyroclastic flows with lava bombs, these were shield volcanoes. Typically much lower and broader, they are formed by the eruption of liquid lava through a crack or fissure, which then flows downhill.

The origins of St Helena can be traced to some unknown point in the past, when a volcanic 'hotspot' pierced the ocean floor and began building the three-mile (5km) high pile of rock that underlies the island. Then, around 12 million years ago, the first eruptions breached the surface around the area between Flagstaff and The Barn. This pale brown ridge is composed almost entirely of dykes, the solidified vertical sheets of lava that flowed upwards from the magma chamber below, with one crossing another and another and another. This first volcano rose to around 3,000ft (915m), though half of it has since been lost to the sea.

As this first volcano was reaching its maximum size, the eruptive centre shifted to the area around the Gorilla's Head, Man o' War Roost and Lot's Wife's Ponds. Larger than the original volcano, this second volcano overlapped the first cone, and the resultant stresses caused several square miles of rock in what is now the Deadwood, Longwood and Prosperous Bay Plain area to slide into the sea on either side of King and Queen Rocks. A further cataclysmic eruption then took place with lava flooding into the hollow left by the collapse in several thick flows; these thick horizontal lavas can be clearly seen in the cliffs around Turk's Cap.

As surface eruptions ceased around 7.5 million years ago, stresses within the volcano caused cracks in the roof of the magma chamber, visible today in three distinct forms: the grey stripes visible across much of the landscape, and typically around Lot and Lot's Wife; a series of intrusions that look like an upturned whisky tumbler, with the most easily seen being High Hill; and 'stick of celery' intrusions, such as the 'smiley face' seen on the seaward face of Great Stone Top.

For an in-depth but highly readable account of the geology, it's well worth seeking out Ian Baker's *The Saint Helena Volcanoes: A Guide to the Geology for Visitors and Walkers* (page 189).

**CLIMATE** Although St Helena is located in the tropics, her climate is kept generally mild by the southeast trade winds. Despite the vagaries of global warming, summers are generally hot and sunny, and winters cool and mild (though locals would say cold and wet!). That said, there are noticeable climatic differences between Jamestown, located on the northern coast, and the interior of the island. Jamestown can be sunny and humid, while at the same time Longwood could be experiencing cool mists and a higher amount of rainfall.

Rainfall, while possible at all times, tends to peak in March/April and August, though this, too, varies considerably with elevation. In the past ten years annual rainfall in Jamestown has averaged 10ins (253mm), a figure that rises to 43ins (1,083mm) at Scotland, in the district of St Paul's, at around 2,130ft (650m) above sea level. Similarly, temperatures vary at different points around the island. In Jamestown, the warmest area on the island, the temperature averages 68–86°F (20–30°C), while in the interior – which is at a higher elevation – it is considerably cooler, with an average of 57–72°F (14–22°C). Humidity varies between 75% and 94%. The windiest areas of the island are around Longwood, whilst Scotland has the least wind but also the least sunshine per month.

Very occasionally, you may be lucky enough to glimpse the all-too-fleeting phenomenon known as a 'green flash', a trick of the light seen at sunset just at the

## ST HELENA: AVERAGE RAINFALL AND TEMPERATURES

| | Jan | Feb | Mar | Apr | May | Jun | Jul | Aug | Sep | Oct | Nov | Dec |
|---|---|---|---|---|---|---|---|---|---|---|---|---|
| **Jamestown** | | | | | | | | | | | | |
| Max temperature (°C) | 31 | 33 | 32 | 31 | 30 | 33 | 25 | 25 | 25 | 26 | 27 | 29 |
| Min temperature (°C) | 21 | 21 | 23 | 21 | 20 | 20 | 18 | 18 | 18 | 18 | 19 | 19 |
| Av monthly rainfall (mm) | 12 | 18 | 34 | 36 | 25 | 45 | 22 | 25 | 9 | 6 | 6 | 3 |
| | | | | | | | | | | | | |
| **Scotland (St Paul's)** | | | | | | | | | | | | |
| Max temperature (°C) | 23 | 24 | 24 | 24 | 23 | 22 | 23 | 18 | 19 | 20 | 21 | 21 |
| Min temperature (°C) | 13 | 13 | 17 | 16 | 16 | 14 | 13 | 12 | 12 | 13 | 13 | 14 |
| Av monthly rainfall (mm) | 68 | 92 | 136 | 120 | 93 | 111 | 87 | 124 | 63 | 47 | 36 | 43 |

To entertain any chance of catching the fugitive shot of green that might appear at the precise instant the final glimpse of the sun disappears below the horizon, absolutely clear and calm weather is best. St Helena may have her share of clouded skies, but on clear nights they offer optimum conditions for a sighting as the sun sets over the Atlantic Ocean.

The rarely witnessed sunset occurrence was first briefly acknowledged in 1869 within a paper presented by British physicist James Prescott Joule, recorded in *The Proceedings of the Manchester Literary and Philosophical Society*. Joule, by profession a brewer, was only ever an amateur scientist, yet he came to be regarded as one of the finest of the 19th century. He noted: 'At the moment of the departure of the sun below the horizon, the last glimpse is coloured bluish-green.'

The peculiarity was taken up a few years later by Jules Verne in his novel *Le Rayon-Vert* ('The Green Ray'), in which he describes an invented Scottish legend said to bestow an extra-sensory perception on anyone who sees the green flash, enabling that person 'to see closely into his own heart and to read the thoughts of others'.

In the 21st century, astronomer Andrew Young of San Diego State University confirms that the green flash is indeed real, a prismatic effect of the sunset more likely to be seen on a low horizon such as a seascape. Theoretically a similar burst of light can be viewed at dawn, though the beam is even less likely to be caught at that hour when it's harder to judge the exact point at which the rim of the sun will appear. Young compounds the issue by declaring the true flash to be yellow, its green colour only an optical illusion. This he says is readily confirmed by photographic imagery of the event.

Whatever the case, those who wish to catch the fleeting green flash are strongly advised not to focus on the setting sun until the final moments before it is to disappear. Even when low in the sky it has the potential to damage eyesight.

point when the sun dips below the horizon. Caused by a refraction of light through the Earth's atmosphere, it occurs in periods of exceptionally dry weather, and generally forecasts a clear spell during the next 24 hours (see box, above).

# HISTORY   *with thanks to Dr Alexander Schulenburg*

**1502–1633: DISCOVERY AND THE PORTUGUESE** In 1502, the Portuguese admiral João da Nova, who was returning home from the west coast of India after defeating a fleet belonging to the Zamorin, came upon an undiscovered island. The date was 21 May, the anniversary of St Helena, the mother of Emperor Constantine. In her honour, he called the island Santa Helena and claimed it in the name of the king of Portugal.

Da Nova anchored on the leeward side of the island opposite a deep valley, where he built a timber chapel. Originally called Chapel Valley, this is now the site of Jamestown, the island's capital. When da Nova set out to explore the island, he discovered seabirds, sea-lions, seals and turtles, but no inhabitants. The interior was covered by dense forest and the cliffs with gumwood trees. The only landbird

As far as anyone can determine, Dom Fernão Lopes, a Portuguese officer who was tortured and mutilated as the leader of the renegades during fighting in Goa between the Portuguese and the local inhabitants, was the first resident of St Helena. In 1515, he set sail from Goa for Portugal, but fearful of his reception, he jumped ship at St Helena. His companions, having searched for him in vain, left some supplies. He made his 'home' by scooping out a cave in the side of a soft bank of earth, and lived on herbs and the occasional fish. Whenever he spotted a ship off the coast, he would hide, yet many of the vessels that stopped would leave behind fresh supplies; one even left a rooster which he adopted as a pet.

Lopes found solace and peace during his self-imposed exile, and over the next ten years, he gained sufficient trust to return to Portugal. From here he made a visit to the Pope in Rome to confess his earlier sins and seek absolution. Yet more and more he longed for his island home and eventually he returned to the peace and solitude of St Helena, where passing ships' crews continued to bring him supplies. He died in 1545 after living on the island for almost 30 years.

he found was supposedly the wirebird (page 42), which remains the island's only endemic bird.

The Portuguese soon realised the significance of this island between the Cape of Good Hope and Cape Verde. For more than 80 years, it served them well as a calling point to replenish supplies of ships sailing home from the east. It was also used to offload sick crew members; those that survived were taken back on board when the ships returned to the island. And in all this time, the Portuguese succeeded in keeping the existence of the island a secret.

It wasn't until 8 June 1588, some 86 years after da Nova first dropped anchor at St Helena, that the English explorer, Captain Thomas Cavendish, arrived on the *Desire* while on the last stage of his voyage around the world. During his 12-day stay on the island, Cavendish described St Helena as 'an earthly paradise' and discovered that Portuguese sailors from the East Indies had regularly used the island. They had built a church, as well as two houses, and there were three slaves living there. Vegetables and herbs (parsley, sorrel, basil, fennel, aniseed and mustard seed) had been planted, and trees such as fig, lemon, orange, pomegranate and date were growing. The island was also home to pigs and goats that had been left to breed to provide food for the crew of passing ships.

The secret was out. Within just four years, King Philip II of Spain and Portugal was warning his fleet not to stop at St Helena on their return from Goa, because since Cavendish's discovery, English captains had learned of the heavily laden Portuguese ships returning from India and were lying in wait to attack them on their way home.

In the meantime, the Dutch, too, developed an interest in the trade route once dominated by the Portuguese, though their fortunes were mixed. In 1613, when a flotilla of four Dutch ships called at St Helena, they decided to attacked two Portuguese carracks that were in the roads. The carracks were broadside to the Dutch and opened fire immediately, hitting the *Witte Leeuw*, which exploded and sank.

Faced with the English and Dutch interlopers, the Portuguese gradually withdrew from St Helena island, and by the beginning of the 17th century, they no longer laid claim to the territory.

**1633–1708: ST HELENA UNDER THE EAST INDIA COMPANY** For some years, no one power formally occupied St Helena, but then on 15 April 1633, the Dutch claimed possession in the name of the United Provinces. In spite of that, there is no evidence that they ever occupied the island, or settled here. Less than a decade later, however, the idea of an English claim to the island was first mooted. The East India Company had identified the potential importance of St Helena for ships on their way home to England from India, so when, in 1657, the company was granted a charter by the Commonwealth, under Richard Cromwell, giving them the right to fortify and colonise any of its establishments, and to transport settlers, stores and ammunition, the decision was formally made to take possession of the island.

In 1659, the East India Company appointed Captain John Dutton as governor-in-chief of St Helena, the company's first settlement. Construction of the first seat of government, as testified by three plaques within the walls, was completed, reportedly, within a month. Originally known as Castle St John, it was soon renamed James Fort (and today is simply 'the Castle'), and the little town that sprang up in Chapel Valley was named James Town in honour of the Duke of York, later King James II.

With the restoration of the monarchy in England in 1660, the charter in the name of Richard, Lord Protector, entitling the East India Company to govern the island, had become of little value. In its place came the first royal charter, from King Charles II, which confirmed the company's right to possess, fortify and settle the island of St Helena on behalf of the Crown. The new charter declared that all people born on or inhabiting the island, and their children, would be subjects of England and would enjoy all liberties within any of its dominions.

Despite this, when Captain John Dutton departed during the summer of 1661, many settlers went with him. His position was taken over by his lieutenant, Robert Stringer, who was left with only 30 men to look after and guard the island.

## Mutiny and a Dutch attack

By 1666, there were only 50 white men and 20 white women left on the island, falling to 48 whites, and 18 negroes four years later. The East India Company did all it could to attract new settlers but with little success; colonists came only in small numbers. At this time, there were no landholders among the island's inhabitants, so instructions were sent to Governor Stringer to give those willing to remain on the island a parcel of land. As a result, the island was divided into 150 parts: 15 for the company, a further five for the governor, and then one for each planter, his wife and his servant. In return, each landholder was required to donate a portion of his produce as rent, to assist in the maintenance of the fortifications and to act as part of the defence force.

In spite of this, by 1671, shortages of food and other necessities were creating grumblings of discontent, and relations between the governor and his people were increasingly strained. Both sides submitted complaints to London, the governor also claiming that, in the event of war, he wouldn't be able to defend his island. In response, the island was sent 80 men, 240 rounds of shot and two barrels of gunpowder. At the same time, thinking of the spiritual needs of its employees, the East India Company sent over the first of many Church of England chaplains, and a modest church was built.

On 21 August 1672, a mutiny broke out. Three St Helena councillors, with the support of the rest of the council, seized the governor and kept him prisoner until October, when they shipped him home. In his place, they elected the island's clergyman, Chaplain Noakes, as governor, but by this time the East India Company had already sent out his replacement, Governor Anthony Beale. A former ship's carpenter and assistant surveyor of shipping, Beale – in response to Charles II's declaration of war against the Dutch – ordered that the island be fortified and that guns be erected as quickly as possible in readiness for an attack.

But preparations started too late: at the end of November, the Dutch decided to launch an attack. When their squadron arrived in December, it took them a few days and several attempts to secure a landing, but – reputedly – on 31 December 1672, they landed a 500-strong party at Bennett's Point. By climbing up the steep Swanley Valley, the men marched unhindered up to High Peak where they overpowered a small English detachment. They then continued without further opposition to Ladder Hill, above Jamestown, and proceeded to descend on the capital. Here, they were at last met with strong resistance and were forced to retreat back to Ladder Hill, where they took possession of the fort, but on 1 January 1673, the Dutch force successfully captured the whole island in an almost bloodless victory. Governor Beale, recognising that the situation was hopeless, escaped with his people on the *Humphrey & Elizabeth* and set sail for Brazil – though not before spiking the guns, so that the Dutch were left with very little booty.

The occupation was short-lived. Two weeks after the Dutch capture of St Helena, Captain Richard Munden set sail for the island from England. A few leagues off, on 4 May, he met up with Beale who, after arriving in Brazil, had immediately hired a sloop to sail back towards St Helena to warn approaching English ships of the Dutch occupation. Munden made plans to retake the island and, on 15 May, forced the Dutch to surrender.

**A new charter and further unrest** The Dutch attack was to represent the only dispute concerning possession of the island. On 16 December 1673, Charles II issued a second royal charter to the East India Company, specifically relating to St Helena and seeking to correct the mistakes that led to the Dutch invasion. In particular, it confirmed more clearly the significance of the island as a fortress, and emphasised its importance to the Crown.

The appointment of Captain Richard Keigwin of the ship *Prosperous* as the new governor was not popular, and in 1674, a second mutiny broke out. The governor was seized and taken to the interior of the island where he was kept under guard without either ink or paper. The mutineers elected Lieutenant Bird to fill the post of governor, and Keigwin was charged with intending to desert the island by the first ship that called, and of abusing the soldiers without cause. When he was cleared of all charges, he was threatened by the soldiers and it took a visiting captain, William Basse, to restore order. Keigwin was reinstalled as governor, but shortly after was replaced by Captain Richard Field, and then in July 1678 – due to the threat of war with France – the company appointed a military man to the post, Major John Blackmore.

Discontent among the inhabitants continued to fester, and in 1684 a minor incident – when a soldier publicly accused the deputy-governor of purposely misconstruing words used in an argument – brought matters to boiling point. Deputy-Governor Holden was cleared of the charges, but the soldier, Adam Dennison, was immediately committed to prison to await the next ship for England. In retaliation, the planters and some of the soldiers drew up a plot to seize and imprison the deputy-governor. They demanded to have Mr Holden delivered to them and when they were refused, they tried unsuccessfully to storm the fort. Six of the rebels were arrested and sentenced to death by hanging.

**War with France brings isolation and harsh times** As a result of the outbreak of war between England and France in 1689, ships no longer visited the island and

Given the level of chance that led to the discovery of St Helena, it's little surprise that many other explorers found their way to these shores, blown along by the southeast trade winds.

Early among them was the English explorer and navigator **William Dampier**, who arrived on 20 June 1691 with his ship *Defence*. Like a modern-day tourist, he stayed just five or six days, but long enough to make the prescient point in his journal that in order to give the inhabitants a decent standard of living, outside support and money would be needed. A decade later, Dampier called again at St Helena in the *Roebuck*, but the ship was in such a poor state that shortly after it sank off Ascension Island (page 148).

The arrival of **Captain James Cook's** HMS *Endeavour* in May 1771 was notable more for his two passengers than for the explorer himself, for on board were the naturalists Sir Joseph Banks and Daniel Solander. Like Dampier, Cook, too, made a second visit to St Helena, in May 1775, this time on board the *Resolution*.

Cook was welcomed by the governor with a 13-gun salute, and was attracted to the island, but in his journal he observed that so much more could be done with the place:

> Whoever views St Helena in its present state and can but conceive what it must have been originally, will not hastily charge the inhabitants with want of industry. Though, perhaps, they might apply it to more advantage, were more land appropriated to planting, corn, vegetables, roots, etc., instead of being laid out in pasture, which is the present mode.

He remarked, too, that the beef on the island was very good and was the only nourishment worth mentioning. And then, after a stay of just six days, he left, calling at Ascension on his way back home to England.

Fast forward another couple of decades, to 17 December 1792, and this time it was **Captain William Bligh** who was welcomed by the governor with a 13-gun salute. On his way to Jamaica with his ships *Providence* and *Assistant*, Bligh presented the governor with ten breadfruit plants so as to provide St Helena with a lasting supply – although they later died from lack of attention. He also left a quantity of mountain rice seed.

necessities ran out. The soldiers' jackets were so worn that they had nothing to cover their backs and no cloth to make new ones. It was to be almost six years before a supply ship was allowed to stop at the island.

In 1693, growing desperation led to another mutiny in which a group of 27 soldiers, led by Sergeant Jackson, seized the fort. The governor was killed and the mutineers took 50 prisoners. Most were held in the dungeon, but five were ordered to go with Jackson and his men as hostages. The acting governor, Captain Poirier, managed to bargain with the mutineers and seven of his men were returned in exchange for supplies. The mutineers escaped from the island on the company ship, *Francis and Mary*.

A year later, it was rumoured that the slaves on St Helena had formed a conspiracy to kill every white man on the island. When word of this plan got around one Friday night in November 1694, panic ensued. By seven o'clock the

**GOLD FEVER**

Towards the end of 1708, while looking for limestone, a member of the council, Captain Mashborne, was believed to have discovered gold and silver deposits. Then a short time later, another soldier discovered what he believed to be gold and copper. On 22 February 1709, Governor Roberts issued a declaration encouraging people to find a gold or copper mine, with respective rewards of £250 and £150. Thus started the short-lived 'Breakneck Valley Goldrush'. Unfortunately, the gold turned out to be iron pyrites, but on the plus side, the prospectors did find a large quantity of lime in Sandy Bay.

following morning, every slave on the island had been taken into custody and the plot thwarted. Although 11 of the slaves were convicted and sentenced to death, in the end only three suffered the death penalty.

In June 1706, the French devised a plot to steal two of the company's ships, by flying the Dutch colours from their own two ships as they approached the island. The resulting confusion was so great that they were able to escape with the stolen vessels before there was any chance of retaliation.

**1708–1815: A NEW COMPANY AND A SUCCESSION OF GOVERNORS** Following commercial rivalries between the original English East India Company and a New East India Company created in 1698, the companies were merged in 1708 to form the United Company of Merchants of England Trading to the East Indies. From now until 1834, the United East India Company were to be Lords Proprietors of St Helena.

The first St Helena-born governor, John Goodwin, took up office in August 1737. It seems that he was governor in name only, because the real power on the council was held by Duke Crispe, who started out as the governor's steward and eventually worked his way up to a seat on the council. Despite reports that he and Goodwin were involved in shady business dealings, Crispe became governor on Goodwin's death, but evidence of embezzlement soon came to light and he was dismissed from the company's service. His successor, Governor Thomas Lambert, established the first hospital in 1741 on the site of the present hospital at Maldivia. And when Charles Hutchinson was appointed governor in 1746, it marked the beginning of a prolonged period of tranquillity and prosperity for the island.

## Another mutiny and military improvements

Despite the relative calm, desertion of soldiers from the garrison was a persistent problem, and measures were taken to try to improve conditions and discipline. The company blamed alcohol for the soldiers' behaviour, so banned them from visiting the punch houses. Things came to a head once more in the 'Christmas Mutiny' when, on 27 December 1783, 200 men armed themselves and marched out of their barracks towards Ladder Hill, where they would have complete command of Jamestown below. The governor, nonetheless, managed to convince them to lay down their arms. The punch houses were once again open to the soldiers, but alcohol consumption was limited. The soldiers demanded more liquor and this time they took over Alarm House, but this was regained by Major Bazett, leading a troop of three officers and 70 men. Although a total of 99 men were condemned to death for their part in the mutiny, in the end lots were drawn and only ten were executed.

Control was finally restored following the appointment in June 1787 of Mr Robert Brooke as governor. Brooke instituted a system whereby known troublemakers were separated from the rest of the soldiers, given the worst provisions and deprived of many valued privileges. This brought the desired effect and with time, he had the military under complete control. Instead of lashings, minor offences were punished by hard labour, which in turn brought some useful improvements. Wasteland was converted into a parade ground for the soldiers, gardens were created, and the appearance of the soldiers greatly improved. Henceforth, men were eager to serve in the garrison.

## Slavery and improved conditions

It appears that slavery was instituted on St Helena around the time of the first settlement by the East India Company, in 1659, when most of them would have come from the Indian Ocean, rather than Africa. Within some 20 years, there were about 80 slaves on the island, but fears of a possible uprising led to restrictions on increased numbers.

Although the majority of slave owners treated their slaves decently, many did not. During his tenure, not only did Governor Brooke improve military morale, he also improved the lives of the slaves. In 1792, he drew up a code of laws for their control and protection, which limited the authority of the master and extended that of the magistrates. The Court of Directors did not totally agree with Brooke's system, but passed a similar set of laws. As a result, a master could punish his slave with 12 lashes, but if the owner felt the offence warranted more severe punishment, it would have to be approved by a magistrate and the governor. The importation of slaves was now forbidden.

Other improvements credited to Governor Brooke include the conducting of water from springs below Diana's Peak to Deadwood, which in turn saved a large stock of the company's cattle during a period of drought by transforming waste ground into good grazing. Brooke also helped arrange a group of St Helena volunteers to support the capture of Cape Town from the Dutch in 1795. After 14 years of service, Brooke retired due to illness and subsequently returned to Ireland.

One of the first actions of his successor, Robert Patton, was to replace the signal guns that had long been used to warn of attack with telegraphs. The governor came under heavy criticism, however, when in 1806, he allowed a group of 282 recruits from St Helena to join a British detachment that attempted, but failed, to capture Buenos Aires.

## Chinese labour

Next in line was Governor Alexander Beatson, who wanted to improve the cultivation of the island, but was hampered by a shortage of labour. As a result, a consignment of Chinese labourers arrived on the island in May 1810, followed by another consignment a year later. At its peak, the total number of Chinese workers on the island reached around 650.

### A MEASLES DISASTER

In 1807, measles was brought to the island on board a slave ship that made a stop at St Helena. Measles was unknown on the island, and there was no warning of the impending danger until the ship had dropped anchor. Even then, it was three weeks before the first families were affected, and there was little initial concern, but the epidemic soon spread. Public and government offices, as well as businesses, were closed, but within two months, 160 people had died, with many more to follow. Until this, the islanders had believed that their climate was much too healthy for the spread of infectious diseases. Theirs was a hard lesson.

At the end of that year, rebellion was once more in the air when the soldiers took against new rules relating to the supply of liquor and provisions, but all the mutineers were captured.

**Education for slaves and a public library** In 1814, a Benevolent Society was founded by Governor Mark Wilks to provide education for the children of slaves, free blacks and the poorer classes of the community. Also credited to Governor Wilks's term in office was the establishment of a public library in Jamestown.

**1815–1821: EXILE OF NAPOLEON BONAPARTE** On 15 October 1815, the British warship *Northumberland* sailed into James Bay with St Helena's most famous visitor on board: Napoleon Bonaparte. Exiled following his defeat at the hands of the Duke of Wellington at the Battle of Waterloo, Napoleon and his entourage were weary after weeks cooped up at sea, but their first impressions were not favourable. As the new arrival scrutinised his 'island prison' with the spy glasses he had used on many a battlefield, he is reputed to have said, 'It is not an attractive place; I should have done better to remain in Egypt.'

For the islanders, Napoleon's arrival also triggered a period of change. Along with his entourage came a significant number of troops to guard him, increasing the population of the island from around 6,500 to 8,000. Accommodation was scarce, so two camps were formed to house the soldiers, one at Deadwood and the other at Francis Plain, and the price of both local and imported provisions soared. Then, to limit the possibility of Napoleon's escape, the government implemented strict measures; even fishing boats were subject to severe restrictions.

On the day of Napoleon's arrival, a crowd of curious people was waiting at the wharf to greet him, but all in vain. It was decided that he should not come ashore until after sundown the following day, in order to avoid unwanted attention. Even then, it required a troop of soldiers with fixed bayonets to force passage for him to the house of Henry Porteous, on Main Street in Jamestown.

The Porteous house had been chosen as a temporary residence for Napoleon but the French, with an entourage of 26 people, were astounded at its meagreness and felt that the Castle, with its vast rooms, or Plantation House (the governor's residence) would have been more suitable. After just one night in these cramped quarters, Napoleon, Sir George Cockburn, and Général Bertrand rode about five

---

## DUKE OF WELLINGTON

Some ten years before Napoleon's arrival on St Helena, Sir Arthur Wellesley, as he was known in 1805, dropped anchor off Jamestown on the *Trident*. Napoleon's future nemesis was on his return voyage to England after victory against the Maratha Empire at the Battle of Assaye. St Helenian tradition has it that both he and Napoleon slept their first nights onshore in the same house – that of Henry Porteous. Others have it that he stayed at the house on Main Street which is now the Wellington House guesthouse. In fact, neither is correct; he actually stayed at The Briars, a house owned by the Balcombes which was, of course, also home to Napoleon for a brief interlude before he was banished to Longwood House. In 1816, Wellington wrote (not in the best of taste) to Admiral Malcolm, Cockburn's successor, 'Tell Boney that I find his apartments at the Elysée-Bourbon very comfortable and I hope he has enjoyed mine at the Balcombes.'

miles to inspect Longwood House, where work on preparations for Napoleon's installation was expected to take two months. Although the house had been used as the summer residence of the lieutenant governor, and Napoleon was assured that it would be transformed into a comfortable residence, he is said to have been disappointed with the dark, low-ceilinged rooms and the bare garden.

It was on the return to Jamestown, when Napoleon decided he could not spend another night at the Porteous house, that he discovered Briars Village. So enchanted was he by the estate that he asked about accommodation here while waiting for the renovations to be completed at Longwood House. The Balcombe family, who owned the house, offered Napoleon the use of their home, but he opted instead to occupy the pavilion, situated on top of a hill just 30 yards (27m) from the main house.

Napoleon spent only two months at The Briars, but they proved to be the most enjoyable of his time on St Helena. His relationship with the Balcombe family was friendly, and he became especially fond of their 13-year-old daughter, Betsy. It was with reluctance and sadness that, at the beginning of December, he left to continue his life in exile at Longwood House.

**Longwood House** Although once just a simple cowshed, Longwood House had long since been transformed into a five-room house. In preparation for Napoleon's stay, a sixth room was added at the front, which was used as a billiard room and ante-chamber. Yet despite the enlargements, the house was still cramped. Over 20 people at a time were living in this limited space, including three of Napoleon's trusted companions: Comte de Las Cases, to whom Napoleon dictated notes on his career; Comte de Montholon, who had also shared the emperor's banishment to Elba, and came to St Helena with his wife and son; and Général Gaspar Gourgaud. (A fourth, Général Henri Bertrand, was based in a separate house with his wife and children.) Napoleon was allowed to walk in the gardens and he had freedom of movement within a specified area, but beyond this he had to be accompanied by an English officer. Today's visitors may think this a pleasant area to live, but Longwood suffers from extremes of weather. In summer it is subject to fierce sun and in winter the

### DAILY LIFE FOR NAPOLEON

Napoleon's life at Longwood broadly followed the same day-to-day routine. He would get up at dawn and, after his morning ablutions, would set out for a ride in the cool of the morning. The limited area in which he was permitted to go alone angered him at times, but to avoid the company of an English officer, he remained within his prescribed boundaries.

Mostly Napoleon lunched alone or in the company of one of his entourage. If weather permitted, he would take his meal in the garden. Then in the afternoon, he dictated his memoirs or other works to one of his companions.

Napoleon still considered himself to be an emperor, and insisted on the observation of strict social etiquette every evening. At 17.00 the officers would assemble in the living room in full dress uniform and the ladies in evening gowns. A game of chess or cards was played until dinner was announced punctually at 20.00. Liveried servants waited on the dining-room table, which was set with gleaming silver and fine porcelain, and the cuisine and wine were always excellent. Coffee was served in the drawing room and then there would be further games of chess or cards, or perhaps some singing or reading. It's not surprising that, over the years, the routine became tedious.

plateau is swirled in mist, bringing high humidity and excessively damp conditions.

In time, Napoleon's constant complaints about the house were addressed by plans to build a more suitable alternative. The 56-room Longwood New House, prefabricated in England, was brought out for assembly opposite the existing building. It was completed in 1821, but Napoleon had never shown any interest in it, and by then was too ill to be moved. The house was demolished after World War II.

**Napoleon as prisoner** Given the constant fear that Napoleon would try to escape from the island, ships were ever present in James Bay, and others patrolled the waters around the island. The island itself was also heavily protected by large numbers of soldiers.

Every attempt was made to treat Napoleon as a prisoner and to demean him. The government censored all correspondence. A curfew of 21.00 was imposed and no-one was allowed to move about the island unless they knew the password. An orderly officer had to report daily that he had personally seen Napoleon, who had to be accompanied at any time if he wanted to go for a ride. During the day, sentries patrolled outside the boundary walls of Longwood, and in the evening they moved in to take up watch in the gardens, close to the house. Napoleon resented being so closely observed, to the extent that he had two peepholes cut in the shutters of the anteroom, which was the largest room in the house, so that he in turn could observe the sentries and attempt to outwit them.

**Lowe versus Napoleon** With the arrival in April 1816 of the new governor, Sir Hudson Lowe, life became even more difficult for Napoleon. From the start, their relationship was strained, mainly because Lowe strictly enforced the regulations and restrictions as dictated by the British government. He expressly forbade anyone to call Napoleon 'Emperor', stating instead that he had to be addressed as Général Bonaparte. The two men met only a few times, the last on 17 August 1816, just three months into the governor's term of office. The following October, the area in which Napoleon was allowed to go out unaccompanied was reduced by a third, and he was also forbidden to speak to anyone outside the house unless in the presence of an English soldier. Now the sentries took up their post close to the house at sundown, instead of at 21.00 as previously.

In the meantime, Napoleon's entourage grew gradually smaller. First to leave was the Comte de Las Cases, who thought of himself as Napoleon's closest confidant, and to whom Napoleon dictated his memoirs. Las Cases was arrested on 25 November 1816 for dispatching secret letters to London through his former servant, and was removed from the island in January 1817.

The departure of Las Cases should have solved the continual jealous rivalry for Napoleon's attention that had existed between him and Général Gourgaud. Yet even

## WILLIAM MAKEPEACE THACKERAY

The famous English novelist was born in India, and was just six years old when his ship stopped at St Helena on a voyage from Calcutta to England in 1817. While he and his servant were walking on the island, Napoleon Bonaparte was pointed out to him. The servant told the little boy that Napoleon ate three sheep a day and 'all the children he can lays hands on'. Thackeray later referred to the incident in a series of essays, the 'Roundabout Papers', published in the *Cornhill Magazine*.

after Las Cases had gone, Gourgaud was still subject to fits of jealousy, becoming quarrelsome and self-absorbed. In February 1818, following a furious exchange with Napoleon in the drawing room, Gourgaud went to Plantation House to request the governor's authority to leave Longwood House. Only after a letter was written claiming illness as the reason for departure, did Governor Lowe permit him to stay elsewhere on the island until passage away from St Helena could be arranged.

**Napoleon falls ill** The year 1818 was not a good one for Napoleon. Plagued by illness, he became moody and irritable. Deep hot baths in his large copper tub, where he had long spent hours reading, lunching and chatting, became increasingly important, while his valets would sleep on the sofa in the adjoining room, ready to respond to Napoleon's every call. Franceschi Cipriani, who was responsible for the smooth running of the household at Longwood House, died after a four-day illness; four other members of staff left with their families; and on 2 August, Napoleon's personal and trusted physician, Barry O'Meara, left the island following a row with the governor.

For a time, Dr O'Meara had had an arrangement with the governor to report on Napoleon and his entourage, but he gradually got tired of the restrictions and his reports stopped. The governor and doctor quarrelled and Lowe attempted to have O'Meara replaced, but Napoleon refused any other physician. Nonetheless, Dr O'Meara resigned, leaving Napoleon without medical care for six months. His condition continued to deteriorate. Although O'Meara had determined that Napoleon was most likely suffering from chronic hepatitis, the governor, afraid that people would feel this had something to do with the unsuitable conditions on St Helena, decided to suppress the information. When a naval surgeon, brought to the island after Napoleon suffered one of his painful bouts of illness, confirmed Dr O'Meara's diagnosis, he was dismissed by court-martial. For several more months, Napoleon refused medical care, and though his mother sent another doctor, as well as a cook, a major-domo and two priests, the newcomers did not live up to the expectations of the exile.

For a brief period over the next few months, Napoleon seemed to be regaining his health. In March 1820, he began to take a keen interest in gardening and drew up plans to remodel the small arid plot at Longwood. With the help of Chinese gardeners, a lawn was sown, flowerbeds were added, orange and lemon trees planted, and a vegetable garden set out in front of the house (although it was ruined by the combined effects of wind, heat and lack of water). Construction of a square pavilion enabled Napoleon to view the sea and follow the progress of ships arriving from South Africa, and he was able to spend time outside in a small parkland area with ponds where he sometimes ate lunch under the arbour.

**Death of Napoleon** Unfortunately Napoleon was not to enjoy his improved health for long, and his bouts of illness returned with increased frequency. His last excursion was on 4 October 1820, when he, Général Bertrand and the Comte de Montholon rode five miles to Sandy Bay to have breakfast on the lawn of Mount Pleasant with Sir William Doveton, the estate's owner.

After this, Napoleon took only short, slow rides in the carriage, and by mid-March 1821, he could no longer leave the house. As his condition worsened, his sickbed was moved into the drawing room, and on 5 May 1821, surrounded by members of his entourage, the former emperor died. Governor Lowe and large numbers of prominent officials were received for the lying in state, and hundreds of people filed through the room to mourn or observe Napoleon in death.

Much controversy exists as to the cause of Napoleon's death. Following an autopsy. the official cause was declared to be stomach cancer and a perforated stomach ulcer. Nevertheless, there has been considerable speculation that Napoleon may have been gradually poisoned by arsenic, which was used in the coloured pattern in the wallpaper in the house, and had seeped out through damp. Yet if this were the case, why were other members of the household not poisoned too? As is often the case, truth may be stranger than fiction (see box, below), though no-one really knows.

## CAUSE OF DEATH: UNKNOWN    *Ian Mathieson*

A 1992 television programme widely screened has given rise to the myth that Napoleon died from ingesting arsenic from the wallpaper of his suite at Longwood. This facile description obscures a much more interesting theory promoted by Sven Forschufvud and Ben Weider based on analysis of a lock of Napoleon's hair. They were able to show that it contained variable amounts of arsenic. From the historical record of the lock they were able to date each section and show that high rates of arsenic coincided with bouts of Napoleon's severe ill health, as recorded by his entourage.

Napoleon's continued existence threatened the Bourbon cause as much as his execution or obvious murder. Only his death by natural causes would permit a sustained restoration of the monarchy. Implicated in the plot were the French commissioner Marquis de Montchenu, who arrived at St Helena in 1816 with his official diplomatic secretary, M de Gros – a member of the Chevaliers de la Foi, a masonic type of organisation of fanatical Royalists established by the Comte d'Artois. David Hamilton-Williams argues that after years of gradual weakening by low-level arsenic poisoning, the trigger for the *coup de grace* was the assassination in 1820 of d'Artois's son, the Duc de Berry, through whom it was hoped to prolong and extend the Bourbon dynasty. His death weakened the Bourbon cause and raised the spectre of Napoleon's return to power.

Ships to St Helena were infrequent and took two months to travel the distance, so the fatal orders didn't arrive until February 1821 aboard HMS *Vernon*. Within three months the emperor was dead.

It is suggested that Napoléon's close confidant, Comte de Montholon had poisoned Napoleon's personal wine supply with low doses of arsenic. He developed a close relationship with Hudson Lowe so that it became relatively easy to arrange for the removal of possibly awkward witnesses such as O'Meara and Las Cases. When more urgent action was required, to remove a possible informant, then the murderer resorted to a massive dose of arsenic. This was the case with the unfortunate double agent Cipriani who, in February 1818 and without warning, collapsed with terrible stomach pains and died within two days; the site of his burial was mysteriously lost.

The end was achieved by mercury poisoning. For some time Napoleon had been given a refreshing drink called orgeat made from bitter almonds – apparently arranged by de Montholon. Towards the end the unsuspecting doctors ordered that an enema was necessary and that calomel was the conventional means for achieving this. A large dose was taken by the reluctant invalid and, according to Weider's chemical knowledge, the mixture of bitter almonds and calomel reacted to produce a lethal dose of mercurial cyanide.

Napoleon was buried in a simple tomb in Sane Valley, a site that the emperor himself is said to have chosen as his final resting-place. As in life, so Napoleon was also guarded heavily after his death. There was a guardhouse stationed close to the tomb and even his coffin was extra secure, with four separate layers. Rather like a Russian doll, the body was placed in a tin coffin, followed by a second box of pine, which itself was sealed into a third of lead, and the whole set into an outer layer of mahogany. On the day of the funeral, the entire garrison lined the route from Longwood House to Hutt's Gate and on to the specially built road to the tomb. Although the tomb is still there, it is now empty; Napoleon's body was returned to France in 1840.

## Hudson Lowe's legacy: the liberation of slaves
Hudson Lowe may not have been suited to act as jailer for the French exiles, but he was considered to be a fine soldier, a good linguist, intelligent, hardworking and kind. During Napoleon's stay on St Helena, he took steps to outlaw slavery on the island. It was following an event in August 1818, when a slave owner was fined for whipping a young slave girl, that Lowe convened a meeting of the inhabitants to urge the abolition of slavery. As a first measure, all children born of a slave woman on or after Christmas Day 1818 were to be free. They were, though, to be considered as apprentices until the age of 18 for boys and 16 for girls, and masters were required to enforce their attendance at church and Sunday schools.

In 1821, after the death of Napoleon, Lowe and many of the island's garrison left the island, but his work bore fruit, and slavery was finally abolished in 1832. Before he departed, the governor was presented with an address from the island's inhabitants. In it, he was praised for his work to abolish slavery and the gratitude and the affection of the people was conveyed to him.

## 1834–1900: THE CROWN TAKES OVER
Under the India Act of 28 August 1833, St Helena ceased to be ruled by the Honourable East India Company that had governed the island for 182 years. In its place, from 22 April 1834, came His Majesty's Government, signalling immediate and radical change. The annual subsidy of £90,000, which it had cost the East India Company to maintain the island, was removed. The garrison was disbanded and the new governor was under orders to cut expenses.

### CHARLES DARWIN

The famous English naturalist, Charles Darwin, anchored off St Helena on HMS *Beagle* on 8 July 1836. Like many before him, he stayed on the island for just six days, but during this time he made a thorough examination of all he saw. To commemorate his visit, he presented to the governor copies of his work, *A Naturalist's Voyage Round the World*, which are now kept in the Castle.

Darwin remarked on the Welsh character of the scenery on St Helena and commented on the poverty of the lower classes and the many emancipated slaves who didn't have work. He also noted that working people could afford only rice and a small bit of salt meat. Darwin liked the islanders, who he found to be gentle and pleasant. He found abundant partridges and pheasants but he failed to sight the wirebird.

On his way home to England, Darwin also visited Ascension and later wrote an account of its geology.

As a result, most people on the island were reduced to a state of near-poverty. Many cases of hardship arose when company servants were dismissed from their posts. Whole families and over 100 young men, finding life so hard and with no prospect of improvement, emigrated to the Cape of Good Hope. With no old-age pensions, friendly societies were founded to provide sickness, death and old-age benefits, as in England. First came the Mechanics and Friendly Benefit Society, followed by the St Helena Poor Society in 1847, the Foresters in 1871, and the St Helena Church Provident Society in 1878.

Early in the new regime, the whale-fishing industry was introduced to St Helena. Like many industries launched to boost the welfare of a place, it wasn't as successful as was hoped. In 1875, another attempt was made to relaunch whaling, but this venture failed as well, probably because the South Atlantic whale fisheries were already in decline.

## Suppression of the slave trade and unwelcome visitors
In 1840, the British government established a Vice-Admiralty Court on the island for the trial of those in charge of ships engaged in the now-illegal South Atlantic slave trade. Over the ensuing ten years, hundreds of these ships were captured and brought to St Helena from the coasts of Africa and Brazil, at huge loss of life to the British sailors on the patrol ships. The captured ships themselves were sold or broken up, while their 'human cargo' of slaves was liberated, fed, clothed and housed at the Liberated African Depot in Rupert's Valley. Conditions on board the ships were atrocious, however, and many of the former slaves died, to be buried in the valley. (Archaeological work in 2008 led to the recovery of 325 sets of human remains, whose final resting place was the subject of much discussion in 2015.) Of the slaves who survived, most were given passage to the West Indies or British Guiana as labourers, but some chose to remain on St Helena as servants, or engaged in various public works.

The work of liberating slaves brought money and employment to the island, but also the scourge of white ants, or termites. These minute creatures were among the timbers on a slave ship from Brazil, which was broken up and stored in Jamestown. So destructive were they, and so great their appetite for timber, books, furniture and paper, that over the next few decades much of the town had to be rebuilt. Among other structural and material damages, the ants destroyed the reception hall at the Castle, and many of the books in the public library.

## Repatriation of Napoleon
On 8 October 1840, two French ships – the frigate *La Belle Poule* and the corvette *Favorite* – sailed into James Bay. On board were several of Napoleon's former companions in exile, including generals Bertrand and Gourgaud, and Comte de Las Cases. A week later the party witnessed the exhumation of their emperor at Sane Valley, and watched as the coffin was placed with appropriate ceremony aboard the French frigate. Thus, 25 years to the day since Napoleon's arrival on St Helena, his body was back on French territory.

In 1858, Queen Victoria granted France the right to buy and hold indefinitely Longwood House and the tomb of Napoleon at Sane Valley. Today, the *tricolore* flies over 'Le Domaine français de Ste-Hélène', and over The Briars, acquired by the French in 1959.

## Governor Hudson Ralph Janisch
In 1873, the second and last St Helena-born governor, Hudson Ralph Janisch, took office. He is most remembered for his *Extracts from the St Helena Records and Chronicles of Cape Commanders*, which

During the 19th century, the St Helenian economy evolved around supplying provisions for shipping and the local garrison. In 1802, a total of 169 ships called at the island, increasing to 367 by 1830, and reaching 1,040 in 1860. The introduction of the steamship, however, was to prove a major blow. Within just five years, the number of ships calling at the island each year had fallen to 850, and the opening of the Suez Canal in 1869 served to seal the island's fate; in 1910, St Helena welcomed just 51 ships.

was printed and published in Jamestown in 1885. It was said that Janisch was a good governor and wanted only the best for his island homeland, but lack of funds prevented him from bringing much benefit to the island. One notable fact of his tenure is the extremely low salary he was paid compared with that of other governors. There is speculation that this was because he was native to the island, but he also had the misfortune to be governing during an economic depression. With the opening of the Suez Canal in 1869, ships called less and less at St Helena. As a result, income fell and the economy suffered, so much so that the island fell into a state of poverty. Nearly a quarter of the poorest section of the community left the island for the Cape in order to escape the economic conditions. Hudson Janisch died in office on 10 March 1884.

**New Zealand flax** With the traditional economic mainstays gone, the island's administrators cast around for some way to make St Helena pay. Over the years, many agricultural schemes had been tried, from viticulture and a silk-worm industry to crops such as cinchona (for quinine), prickly pear (for cochineal), and aloes (for aloe vera). None were successful and some had disastrous consequences, the worst of the lot being *Phormium tenax*: New Zealand flax.

Serious development of the flax industry started at the end of the 19th century, despite the failure of an earlier attempt at developing production. Flax was grown to produce fibre, which could be used to make a variety of products, but success was normally based on large-scale production with a high degree of mechanisation. St Helena's topography did not lend itself to this approach, and its flax industry was only really profitable during the two world wars, and in the Korean War, when supplies of the competing and superior-quality jute were interrupted.

Even when it was profitable, flax production had its downsides. First, clearance of land for its production had negative consequences for the endemic flora, particularly towards the Peaks where the vegetation had already been affected by earlier attempts to grow cinchona. The impact of flax production was also social, with the flax mills presenting St Helena with their own 'dark satanic mills'. The industry continued until the mid 1960s, when the government – faced with a loss of contracts – finally acknowledged that it was no longer viable and withdrew the wage subsidy. Within days, the flax mills closed permanently and the islanders did not mourn their passing.

**More exiles** The island's next prisoner arrived in 1890. Following the Zulu Wars, Chief Dinizulu, son of Cetawayo, and his family were exiled to the island for seven years. Unlike Napoleon, Dinizulu was considered to be very co-operative during his captivity and readily made friends. He became a convert to Christianity, and was baptised and confirmed by the bishop. It wasn't until 1957 that the last exiles

1

arrived: three Bahraini nationalists, who remained on the island until 1960, when they were released by a writ of habeas corpus.

**THE 20TH CENTURY** In November 1899, in the dying stages of the 19th century, the first submarine cable was landed on St Helena by the Eastern Telegraph Company. Initially connecting the island with Cape Town, it was the first stage in the link north to Ascension and then to Europe and England, signalling the onset of international communications that was to bear fruit over the next hundred years.

The century was barely underway when in April 1900, St Helena once again became an international place of imprisonment, this time to some 6,000 South African Boer War prisoners. During the next two years, ship after ship arrived bringing new prisoners, who were interned first at Deadwood Plain, then at a second camp at Broad Bottom. As the population reached its all-time record of 9,850, the island experienced a temporary wave of economic improvement, but it was short-lived.

Meanwhile, another money-making venture – lace making – was introduced to the island. The potential was there for some of the neediest women on the island to earn money to support their families, but the fledgling industry was neglected and the Government Lace School was closed. Then, in 1909, a private investor established a mackerel-canning factory, but to everyone's dismay, the fish did not appear to order, and this venture, too, was shut down.

**World War I** With the outbreak of the Great War in 1914, the defunct St Helena Volunteer Corps was re-established, and the following year, the Imperial Government constructed certain military defences and enlarged the wharf. This in turn brought badly needed employment, which was boosted when, as a result of the war, the price of flax fibre soared and new mills were constructed. But now, with money in their pockets, the islanders chose to neglect growing their own produce, in favour of importing their food at exaggerated prices.

After the war, in 1922, the island of Ascension became a dependency of St Helena, and was leased out to the Eastern Telegraph Company (later Cable and Wireless). This presented new opportunities for the islanders, the first of whom left to take up employment on Ascension as servants and labourers. More frivolously, 1928 saw the introduction of the Motor-Car Ordinance, which made it legal to import automobiles to the island. In readiness for the first vehicle, owned by the Honourable H W Solomon OBE, 60 miles (97km) of road were prepared.

**World War II** World War II brought a second period of prosperity for the flax industry, but very little hardship to St Helena itself, which maintained a garrison and a local defence force. However, the war did come uncomfortably close to the island when the Royal Fleet Auxiliary ship HMS *Darkdale* was torpedoed off Jamestown by a German submarine, killing 41 people. In another incident, a German naval vessel, the *Graf Spee*, was sighted off Jamestown, but it disappeared again without incident.

**Post-war St Helena and economic decline** Over the next few years, the price of flax increased, reaching its peak in 1951. In that year, the island's exports exceeded its imports, the first and only year that this occurred. During the later years of the decade, things started to take a downward turn. A fish cannery, which was opened in 1957, was forced to close. In 1958, the Union-Castle Line decided to cut its passenger-carrying schedule so that only one in three vessels southbound

With its allegiance to the British Crown, St Helena has long had links with royalty. The first royal visit took place in September 1860, when **Prince Alfred**, second son of Queen Victoria, arrived on the HMS *Eurylaus* to present new colours to Her Majesty's St Helena Regiment.

It was to be almost 90 years, after World War II, before the island was again graced with royalty, but this occasion was of even greater significance. On 29 April 1947, during a royal tour to South Africa, **Princess Elizabeth**, later to be crowned queen of the United Kingdom, and **Princess Margaret**, arrived with their parents **King George VI** and **Queen Elizabeth**, aboard the HMS *Vanguard*, and were welcomed by the acting governor, Colonel Gilpin. Their time on land was all too brief – just three hours and 25 minutes – before they left for a very brief stop at Ascension. At Longwood House, the King signed the visitors' book, and later commented to the French ambassador on the parlous state of the building. In 2002, on the occasion of the quincentenary of the island's discovery, Queen Elizabeth II recalled her visit:

> I have an abiding memory of the arum lilies, understandably the island's national flower, growing in the wild as we drove to Bamboo Hedge and back to Plantation House. There we met Jonathan, still the oldest living inhabitant of St Helena, and many Saints. The warmth and informality of our welcome remain with me to this day.

Ten years later, her husband, **Philip, Duke of Edinburgh**, made a stop at the island during his round-the-world tour on the Royal Yacht *Britannia*. Then, in 1984, their second son, **Prince Andrew**, visited St Helena to celebrate with the Saints 150 years under the Crown. Announcement of the approval of funds to build Prince Andrew School was scheduled to coincide with the visit. And most recently, in 2002, the Queen's daughter, the **Princess Royal**, followed in her mother's footsteps to mark St Helena's quincentenary in person.

and two of three vessels northbound made a call at the island. Then, in 1966, the flax industry collapsed, as the cost of subsidy was simply too high to be sustainable. The island slipped into further economic depression, a situation that was compounded in 1977 when Union-Castle ceased servicing the island altogether. Now, to add to the financial burden, the British government acquired the first RMS *St Helena*. By the end of the 20th century, the island was left with fewer transport links to the rest of the world than it had had 200 years earlier.

**The Falklands conflict** During the Falklands conflict, in 1982, the first RMS *St Helena* was requisitioned by the Ministry of Defence, and sailed south with many of the crew volunteering for duty. Her role, as a supply and support vessel, continued for some time after the war was officially over.

**Saints stripped of British citizenship** On New Year's Day, 1983, the Saints were dealt a hard blow when the British Nationality Act of 1981 came into effect, stripping all citizens of British Overseas Territories of their right to full British citizenship. The intention was to prevent the anticipated influx of UK passport holders from Hong Kong when the island was returned to China, but the Saints, too, were caught in this legislation and found themselves effectively excluded from

In 2000, a 16-year-old boy from the tiny central African country of Burundi stowed aboard the RMS *St Helena* while she was docked at Cape Town. When he was finally discovered, the afternoon before the ship was to arrive at St Helena, he had a sad tale to tell of the atrocities he and his family had suffered. The ship's passengers held a collection and it was decided that the young man should apply for political asylum on St Helena.

He was warmly received on the island, and government officials did everything they could to assist and make him comfortable. After much effort and much interviewing, however, the youth decided to withdraw his application for asylum. When he first decided to stow away aboard the RMS, he saw 'London' written on the stern and thought it was headed for the United Kingdom. When he arrived on St Helena, where he didn't speak the language, he was surprised and disappointed, and became very homesick. He was eventually transported to the UK – thus ending the story of St Helena's first, and so far last, political refugee.

the UK for nearly 20 years, undermining the royal charter of 1673 that had been granted to them by King Charles II. The fight was on. Support for the Saints' cause came from the Bishop's Commission on Citizenship, which was established in 1992 by the Anglican bishop of St Helena, Bishop John Ruston, but it was to be a long, drawn-out struggle.

**THE NEW MILLENNIUM** For St Helenians, the new millennium started with long-awaited news on two fronts. The first was the return of full British citizenship, which was granted by the British government to all Overseas Territories from 21 May 2002, in part to commemorate the 500th anniversary of the discovery of the island. The second was the announcement in 2004 that the government was at last going to build an airport on St Helena. Within a few months, the first piece of news caused around 1,500 Saints to leave the island for more prosperous pastures overseas. Whether the second will bring them back again is a matter of considerable conjecture.

**FURTHER INFORMATION** Those interested in island history would do well to make their way either to the St Helena Archives (page 94) or to the St Helena Museum (pages 93–4), both in Jamestown, or to contact the Friends of St Helena (page 193). See also pages 187–9.

## GOVERNMENT AND ADMINISTRATION

Together, St Helena, Ascension and the Tristan da Cunha group make up a single UK Overseas Territory, one of just 14 worldwide. Known until 1 September 2009 as St Helena and Dependencies, the territory was then renamed St Helena, Ascension and Tristan da Cunha, affording equal status to each island or island group. The group has a single governor, based in St Helena, who is appointed by the British government to act on behalf of Her Majesty the Queen. Ascension and Tristan da Cunha also have their own administrators, who in turn act on behalf of the governor.

**ADMINISTRATION** It is sobering to think that elected representatives from within the small population of St Helena – no larger than that of a village in the UK – have responsibility for an annual government budget of some £20 million, about half of which is raised locally.

Under the terms of the constitution, which was last revised in September 2009, St Helena is administered by the governor with the help of a Legislative Council and a smaller Executive Council. The former has 12 elected members, plus a further five non-voting members: a speaker, a deputy speaker, and three ex officio members – the chief secretary, financial secretary, and attorney general. Elected members of the Legislative Council vote five people from among their ranks to the Executive Council, which also comprises the three non-voting ex officio members. The governor, in the chair, has no vote, but does have the right of veto, subject to British government approval. There are no political parties, so all councillors are independent. Elections are held every four years.

**LAW** The island is empowered to make its own laws, known locally as 'ordinances', along with various rules, regulations and orders. For the most part, legislation is the responsibility of the Legislative Council, subject to the approval of the governor. In default of local laws, the islanders are subject to English law.

The judicial system, too, is similar to its counterpart in the UK, although there are no juries. A weekly Magistrates' Court hears minor cases, while more serious offences are referred to the Supreme Court, usually held twice a year. The Supreme Court is presided over by a non-resident chief justice, supported by the island sheriff. In 1989, the first Court of Appeal was held, consisting of a president and two justices of appeal, all of them non-resident.

There is a resident attorney general who is responsible for legal matters relating to the St Helena government. For most individual court cases, a public solicitor supported by lay advocates provides legal advice, assistance and representation to the public. In the event of a serious case, a lawyer for the defendant is sent out from the UK.

In exceptional circumstances, such as the public enquiry into child abuse in 2015, a full legal team will be brought over from the UK.

The St Helena police force is based in Jamestown and also has responsibility for immigration and prison services. The force is staffed largely from the local population with assistance from serving police officers from the UK, particularly in specialist roles.

## ECONOMY

Virtually every visitor to St Helena has an instant solution to the island's challenges but, as the American journalist H L Mencken famously said: 'For every complex problem, there is a solution that is simple, neat and wrong.'

When first settled by the East India Company, St Helena was originally intended as a military and supply base; it was never the intention that the island become self-sufficient. The decline of shipping during the 19th century, however, put paid to that role, and since the demise of the flax industry in the 1960s, the island has become increasingly dependent on British support.

**TRADE AND SUBSIDY** St Helena imports a large percentage of its goods, valued at £13 million in 2011/12. These emanate primarily from the UK, with South African goods representing a substantial minority. Exports, conversely, brought in just £852,000 in revenue in the same period.

Fishing is the greatest earner, but current income reflects only a fraction of its potential. In spite of an established 200-mile fishing limit around the island, the local fishing fleet is not currently able to maximise opportunities, with only a few vessels having the capability to fish offshore. And while there's a fish-processing factory in Rupert's Valley, it has been some time since the plant was working to full capacity.

Tourism, too, is in its infancy, with visitor numbers in 2014 reaching just 736, plus a further 3,355 cruise-ship passengers. Much of this lies at the door of the RMS *St Helena*, whose current schedule means that most visitors stay for just eight days, after which there is a gap of two weeks before the next ship. Once the airport is open, however, the aim is for numbers to rise incrementally, reaching around 600 visitors a week, or 30,000 a year, within ten years or so – a challenge that not everyone believes is realistic or even advisable. In 2012, 41% of visitors were from the UK, and a further 28% from South Africa, but the introduction of flights from Johannesburg could well see this balance change considerably.

At present, the island's trade deficit is met by the British government, which in 2011/12 subsidised St Helena to the tune of £26.32 million a year. This is broken down into four main categories: budgetary aid, which supports the budget of the St Helena government; a shipping subsidy covering the loss on the RMS *St Helena*; development aid, which finances all capital projects; and technical co-operation, which finances expatriate contract officers, consultants and overseas training for Saints.

Although the St Helena government raises money through taxes, passenger permits, import duties and fishing, it was largely to address the mounting cost of

## AIRPORT PROJECT

Building an international airport on St Helena was first mooted as far back as 1942, following development of the airstrip on Ascension. For many years it was deemed impossible, as St Helena's hilly and rocky terrain means that there is virtually no flat land, and the lack of infrastructure along with high costs resulting from extreme logistical challenges combined to make the project appear a non-starter. In the meantime, economic problems on the island were mounting. Lack of opportunity meant that more and more people were leaving the island, resulting in a diminishing and ageing population. In 2002, a referendum to the St Helenian people found in favour of an airport, and the following year, the UK government's Department for International Development (DFID) decided to investigate the possibility of a joint public–private partnership.

The site selected for the airport was Prosperous Bay Plain, arguably the only area that could reasonably incorporate a runway suitable for jet aircraft such as the Boeing 737-700. Nevertheless, the location posed some serious engineering challenges, prime among them being a valley – Dry Gut – that would have to be filled to give the requisite length for the runway, and a suitable safety margin.

In the initial stages of tender, the St Helena Leisure Corporation (SHELCO), a consortium backed by the Indian Oberoi hotel group among others, put in a proposal to build an upmarket resort with hotels, golf courses, houses, etc, to partly finance the airport, and to run an airline. DFID then decided to seek other potential partners, resulting in a further four proposals being submitted. Despite this, these last three pulled out once they had evaluated the risks involved, but delays were incurred and costs were rising.

In 2008, in an apparent change of tack, the government announced that their preferred bidder was an Italian consortium, headed by Impregilo. Later that year, however, negotiations were put on hold as a result of the global recession. By 2009, costs were estimated to have risen to more than £200 million.

the subsidy that the British government finally agreed to finance an airport. At its simplest, the aim is to encourage growth in several sectors, leading in time to full economic self-sufficiency – though it's likely to be a rocky road.

**AGRICULTURE** Ever since St Helena was first discovered, the environment has suffered. As fertile valleys were denuded by the introduction of animals – goats, pigs and the like – so the plants that thrived – among them fig, lemon, orange, pomegranate and date – were lost. In time, erosion set in and the land dried out and became stony. Today's islanders are faced with the legacy of those centuries of neglect, and little produce is grown locally, bar a few vegetables and fruits for local consumption, including bananas. Despite that, the tide is beginning to turn. Pigs, cattle, goats and chickens are providing at least some local meat, but the poor grass is lacking in nutrients, and there is no dairy industry; EU regulations put paid to that some time ago. The value placed on fresh produce has encouraged the establishment of polytunnels, to grow salad crops, herbs and produce such as melon and aubergines, and a few of the island's hotels and restaurants are managing their own smallholdings. As such initiatives take hold, it may be just a matter of time before the reliance on imported fresh produce is stemmed.

In order to prevent the spread of diseases or pests, St Helena imposes very tight security measures on goods brought to the island, from the examination of every

It was to be another two years before the contract was finally awarded, but at last, on 3 November 2011, the formalities were agreed with the South African company, Basil Read, one of the initial bidders for the project. On 14 November 2012, once the company was established on the island, work started to fill Dry Gut. Operating around the clock, six days a week, it took 22 months to fill the valley with 450,000 truckloads of material. Attention then turned to the runway, the terminal buildings, and airport logistics. As St Helena looks forward to the arrival of its first passenger plane in 2016, the die is cast.

The cost to the British taxpayer of the first phase of the airport, including a permanent wharf at Rupert's Bay, is estimated to be on budget at nearly £201 million, or roughly the equivalent of ten years' subsidy. Following completion, Basil Read will retain the contract to operate the airport for ten years, subsidised by the British government, but the long-term aim, based on economic growth through tourist development, is for the island to become entirely self-sufficient.

While many Saints are sceptical about the impact of the airport, others are more sanguine, and some are already taking advantage of the increased business potential. Inevitably, though, it's not all good news. Environmentally, although it is incumbent on Basil Read to restore the habitat around the airport, and there is no doubt that this is being taken seriously, there are concerns about its impact on St Helena's already fragile ecosystem. The loss of 'their' ship is a hard blow to many St Helenians, and along with this will be a consequent loss of jobs, although new opportunities may well offset this. There are also fears that property prices will rocket as wealthy visitors buy or build their place in the sun. But perhaps of greatest concern to many is that the island will lose some of its alluring qualities as a unique destination while their gentle pace of life will be destroyed forever.

cargo load of imported fruit to pest-eradication programmes targeting insects such as the fruit fly.

**EMPLOYMENT**  Some 48% of the workforce is in government employ, where wages are notoriously low. With a minimum adult wage of £2.60 an hour, a typical worker might earn just £75–100 a week. The average income in 2013/14 was £7,640 a year. Many employees, including teachers and nurses, have quit their jobs for more lucrative, if lowlier, employment overseas, particularly in the Falklands, Ascension and the UK – though remittances from that employment are a considerable boost to the island economy.  In their place, the government has had to bring in staff from the UK and South Africa, often on short-term contracts and at a much higher cost. It's a cycle that causes inevitable resentment, but is as yet showing no sign of easing.

In the private sector, a boost to jobs has come from construction of the airport, making Basil Read the second-largest employer of local labour. As a result, the island is in the unusual situation of zero unemployment, in marked contrast to the lack of jobs at the beginning of the millennium. Even so, a proportion of employees on the airport project has had to be brought in from abroad, some from South Africa and some – many of them with specialist skills – from Thailand.

**COST OF LIVING**  Inflation in December 2014 stood at 3.3%, with a very small rise projected over the following year. Nevertheless, the cost of living is very high for most Saints, especially considering the low salaries. Prices of most consumer goods are subject to freight charges and 20% customs duty, and are also affected by inflation in the country of origin – usually the UK or South Africa. The cost of electricity, too, is exceptionally high. Income tax stands at 25%, but there is as yet no VAT.

**ENTERPRISE ST HELENA (ESH)**  (*www.investinsthelena.com*) Fundamental to the government's aim to promote sustainability and eventual economic self-sufficiency on St Helena, Enterprise St Helena plays a major role in inward investment and the development of new projects.

A key part of the agency's mission is a series of targeted growth sectors, prime among them being tourism, fisheries and agriculture. In the field of tourism, its remit ranges from facilitation of new businesses and training, to international promotion of St Helena as a holiday destination on low-volume, high-value lines. In fisheries, consideration is being given not just to commercial development of the island's under utilised fishing waters but to the promotion of wealth-generating sports fishing. And on the agricultural front, the aim is to tackle St Helena's current high dependency on imported produce by improving on-island practices and usage of agricultural land.

ESH is also tasked with enhancing the island's green credentials, in which they have supported paper and cardboard recycling initiatives by SHAPE, and the installation by Basil Read of a new waste segregation facility at Horse Point – which in turn creates the potential for further recycling.

## PEOPLE

As the races become integrated on our tiny island, so may it be in the world of the future, when prejudice is no more.

Barbara George
from *St Helena: The Chinese Connection*

Since the 1980s, the population of St Helena has seen a steady decline, in part due to falling birth rates, and in part because many Saints have chosen to leave the island to work overseas. Work on the airport, however, has seen a reversal of this trend, with an estimated increase in population from 4,077 at the time of the 2008 census to an estimated 4,600 in 2015. Included in this latest figure are some 4,100 St Helenians, with the others made up of expatriate workers.

But statistics tell nothing of the people themselves. St Helenians represent a mixture of many different nationalities and influences from different parts of the world: European settlers, with their slaves from the Far East, Chinese labourers, African slaves, and prisoners from the Boer War. They are gentle people, who fiercely defend their traditions and their right to be full British citizens, yet as David Smallman, a governor of St Helena in the 1990s, wrote in his book, *Quincentenary: A Story of St Helena 1502–2002*:

> the veneer of Britishness is often quite thin. First impressions can be deceptive. St Helena is not a few acres of Britain in a sub-tropical environment. Its remote location and history have conspired to produce a breed of people without equal who, given their lack of natural resources and the relationship with those responsible over the centuries for their governance, have developed a unique personality of their own.

St Helenians are also proud of their identities as Saints *per se*. Indeed, in some ways they are very un-British. In particular, their friendliness is most unlike the traditional British reserve, with a natural instinct to greet everyone, whether friend or stranger. Theirs is a close-knit community, used to sharing resources, to working together – whether in bringing up a family, tilling the land or building the family home. As islander Basil George wrote in his poem, 'Carry Stone Cottage', St Helenians are a people who 'think with their hands'.

## SAINTS ABROAD

There are around 5,000 Saints permanently settled in the UK and many others carrying out contract work on Ascension and the Falkland Islands. In fact there are so many St Helenians in Swindon, a prosperous medium-sized town in the southwest of the UK, it has been nicknamed Swindolena.

While the government does help and support its people, it hasn't until recently encouraged them to stand on their own feet. Young Saints in particular feel the lack of opportunity and many make plans to leave, be it to study, serve in the military, or take up employment offshore.

The chances of these migrants returning permanently to the island for a wage of less than £100 a week and a severely limited choice of consumer goods are not high. Yet they often maintain or build homes on the island and import modern cars, and such remittances have become an important non-governmental source of revenue.

Even if they have no intention of returning home permanently, Saints abroad don't forget their roots. Every year, for example, the St Helena Association, a UK-based group of Saints who are long-time UK residents, organises the Reading Sports on the last Sunday of August. Up to 1,500 Saints and their families gather together for a day of sporting events, dancing and partying late into the night. The association also organises an annual dance in London which raises considerable sums of money for St Helena charities.

Every person on St Helena has a story to tell, each interesting in its own right, but they're often reluctant to speak publicly. Centuries of dependency on Great Britain has certainly had its effect. Despite this, many St Helenians are committed to their island, and work tirelessly for the good of the community in the fields of education, local history, music, arts and craft, as well as in government positions. Others spend considerable time fundraising for local charities. There are thriving youth groups on the island, including organisations affiliated to the Scout and Guide movement. But perhaps just as important is the contribution made by those who are prepared to share their knowledge and love of the island with visitors, drawing them into the island's way of life.

## LANGUAGE

English is the only official language of St Helena, typically spoken with a kind of musical lilt, not dissimilar to that of the West Indies. The local dialect combines remnants of older English with some South African influence, and you may still hear phrases such as 'How is you be?' For a more detailed feel for the language, it's worth finding a copy of a book by the St Helena Creative Writing Group, *Speaking Saint* (page 192).

## EDUCATION

Education on St Helena largely follows the British system, with local variations as appropriate. Students work towards the international GCSE and A level examinations, as well as NVQs – locally known as a certificate of vocational studies (CVS). There are just four schools on the island: three primary schools, and one secondary – Prince Andrew School (*www.pas.edu.sh*) – plus a nursery for younger children. Education is compulsory up to the age of 16. Students with learning difficulties are integrated into main school activities and also provided with specialist education and support at the school's learning support centre.

As a community school, Prince Andrew's has a wider remit in providing community education, as well as offering part-time exam courses and evening classes. For school leavers, there are some opportunities on the island to learn a job or trade, but others attending training school or university overseas, some on a scholarship basis.

In recent years, a combination of shrinking school rolls and low salary levels has created considerable educational challenges. While many of the teachers are still Saints, teachers have had to be brought in from overseas to make up for the shortfall caused by the departure of local teachers for better-paid jobs offshore.

## RELIGION

Many Saints have strong, if varied, religious views; less than 1% profess no faith at all, which is perhaps appropriate as St Helena was known for her piety. For such a small population, there is an extraordinarily broad range of churches: Anglican, Baptist, Catholic, Salvation Army, Jehovah's Witness, Seventh-Day Adventist, New Apostolic and Baha'I. Details of services are published in the weekly *Sentinel*.

That said, the majority of people belong to the Anglican Church within the Diocese of St Helena. Established in 1859, the diocese now includes the islands of Ascension and Tristan da Cunha, but until 1869 also embraced the British residents of Rio de Janeiro and other towns on the eastern seaboard of South America, as well as the Falklands. The Bishop of St Helena resides on the island, administering to 11 churches in four parishes. The Baptists were introduced to St Helena in 1845 by a Scottish evangelist from the Cape, who purchased a Baptist mission house a year later; by 1854, there were four Baptist churches here. Catholicism arrived at the same time, with a succession of Catholic priests since 1852, many initially sent to St Helena as military chaplains.

## CULTURE

The Saints are a sociable people. Dances, festivals, pageants, fundraisers: all are well attended, with considerable enthusiasm and plenty of noise and spectacle.

On the music scene, country and western is a perennial favourite, as you'll soon find out if you're close to any of the pubs or clubs on a Friday or Saturday night, but local rock bands are in the mix too. Amongst them is the local Gettogethers, which plays at various functions.

While St Helena doesn't have any great literary tradition, it does have in Basil George a thought-provoking poet, some of whose work was published to coincide with the Commonwealth Games in 2014. Basil also writes children's books (page 192).

## SPORT

Cricket, football, skittles, golf, rifle shooting: sport on St Helena is pretty mixed and very popular, even if facilities are limited.

Francis Plain is the home of most team games, including **football** – played in two divisions from June to November – and a highly competitive **cricket** league made up of eight teams. While the carpet wicket may not be up to the turf you would find in South Africa or England, the standard of play is pretty high. Regular fixtures are played at weekends.

**Golf** is popular, too (page 76), as is **skittles** – a form of bowling using wooden pins and rubber balls. It might sound a lot of fun, but if you decide to participate in a skittles match on the RMS, don't underestimate the competitive nature of the Saints.

On the **water**, fishing (pages 79–80) is a source of both pleasure and income for some islanders. Sailing, while relatively low key on the island, is important in terms of two international races: the bi-annual Governor's Cup between Cape Town and St Helena (page 79), and the annual World ARC rally, a 15-month round-the-world event following the tradewinds that takes in St Helena.

St Helenians became involved in **international sport** in 1985 when they participated in the newly organised Island Games held on the Isle of Man. The Governor's Discretionary Fund as well as voluntary donations and various fundraising activities helped send a team of athletes and a manager to the inaugural games, when a 100m runner from St Helena won a bronze medal. Two years later, another team was sent to the games on Guernsey, but financial constraints prevented further participation until 1997, when funds were raised by people on the island of Jersey. Since then, with the help of numerous fundraising initiatives on the island, a small team of Saints has competed regularly in the bi-annual games, and in 2015, again in Jersey, a team of ten participated in shooting, swimming, athletics and golf events.

On a bigger stage, the 2014 Commonwealth Games in Glasgow saw a much-heralded team from St Helena compete in swimming, shooting, badminton and athletics, and in September 2015, young Saint competitors were set to take part in the Commonwealth Youth Games in Samoa.

1

# 2

# Natural History and Conservation

## FLORA  *with David Sayers*

More than any other of the world's isolated oceanic islands, St Helena is most famously associated with rare and endemic plants, thanks to well-documented conservation work by the WWF (World Wide Fund for Nature), the Royal Botanic Gardens at Kew and other organisations. Plant species have been pulled back from the very brink of extinction, and the island is a showcase for the international conservation role of botanic gardens.

That said, almost from the moment that the first man set foot on land some 500 years ago, destruction of the original vegetation began. Today, barely 1% of the indigenous forest is left, almost all on Diana's Peak ridge. Some 60% of the island is now bare, eroded rock, colonised in places by a few tough alien plant species.

Although much of the interior of the island remains green, this is largely due to imported exotic vegetation: over the years, more than 1,000 plants have been introduced. Many have brought welcome colour and balance to garden environments, but others – such as New Zealand flax (*Phormium tenax*) and whiteweed (*Austroeupatorum inulifolium*) – have proved to be botanical thugs, invading areas where endemic plants are hanging on, and preventing these less-hardy plants from retaining – or regaining – a foothold.

**HISTORY** Approaching the island and seeing today's bare rocky cliffs ascending from the sea, one can only conjecture as to how these impressive cliffs appeared to the first Portuguese who landed here in the early 1500s. There are no contemporary descriptions of the native vegetation, and destruction of the forests was rapid. It was not until 1771, when Captain James Cook's *Endeavour* called at the island on the way back from Australia, that the discovery of St Helena's botany really took off. On board were the great naturalists, Banks and Solander, who collected many specimens and brought them back to Europe.

Most of the native forests had already been well cleared earlier in the 18th century, before their visit, so there are no scientific accounts of the flora as it was originally. By carefully looking at historical references in various sources, allied with knowledge of the distribution of the indigenous flora from the few remaining locations, botanists today have been able to picture what the island might have been like. Much of the now barren rocks towards sea level would have been covered with scrubwood (*Commidendrum rugosum*) and ebony (*Trochetiopsis ebenus*). Above these, from about 1,300ft (400m) to 2,000ft (600m), a low forest of gumwood (*Commidendrum robustum*), with a canopy height of about 6m, would have covered the island with other associated species. Between 2,000ft (600m) and 2,500ft (750m) you would have had to ascend through a woodland of cabbage trees – the false gumwood

(*Commidendrum spurium*), the she cabbage tree (*Lachanodes arborea*), whitewood (*Petrobium arboreum*), redwood (*Trochetiopsis erythroxylon*), now extinct in the wild, and finally the he cabbage tree (*Pladaroxylon leucadendron*) – before emerging between 2,300ft and 2,600ft (700–800m) into a landscape dominated by the endemic tree fern (*Dicksonia arborescens*). We know the species that have become extinct since scientific records began; what we cannot know is how many more species became extinct before this, although it is estimated that they numbered around 70 or more.

With no natural browsing animals on St Helena, most of the endemic plants evolved without the ability to regenerate. If they were nibbled, for example, there was no chance of the shoots resprouting. Even the grasses fall into this category, making them extremely vulnerable to introduced mammals.

Yet today, in spite of the ravages caused by humans and their animals, there remain extant in tiny, isolated and often almost inaccessible refuges, around 45 endemic species (including ten genera) of ferns and flowering plants that occur naturally only on St Helena and nowhere else in the world. Some of them have grown on St Helena for more than eight million years, surviving while their relatives on distant landmasses became extinct through climate change.

So, how did St Helena, with an unspoiled environment, so quickly change by human incursion into one of the world's most spectacularly eroded islands?

For voyagers into largely unknown seas and facing numerous hazards, this island was understandably viewed as a source of supplies on a very long voyage. Although the Portuguese did not establish any permanent settlement, they planted large numbers of fruit trees, especially lemons, limes and oranges, and introduced pigs and, significantly, goats. These animals are the curse of botanists the world over, for their appetites are voracious; they bred well and quickly and at one time were said to be in their thousands. Culinary herbs and vegetables were also brought, such as parsley, fennel, mint and purslane, melon and pumpkin that thrived and spread, alongside the various weeds unwittingly introduced. It must have seemed a paradise garden to the sailors, a mid-ocean supply of fresh fruit and herbs, and abundant meat for the shooting. Indeed, as sea traffic increased with the development of trade, it later became the equivalent of a motorway café on the run between the East Indies, the Cape and Europe.

From 1588, with the ascendance of Dutch and British naval power, these two nations continued where the Portuguese left off, except that they took what was there and ceased to care for the plantations. As a consequence, produce and pigs declined and the Dutch came to prefer their new Cape of Good Hope settlement, established in 1652.

When the East India Company annexed the island in 1659, they promptly encouraged settlement and change accelerated as the remaining forests were felled for fuel, or their bark used for tanning leather, or cleared for pasture. They also introduced seeds of plants, such as various grasses, English oak, and gorse (*Ulex europaeus*), for fuel wood and hedging.

Early houses were of a simple design, made of roughly dressed volcanic rock, usually bound with a mud or lime mortar mixed with the cut leaves of hair grass (*Eragrostis saxatalis*). This is now one of St Helena's rare endemics, found only on inaccessible cliffs and rocky places, but must once have been widespread. The roof was thatched with an indigenous sedge (*Scirpus nodosus*). Native timbers known to have been used in house construction included redwood (*Trochetiopsis erythroxylon*), she cabbage (*Lachanodes arborea*), he cabbage (*Pladaroxylon leucadendron*), black cabbage (*Melanodendron integrifolium*), and gumwood (*Commidendrum robustum*), all endemic species.

By 1700, a serious timber shortage had been created by the overuse of the native forests, but another 50 years had to pass before the introduction of the first successful timber-producing species, the maritime pine (*Pinus pinaster*), a native of the Mediterranean region which today may be seen planted in many parts of the world. When Joseph Banks returned to London he influenced the establishment of a small botanic garden on the island, located on a site below the present hospital in Jamestown; the large Indian fig trees are its most obvious legacy. This was simply another link in what became an empire-wide chain of gardens designed to facilitate the import and exchange of useful plants. New introductions came from the Calcutta Botanic Gardens, Kirstenbosch Botanic Garden in Cape Town, the Royal Botanic Gardens at Kew, and other colonies, and included grapefruit, coffee, quinine (*Cinchona succirubra*), sugar and many others.

Either by accident or by intent, other species were introduced that escaped and became dreadful weeds, such as Madagascar's attractive endemic butterfly bush (*Buddleja madagascariensis*) and the South American bugweed (*Solanum mauritianum*), a poisonous plant known locally as bilberry, and now seemingly in every corner of the world. From a legacy of plant introduction during the past 500 years there are now some 276 species firmly naturalised on the island. These have not only created new vegetation types on the lands previously cleared of native forest, but they also seriously compete with what little remains of the native flora and further threaten its survival. The goats that at one time were numbered in their thousands were, after many attempts, finally controlled in the 1960s, so at last allowing the vegetation to begin to regenerate.

**THE PRESENT VEGETATION COVER** Again, beginning at sea level with those bare and eroded hillsides, one may find the Hottentot fig (*Carpobrotus edulis*), an evergreen succulent ground creeper from South Africa that can form extensive patches with large, quite spectacular, flowers and edible fruit. Also to be found are its Cape relative, the ice plant (*Mesembryanthemum crystallinum*), another succulent but with tiny pink flowers, and the pretty Madagascar periwinkle (*Cantharantus roseus*), or Venus rose, all now pan-tropical weeds.

At higher elevation, but before you reach the good agricultural land, there is a scrub zone dominated in different places by different species; perhaps prickly pear (*Opuntia* spp.) or elsewhere Brazilian mastic (*Schinus terebinthifolius*), with its showy holly-like berries, or that dreadful red-and-yellow weed, lantana (*Lantana camara*), a Mexican plant much loved by gardeners with conservatories in cold countries. Other common species include the tree tobacco (*Nicotiana glauca*), the sweet pittosporum (*Pittosporum undulatum*), the wild olive (*Olea africana*) and more. The cultivated landscape includes grasslands of introduced species, mostly kikuyu grass (*Pennisetum clandestinum*), in the moister areas, while the woodlands are of pine species.

Unmissable are the extensive areas of pure New Zealand flax (*Phormium tenax*); its successful naturalisation and aggression probably identifies it as the greatest killer of what was left of the indigenous flora. During the late 19th and into the following century, it was widely planted on the central ridge to produce fibre for cordage and sacking, and was the island's main industry until the 1960s. Finally, and above 2,300ft (700m) or so, are the few hectares of what remains of the tree-fern thicket and cabbage tree woodland, the vegetation that covered the high central ridge and particularly Diana's Peak and High Peak. Here one finds endemic dogwood (*Nesohedyotis arborea*), black cabbage (*Melanodendron integrifolium*), and whitewood (*Petrobium arborea*). Even here, though, New Zealand flax threatens, along with other invaders, including the trailing fuschia (*Fuchsia coccinea*).

**ENDEMIC FLORA** Although many of St Helena's endemic plants are now extinct, the island still boasts at least 45 species unknown anywhere else in the world, most of them related to the daisy family. The exact number is hard to quantify, though, as the occasional variety of these 'extinct' plants will be found, sometimes quite unexpectedly. The St Helena olive (*Nesota elliptica*), for example, was found in 1977, and the endemic flowering shrub, the dwarf ebony (*Trochetiopsis ebeneus*), believed to have been extinct for over a century, was 'rediscovered' in 1980. As recently as 2009 came the rediscovery in the wild of the bastard gumwood (*Commidendrum rotundifolium*).

Very rare and often extremely slow growing, the endemics are protected by law and you should take great care to minimise your impact upon them and their habitat. Indeed, unless you have a serious interest in botany, these rare plants are better and certainly more easily seen in protected areas such as the Millennium Forest and the George Benjamin Arboretum.

Places that are inaccessible to humans and goats still support many of the rarities, so that any cliff vegetation is always worth scanning carefully to see what you might recognise or see in flower. Content yourself with binoculars, however, since attempts at closer inspection can be hazardous. Peak Dale is a good place to see gumwoods, and hikers on Diana's Peak may see species that include tree ferns (*Dicksonia arborescens*), black cabbage tree (*Melanodendron integrifolium*), he cabbage tree (*Pladaroxylon leucadendron*) and the she cabbage tree (*Lachanodes arborea*), along with ferns, mosses, grass and other rare endemics.

Details of 25 of the key endemics are included below.

**Babies' toes** (*Hydrodea cryptantha*/Aizoaceae) Large numbers of babies' toes still thrive on St Helena, mostly in barren, arid and rocky areas such as Sandy Bay, Turk's Cap and Prosperous Bay Plain. Sometimes these plants can be found right up to the sea's edge. A distant relative of the more common 'creeper' (or Hottentot fig), this is a small plant adapted to growing in very dry conditions. It stores water within its tissues, giving the stems and leaves a fleshy appearance. When the young plants first appear after the winter rains, from July to August, they are bright green in colour, turning yellow with age and finally drying up around November to December as the weather becomes hotter. Small flowers, which appear around August to September, are much like those of the ice plant, also a distant relative and a very common species on St Helena. A single plant seldom spreads more than 15in (38cm) in diameter, and reaches only 1–2in (2–5cm) in height. The plant is so succulent that it will not support its own weight, so it spreads across the ground in a compact mass.

**Bellflowers** (Campanulaceae) There were once four species of bellflower endemic to St Helena, of which two are now extinct. Of the remaining two, the endangered **large bellflower** (*Wahlenbergia linifolia*) has a habit of spreading and can reach a height of about 20in (50cm). It has long narrow leaves up to 2in (5cm) in length that are slightly edged with notched, tooth-like projections. The flowers are white, bell-shaped and a little less than 1in (2.5cm) in diameter. Flowering occurs all year round with the main flowering period in the months of July and August.

The large bellflower naturally grows out of the live trunks of tree ferns and cabbage trees, but is also found on exposed cliff sites. It once grew commonly amongst the tree ferns of the Peaks, and in the mid 1800s Melliss recorded it as quite common on the Sandy Bay side of the ridges. He even commented on how well its white flowers contrasted with the red flowers of the fuchsia, a species which had escaped from people's gardens after being introduced to the island. Today, instead of large bellflowers growing out from the trunks of the tree ferns and cabbage trees, it is the fuchsia that grows in great profusion and has become a serious weed on the Peaks.

In the mid 1800s, Melliss described the **small bellflower** (*Wahlenbergia angustifolia*) as 'quite rare', but today it grows abundantly in many different areas, usually at altitudes of 1,800–2,400ft (600–800m). A small creeping plant, it can be seen growing in rock crevices and along grass verges at the roadside. It is similar to the large bellflower except that it is much more spreading in habit. The narrow leaves are a little less than 1in (2.5cm) in length and can also be slightly serrated. The small, white, bell-shaped flowers are ½in (12mm) in diameter and can appear almost all year round, although the main flowering months are July to August. The small bellflower can be found growing at Man and Horse Cliffs, Peak Dale, Deep Valley and many other sites around the island.

**Boneseed** (*Osteospermum sanctae-helenae*/Asteraceae) A rough hairy herb with thin straggling stems that creep along the ground, boneseed has long narrow grey-green leaves. Unlike most of the endemics, the flowers are yellow, about ½in (12mm) in diameter and daisy-like. The fruit is star-shaped. The seeds are less than ¹⁄₁₀in (2mm) long, and are hard, angular and sticky due to the short hairs which cover them. Boneseed grows in the very dry outer parts of the island, generally between 160ft and 820ft (50–250m) above sea level, but occasionally as high as 1,800ft (550m). It appears after the onset of the winter rain in July and August, then grows quickly to produce flowers and then seed, before dying back in the summer.

Little is known about the history of this species, which was described as 'not uncommon' by Melliss in 1875, but 'very rare' by Kerr in 1970. Small populations of boneseed can be found around the Sandy Bay area between the old lime kiln and Lot's Wife's Ponds. Other sightings are recorded in Turk's Cap Valley, near Flagstaff, Bencoolen, the Asses Ears, and South West Cliffs. The plants spread down the slopes, often down small, steep 'guts'. They grow alongside a mixture of native species – babies' toes, French grass, salad plant and samphire – and exotic species, including ice plant, creeper, Venus rose and atriplex.

**Boxwood** (*Mellissia begoniifolia*/Solanaceae) The St Helena boxwood, until recently thought to be extinct, once grew on the southeastern side of the island, at Long Range and Great Stone Top. In early 1998, a single boxwood was found growing near Lot's Wife. The number of plants at this site fluctuates from year to year, and although seed has been collected and germinated successfully, the species remains on the brink of extinction.

The boxwood grows to a height of about 8ft (2.5m), its crooked, branching stems seldom exceeding 2in (5cm) in thickness. It flowers through most of the year, but the flowers are hidden under the leaves and are barely visible without lifting them up.

**Cabbage trees** (Asteraceae) Members of the daisy family, the four species of cabbage tree are all shade lovers, but have very different characteristics.

The most common is the **black cabbage tree** (*Melanodendron integrifolium*), a spreading tree with a trunk that's permanently moist and usually supporting a dense growth of mosses, lichens and ferns, giving it a dark appearance. Once it grew possibly to 26ft (8m) tall, but present generations are 13ft (4m) at most. The smooth dark green leaves are thick and fleshy and crowded towards the end of the branches, having an appearance similar to cabbages. During October and November, daisy-like flowers about ½in (12mm) across are borne in clusters on the ends of the branches, surrounded by the leaves. The seeds germinate well on the tree ferns in the moist habitat of the peaks. As the cabbage tree grows, it is supported by the ferns; although its weight eventually causes the ferns to fall over, both continue to grow, demonstrating their interdependence.

The black cabbage once grew in great abundance amongst the tree-fern thicket (*Dicksonia arborescens*) of the island's central ridge, at altitudes between 2,300ft and 2,700ft (700–820m) above sea level. Numbers have declined considerably as a result of clearance of natural vegetation and the invasion of alien plant species, in particular flax. The black cabbage can today be found scattered across The Peaks National Park.

Fast-growing and quickly maturing, the **she cabbage tree** (*Lachanodes arborea*) has a slender, upright habit. Within ten years it can grow up to a height of 24ft (7.5m). It has a single, unbranched stem up to 9ft (3m) tall with very large leaves clustered on the top, much like a cabbage. As the tree ages it begins to branch.

Before 1977, the she cabbage was considered quite rare, or possibly even extinct in the wild. In 1977, however, a group of mature trees was discovered within a hedge line of thorn trees (*Erythrina caffra*). Surrounded by pastureland, the trees were growing in grass, along with a number of exotic trees and scrubs, instead of surrounded by other endemics (tree ferns, redwoods and false gumwoods) in a moist rich organic soil. Over the next three decades, many died, and those few trees that survived were suffering from attack by the Lepidopteran moth larvae. It is not yet clear whether this is the primary cause of death in the trees, as it is possible that they are initially attacked by a fungus or bacteria. Reintroduced populations of she cabbage can be found at the beginning of the Diana's Peak Postbox walk, as well as at the George Benjamin Arboretum, the Clifford Arboretum, Napoleon's tomb and other locations.

The **he cabbage tree** (*Pladaroxylon leucadendron*) is a small, spreading tree growing to a height of 10–13ft (3–4m) with a characteristic di- or trichotamous branching habit, and grey-green bark. The leaves are longer than they are wide and are clustered towards the end of each branch and vary greatly in size, growing up to about 12in (30cm) in length. They are pale green and rougher than those of the black cabbage and have slightly toothed edges with very prominent veins. The white composite flowers, appearing from June to August, form terminal clusters on the branches, resembling the head of a cauliflower.

The he cabbage was once abundant amongst the cabbage tree woodland, growing alongside whitewoods and she cabbages, but is

now considered to be very rare. The few trees that survive today can be found growing within The Peaks National Park.

The smallest of the cabbage trees, the **whitewood** (*Petrobium arboreum*) also grows up to 10–13ft (3–4m). It is more upright and less spreading than the black cabbage tree, with smaller leaves. Borne in opposite pairs, these are up to 3in (7cm) long, broadly oval in shape and with a slightly serrated edge. The young leaves appear bronze in colour. The flowerheads are borne at the ends of the branches in groups of six to eight, with male and female flowers on different individual trees. The flowers, each about ⅓in (8mm) across, have a composite structure of ten to 12 white florets. Flowering occurs from March to June.

The whitewood is mainly restricted to remaining areas of high-altitude vegetation within The Peaks National Park, growing among tree ferns, cabbage trees and dogwoods. A widely scattered species, like the dogwood, it is primarily threatened by the fragmentation and degradation of its original habitat. Specimen trees have also been planted in the George Benjamin Arboretum.

**Dogwood** (*Nesohedyotis arborea*/Rubiaceae) The dogwood is a species of the tree-fern thicket and can be found growing at the highest elevations on the island, alongside tree ferns, black cabbage trees, whitewoods and ferns. It is a small, often multi-stemmed tree up to 10ft (3m) tall with upright branches and leaves with a down-turned drip-tip. It forms a dense, spreading canopy that is able to catch the mist quite often surrounding the Peaks, which then drips from the leaf tips on to the ground. The leaves are lance-shaped, smooth and glossy green in colour. The flower-cluster is found at the tips of the branches and made up of many small bunches of greenish-white flowers measuring only about ¹⁄₁₀in (2–4mm) across. These trees bear either male or female flowers and hence the dogwood is dioecious. Flowering takes place from December through to March. The fruit is a small dark brown capsule. Like many of St Helena's endemic plants, the dogwood was named for its resemblance to a common European species, in this case the European dogwood, but it is not in any way related to it.

The dogwood is the second most common tree species left on the Peaks after the black cabbage. More than 300 specimens can be found growing within The Peaks National Park,

**Ebony** (*Trochetiopsis ebenus*/Sterculiaceae) According to historical records, the ebony was once an abundant tree on the southwestern parts of St Helena but grazing goats largely caused its demise. Occasionally dead wood or roots may still be found exposed by periodic rains, or a piece of the once-prized wood washed up on the southwestern shores. Destruction of the ebony was so immense that in some places, dead stumps were soon all that remained, and these in turn were then used for the burning of

lime. By 1850, the tree was finally assumed to be
extinct. In November 1980, however, a small
bush was rediscovered by George Benjamin
on the cliff between Lot's Wife and the Asses
Ears. Cuttings were successfully rooted
and from these, thousands of plants now
thrive, including at High Peak and in the
Millennium Forest.

Records show that the ebony once grew
to a height of up to 15ft (5m), but currently
it grows more in the style of a low-spreading
shrub, with horizontal stems. The leaves are
heart-shaped, longer than broad, with brown hairs on the underside.
The flowers are large, 3in (8cm) when open, bell-shaped, white with a dark centre
and spreading widely from the stem. They appear throughout the year, peaking
from June to August. As the flower ages, it turns pink before forming a seed
pod. The flowers are not to be confused with those of the similar-looking rebony
(*Trochetiopsis* x *benjaminii*), a cross between the ebony and the redwood, which
have a purple centre.

**Gumwoods** (Asteraceae) There are place names on the
island which give a strong indication of the once plentiful
forests of which the gumwood was the dominant
species: Deadwood, Longwood, Bottom Woods,
Levelwood, Woody Ridge, Woody Point,
Woodlands, Gumwoods and Thompson's
Wood. Indeed, gumwood woodland
once stretched across approximately a
third of the island, along the mid-altitude
zone from 1,200ft to 1,800ft (400–600m).

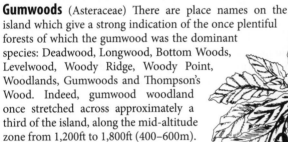

Like all the original woodland trees, the
**gumwood** (*Commidendrum robustum*),
at 26ft (8m), was once much taller than it
grows now. It has a branching structure, forking low and producing an umbrella-like
canopy. Its gnarled and crooked stems and domed crown make this a distinctive and
picturesque tree, popular for sketching. The leaves are 3–4in (7–10cm) long and vary
from grey-green to dark green on the top, with a white cottony appearance below.
They are thick and hairy, giving a wrinkled appearance, and are borne in tight whorls.
Flowerheads are off-white, on a long drooping stalk at the ends of the branches, and
are usually borne during winter and spring. Seeds germinate freely to produce a
carpet of seedlings under the canopy of the parent plants.

Almost all the original gumwoods have been destroyed through grazing and
collection of firewood. The awkward location of most of the remaining trees,
growing close to or actually out of the cliffs, has probably contributed to their
survival. Then, in 1991, the Peak Dale gumwoods were attacked by the jacaranda
bug (*Orthezia insignis*), which swept through the population, killing hundreds of
trees. The jacaranda, which looks a little like a whitefly, is a sucking insect that takes
the sap from the tree. A black sooty mould covers the branches, attracted by the
honeydew produced by the bugs. Fortunately, a ladybird, *Hyperaspis pantherina*,
introduced from Kenya, brought the infestation under control, although it has not
been eliminated altogether.

Very similar to the gumwood, the **bastard gumwood** (*Commidendrum rotundifolium*) is smaller in height. None of the trees known today are taller than 10ft (3m) and all have weak growth. The leaves are of a mid-green colour and are about 2–3in (5–7cm) long. Flowering is throughout the year. The flowering heads form in clusters between the leaves near to the ends of the branches. They are whitish, turning brown with age.

A single bastard gumwood was known to have grown at Black Field, Longwood, in 1868, but after the death of this tree, the species was thought to have become extinct. In 1982, however, a single tree was discovered by Stedson Stroud, growing out of a cliff close to Horse Pasture, and was identified by the island's resident botany expert, George Benjamin. The tree died in 1986, but not before a cutting and seedlings had been raised. Although the cutting, too, died – it has now been determined that the tree is not self-fertile – seedlings were successfully planted. Then, in 2009, a further wild specimen was identified on a cliff face near the beginning of the South West Point Walk.

A third species, the **false gumwood** (*Commidendrum spurium*), was once common in moist gumwood woodland, growing at altitudes of about 1,500–2,000ft (500–650m) above sea level. Another small tree, reaching a height of 10ft (3m), it has a branching pattern like that of the other gumwood species. The leaves, which are light green and slightly hairy, form clusters at the ends of the branches and are toothed. The flowerhead is densely packed with tiny petals (ray florets) and a yellow-green centre (disc florets). Flowering occurs from December through to March or April.

By 1875, the false gumwood was recorded as 'very rare' by Melliss, and only about six trees now survive in the wild, in the centre of the island. The false gumwood appears to have few practical uses, so its rarity is probably due to loss of habitat. Fortunately, the tree does not appear to have reproductive problems – over 2,000 seedlings have been raised to date!

## Jellicos (Apiaceae) These two umbelliferous plants vary considerably. The beautiful **jellico** (*Berula bracteata*) grows to a height of 6–9ft (2–3m). It has thick, fleshy, hollow green stems, and spreading compound leaves about 3ft (1m) long with many spike-edged leaves. The flowers are borne at the tops of the plant in a large spreading umbel of many hundreds of small white flowers, which produce small green fruit. Flowering usually occurs in December but, depending on weather conditions, it may flower at different periods.

The large jellico can be found in several 'guts' on the Peaks, and is often the dominant vegetation type where it is present. These stalk-like plants most probably once grew abundantly, but have declined due to the invasive growth of flax and bilberry on Diana's Peak and High Peak and along the central ridge. The stems of this plant were once eaten raw by the islanders and could be bought at the local market.

By contrast, the **dwarf jellico** (*Berula burchellii*) grows only to some 24in (60cm) in height. It, too, has thick, fleshy, hollow green stems, but its compound leaves reach only 12in (30cm) in length. The flower bears umbels of white flowers, which produce small green fruit in December. Seeds are fertile and sometimes fall on to the tree ferns, where they germinate freely.

This plant was recorded as being 'very rare' in 1875, but there are scattered populations still growing in the wild in The Peaks National Park and on Sandy Bay Ridge.

## Old father live forever (*Pelargonium cotyledonis*/Geraniaceae) Named by St Helenians because of its ability to stay alive for months without either soil or

water, the perennial old father live forever is related to the garden geranium. It grows up to 12in (30cm) with gnarled, chocolate-brown, fleshy rough-barked, often prostrate stems, and roundish, heart-shaped leaves clustered at the branch tips. It is sometimes difficult to distinguish it from the rock upon which it grows.

The plants can be leafless for much of the year. White flowers, up to 1in (25mm) across, first appear after the summer rains, about May or June, when the stems are still leafless. The leaves, which are light green, rounded and thick, sometimes hairy underneath, die away so that for much of the year they resemble a knotted mass of old fir tree roots. Old father live forever produces pointed fruit and small seeds which disperse in the wind.

Old father live forever occurs naturally in the dry outer parts of the island, often in the most inaccessible places where little or no other vegetation grows. Other endemic species with which it is associated are the tea plant, plantain, salad plant, scrubwood and hair grass. There are a number of patches of old father live forever on the rocky cliffs at South West Point, the Asses Ears and Turk's Cap. The plant is regenerating naturally in small, scattered populations and, since the removal of goats from the Crown Wastes, numbers appear to be recovering.

**Redwood** (*Trochetiopsis erythroxylon*/Sterculiaceae) When St Helena was first discovered, redwoods were growing in large numbers in upland areas below the tree-fern thicket. They grew with a straight trunk, resulting in a medium-sized tree of about 20ft (6m) tall. Today redwoods grow only to about 10ft (3m), some with a straight trunk but others considerably dwarfed and misshapen. The leaves are pale green, about 3in (7cm) long and about 2in (5cm) wide. Older leaves quickly turn yellow and speckled and fall to the ground. Although flowers can be produced throughout the year, the main flowering season is in November. They are about 3in (7cm) long and open up to 2in (5cm) in diameter and hang down from the tree. At first they are pure white, turning pink with age, until eventually the dying flower turns a deep red.

The redwood was the most valuable endemic tree to settlers on the island because it produced a fine hard grain timber and its bark was used for tanning the hides of cattle. Very quickly, nearly all the trees were cut down or stripped of bark, which resulted in near-extinction as early as 1718. Since then, redwoods have remained very rare, being recorded only near Diana's Peak and High Peak. By the 20th century, just a single redwood tree was growing near High Peak, and today the tree is extinct in the wild.

**St Helena lobelia** (*Trimeris scaevolifolia*/Campanulaceae) This fleshy-stemmed shrub has thin, conspicuously scarred leaves about 3in (7cm) long, with both leaves and stem a bright light-green colour. The white flowers with a yellow centre and are about 1in (25cm) in diameter and may be present through much of the year, through rarely in the summer.

In 1875, there was an abundance of this plant on the central ridge from High Peak to Diana's Peak, but numbers have considerably declined and today the lobelia is found only in small scattered patches on the Peaks.

**St Helena plantain** (*Plantago robusta*/Plantaginaceae) Related to the ground plantain (*Plantago major*), the St Helena plantain is a rare and very localised species. Considered the largest of the plantains, it varies in size from 6in (15cm) to over 3ft (1m) long. The plant forms a rosette with narrow, strap-like leaves up to 16in (40cm) long. When the flower stalk rises from the centre of the rosette, it resembles a thick rat's tail, clustered with many small, insignificant, green flowers, which appear throughout the year, but less so in summer. Small, round fruit are produced containing minute, flat seeds. It grows in the drier parts of the island, mainly in the far southwestern corners, in loose soil, on rocky outcrops and in crevices, and is associated with plants such as the tea plant and scrubwood.

**St Helena rosemary** (*Phylica polifolia*/Rhamnaceae) The St Helena rosemary, a straggling or upright herb, resembles the British herb from which it takes its name. The leaves are bright green on top, with dense white hairs on the reverse giving them a silvery appearance. Small, green, inconspicuous flowers are borne for much of the year, followed by round green fruit, about the size of a pea, which turn black when mature. The fruit contains viable seeds.

The St Helena rosemary is one of the island's most endangered plants. It has been recorded growing wild at Lot amongst wild mango, scrubwood and the cabbage palm fern (*Phlebodium aureum*), and other bushes grow at High Hill Cliffs amongst the fir trees (*Pinus pinaster*), gobblegheer, wild coffee, wild carrot, cow grass, bilberry, small bellflower, hair grass and ferns.

**St Helena salad plant** (*Hypertelis acida*/Aizoaceae) The salad plant, or Longwood samphire, is named for its succulent leaves, which have a salty acid flavour. A small, low-growing bushy plant, it survives in the hot dry conditions of the coastal zone, and is associated with scrubwood, tea plant, creeper and ice plant. It grows to about 8in (20cm) tall, but can reach up to 3ft (1m) in diameter. The succulent, slightly swollen leaves are about 2in (5cm) long and bluish-grey in colour. Pure white flowers with yellow centres are borne from July to September in groups of two to three at the top of the 3–4in (7–10cm) flower stem.

A few scattered populations of salad plants grow in rocky, inaccessible areas of the southern cliffs between the Asses Ears and Great Stone Top. Although there is no immediate threat to them, their habitat makes them vulnerable to natural events like rockfalls and landslides.

**St Helena tea plant** (*Frankenia portulacaefolia*/Frankeniaceae) Despite the name, there are no records of this plant ever having been used as a substitute for tea, but its tiny round leaves turn brown with age and fall to the ground, resembling dried tea leaves. A crooked, wiry-stemmed plant, it is brittle with branching stems, and grows to a height of 3–5ft (1–1.5m). Small white flowers often cover the bush and produce minute seeds. The wood is hard when dried and mahogany in colour.

Small populations grow in the wild at The Barn, Gregory's Battery, Turk's Cap and Prosperous Bay, as well as along the cliffs of Man and Horse, where they are supported by hair grass and scrubwoods. Like other dry-land species, the tea plant is starting to regenerate naturally, although the small size of these isolated populations and the low rate of seed germination poses a threat to their future survival.

**Scrubwood** (*Commidendrum rugosum*/Asteraceae) This long-surviving shrub can tolerate both the semi-desert climate and the saline soils of the Crown Wastes – St Helena's eroded coastal regions – where its ability to capture moisture from the sea mist allows it to grow out from the sheer cliffs. A low-spreading shrub, it grows to about 3ft (1m) in height and is often wider than it is tall. The branches are dark brown in colour and are scattered with leaf scars left after older leaves have fallen. The toothed leaves are somewhat sticky and grow up to 2in (5cm) long in tight rosettes. When they fall under the protective branched canopy, they provide a mulch that helps to develop the scrubwood's own pocket of soil. Large, white and yellow, daisy-like flowers, about 1in (2.5cm) in diameter, are borne at the tips of the branches almost throughout the year. With age they become tinged with red.

In earlier days, scrubwoods would have survived in large numbers throughout the dry outer parts of the island, growing among the ebony, tea plant, old father live forever, plantain and salad plant. Today only fragments of the larger populations survive, including at Man and Horse Cliffs and Great Stone Top, still growing beside other endemics with the exception of the ebonies. The scrubwood has been the most successful of all endemic plants to recover in numbers. Several populations are naturally regenerating, from Flagstaff to the cliffs of the southwest.

**Tree fern** (*Dicksonia arborescens*/Cyathaceae) The tree fern is very easy to recognise as it is the only fern on the island with a distinct trunk, from the top of which grow fronds, giving a rather palm-like appearance. The trunk, which is covered with hair-like roots, is 6–8in (15–20cm) in diameter and grows 16–20ft (4–6m) in height. The fronds are dark green and over 3ft (1m) long. When young, the plant is hairy and looks like a monkey's tail. Fallen tree-fern trunks can sprout along their length to form new growth.

Tree ferns once formed a thicket covering St Helena's highest peaks, up to 2,690ft (820m) above sea level. Small pockets and isolated tree ferns can still be seen along the roadside, particularly along the ridges of Sandy Bay and in the Cason's area. Although the plant is not threatened, in 1995 it was estimated that tree-fern thicket was being lost at a rate of 5½ yards (5m) a year, mainly because of the invasion of flax, wild fuchsia and bilberry, but today it is gradually being replanted along the central ridge.

## FAUNA

The first Portuguese who explored the island found an abundance of seabirds, sea-lions, seals and turtles, but no strictly land animals. Today, the fauna on the island largely comprises introduced species: cattle, sheep, goats, donkeys, cats, dogs, rabbits, mice, rats and various types of fowl. There are no snakes, but there is one type of frog, which was probably introduced to St Helena along with the mynah birds in 1885 by Miss Phoebe Moss, a naturalist. There is, however, a good variety of endemic invertebrate fauna, including some particularly interesting examples of their types.

**BIRDS** The only remaining bird that is indigenous to St Helena – now critically endangered with a population of around 400 – is the wirebird. All other native species of birds died out long ago at the hand of rats, cats and humans, and the environmental changes that these brought to the island. Although they can be just as interesting to observe for the avid birdwatcher, all other birds now to be seen were introduced to the island from overseas.

**Wirebird** (*Charadrius sanctae-helenae; 8in/20cm*) The critically endangered St Helena plover, or 'wirebird' as it is more popularly known, is St Helena's only surviving endemic bird, one of at least six species that once lived only on this remote island. A small, long-legged, grey-brown plover with white underparts and a black mask extending to the sides of the neck, the wirebird prefers flat areas of short grassland with patches of bare ground. They eat mainly caterpillars, beetles and snails. They breed throughout the year, but most nesting occurs during the drier months, from October to March. They usually lay two eggs at a time.

Over the years, wirebirds have suffered significantly from three major threats: habitat degradation caused by reduced cattle grazing, the proliferation of invasive plants, and predation, especially by feral cats. By 2006, the population had been reduced to just 220 adults. It was only in 2008, with the introduction of an intensive monitoring programme by the St Helena National Trust (SHNT), with the backing of the Royal Society for the Protection of Birds (RSPB), that this downward trend started to level out. Key to the programme was the establishment of a trial pasture restoration project on Deadwood Plain, one of the main breeding sites for the wirebird. Fencing was repaired, invasive weeds removed, feral cats controlled during the breeding season, and a properly managed pattern of grazing formulated. By 2015, with careful monitoring, the wirebird population had stabilised at more than 430 adults. During that year, five 'important wirebird areas' – Deadwood Plain, Bottom Woods, Upper Prosperous, Man and Horse and Broad Bottom – were designated under an umbrella conservation initiative that bodes well for the future.

**Other landbirds** The wirebird may be the island's only endemic, but keen birdwatchers won't otherwise go unrewarded, for St Helena boasts many a colourful creature that's found its way here from distant climes. One of the most common – and the smallest of the bird species on the island – is the tiny **common waxbill** (*Estrilda astrild; 4in/9.5cm*), known locally as the avadavat. These members of the finch family originate in tropical and southern Africa, but no-one knows for sure when they were first introduced to the island: most likely some time during the 19th century. The waxbill has very pronounced dark, cross-barring on its pale-brown upperparts and flanks, a brown rump and a dark-brown tail. It has a beautiful scarlet colour down the centre of the belly, a waxy, coral-red bill and a crimson stripe through the eye. Usually seen in flocks of up to a dozen birds, these waxbills inhabit open grassland, farmland, cultivated fields, marshes, grassy clearings in forests, and areas near human habitation, especially abandoned farms.

Not much larger is the **yellow canary** (*Serinus flaviventris; 5in/13cm*), a native of southern Africa and also quite common throughout the island. The more attractive male has streaked green upper parts with a yellow breast-belly and band above the eyes, whereas the female is streaked grey-green. Mainly seedeaters, with a short stubby bill, they also feast on fruit and insects.

Adding a vivid splash of colour to the spectrum is the **Madagascar fody** (*Foudia madagascaniensis; 5½in/14cm*). Known on the island as cardinals, robins or red birds, these small birds are easily recognised during the breeding season, around October to March, when the head and breast of the male turn an intense scarlet. At other times, they – and the females – are relatively undistinguished, their streaked grey-green colouring easy to confuse with the female yellow canary.

Another introduced species, this one brought from Indonesia in the early part of the 19th century, is the **Java sparrow** (*Padda oryzivora; 6in/15cm*). Attractive bluish-grey birds, with their distinctive black head and tail, white cheek patches, lilac breast and heavy red bill, they are now relatively common on St Helena.

St Helena's most common bird, however, originated from India. The noisy **common mynah** (*Acridotheres tristis; 10in/25cm*) was introduced to the island in 1815 in order to try to control cattle ticks and other pests. By 1875 they had almost totally disappeared, but in 1885, five mynah birds were brought from India by a Miss Phoebe Moss, who released them near her home at The Briars. This time, the birds multiplied out of control, and are now considered a pest, not least as they pose a serious menace to fruit-growers. Their bodies are black and brown with white wing patches and the bill is an orange-yellow.

The pigeon family is represented by two species. The **rock dove** or **feral pigeon** (*Columba livia; 13in/33cm*), is found in limited areas such as the cliffs of Briars Valley. It has a dark bluish-grey head, neck and chest, with glossy yellow, green and reddish colouring along its neck and wing feathers, and a dark greyish-pink bill. Two dark bands across the wings are seen in most birds of this species, with one bluish-grey band across the tail. Rather smaller is the **peaceful dove** (*Geopelia striata; 10in/25cm*), locally called the turtle dove: dusty-grey birds which were probably introduced from Australia during the early 18th century. With a preference for drier areas where open woodland and scrub predominate, they can often be seen along the wooded roadsides in the centre of the island, and picking up fallen seeds in the public gardens in Jamestown.

The arrival on St Helena of two game birds is thought to date back to the 16th century. First mentioned by the English explorer Captain Thomas Cavendish when he visited the island in 1588, both the **Chukar partridge** (*Alectoris chukar; 13in/33cm*) and the **ring-necked pheasant** (*Phasianus colchicus; 22–23in/55–58cm*) are thought to have been originally introduced by the Portuguese – the partridges from the Persian Gulf area, and the pheasants from China. Today, Chukar partridges can be found in the more remote parts of the island, preferring very arid areas. They are mostly grey all over with a black band from the eyes down to below the neck, several black bars on the flanks, and a bright red bill and legs. The females are smaller than the males, and have a smaller knob on the legs. By contrast, there is still a healthy population of pheasants, even though they are actively hunted during the open season. They are not easy for the casual passer-by to spot, though, as they prefer the thick cover of the woodland. As with most pheasants, the female – a dull greyish-brown colour – is eclipsed by the male, whose green, red and copper hues are finished with a swagger by a long tail.

**Seabirds** Just eight species of seabird breed on the island, but you don't need to have all the latest kit to spot most of them.

The favourite of many a bird lover, **terns** are the dancers of the air. Of the four found on St Helena, the **white tern** (*Gygis alba; 12in/30cm*) is considered the most elegant and beautiful of all seabirds. Locally called **fairy terns**, they are pure white, with delicate, translucent wings and large, jet-black eyes. Fairy terns build no nest, but instead lay their eggs in trees, usually precariously balanced in the hollow of a branch, or on buildings or cliff faces. Eggs have even been found on the window ledges of St James' Church in Jamestown. Fairy terns are extremely inquisitive and will often fly close over the heads of passers-by.

The beautiful **sooty terns** (*Onychoprion fuscata; 28in/44cm*), also known for their call as 'wideawakes', have long narrow wings and a forked tail. They are black on the upper parts, legs and bill, with white underparts, a white patch on the forehead, and a white face with a black stripe running across the eyes to the base of the bill. They skim the water to obtain their food, primarily fish and squid.

Sooty terns are widely distributed in tropical latitudes, nesting every ten months on coastal flats. They are heavily affected by predators, such as feral cats, but while they are still numerous on Ascension Island, on St Helena they are relatively rare. Their nesting sites are now largely confined to Speery Island and other predator-free stacks, where you'll occasionally hear the distinctive call that gave rise to their local name.

Two species of noddy complete the tern family. The **black noddy** (*Anous minutus; 12–14in/30–35cm*) is actually a very dark brown, with a white cap and a long fine bill. They build their nests on sheer cliff faces out of guano and seaweed. The larger **brown noddy** (*Anous stolidus; 15in/40cm*), is a sleek, grey-brown tern with blackish flight feathers and a greyish-white cap extending from its forehead to its crown. Normally they prefer sandy beaches and trees, but on St Helena they, too, usually frequent rock crevices or ledges. Both species congregate on Egg and Speery islands whey can be readily seen from a boat.

One of the rarer seabirds to be found on St Helena, the diminutive **Madeiran storm petrel** (*Oceanodroma castro; 8in/20cm*) is also known to breed on Egg Island. It is mainly dark brown below, with a black back and a distinctive white patch on the rump. The bill is short and black and the tail slightly forked. Madeiran storm petrels nest in crevices in rock piles and stone walls, or burrow in soft earth. At sea, they like to fly close to the tops of the waves, and though rarely seen away from their breeding grounds, occasionally one is spotted in James Bay at dusk. It is possible that the St Helena population is an undescribed endemic subspecies, and tests are currently being undertaken to see if this is actually the case.

The **red-billed tropicbird** (*Phaethon aethereus; 37in/95cm*), with its dagger-like scarlet bill and spectacular long white tail streamers, is unmistakable. Called 'trophy birds' by Saint Helenians, these pelagic birds, whose diet consists of small fish and squid, come ashore on St Helena and Ascension Island only to breed, usually on almost inaccessible cliffs such as those between Breakneck Valley and Jamestown. They are about the size of a large gull, with a white head and body, black outer wing feathers, and fine black barring on the back. A dark patch around the eye sometimes extends across the nape. Look out for them from the top of Jacob's Ladder in the late afternoon, or from Munden's Point.

Two members of the **booby** family bring added avian interest to the skies. Brilliant white in colour, with deep-black wing markings and a distinct bluish face-mask, the aptly named **masked booby** (*Sula dacylatra; wingspan 5ft/1.5m*) is a member of the gannet family, and the largest and farthest-ranging of their genus around the world. Juveniles are easily mistaken for the **brown booby** (*Sula leucogaster; wingspan 4ft 6in/1.4m*), which is brown on top with white underparts, and dives from quite a height. The brown booby, however, dives for fish at a shallower angle. These are the birds that are likely to be following the fishing boats, though sometimes the masked booby will do so, too. On land, boobies are heavy and awkward birds, requiring the aid of gravity to take off into full flight, so their nests are often located near cliffs or steep slopes. Boobies breed all year, and don't have a regular breeding cycle. The young are usually born in pairs, with the larger chick frequently killing the smaller within a few months of birth. As they grow larger while still retaining their downy coat, juvenile masked boobies often look much bigger than their parents.

From September to March, the island is also visited by **Arctic** and **pomarine skuas** (*Stercorarius parasiticus* and *S. pomarinus*), large, dark-brown, gull-like birds which migrate from their breeding grounds in the Arctic to avoid the northern winter.

**INVERTEBRATES** Of more than 1,350 species of bugs recorded on St Helena, it is estimated that an incredible 456 are endemic, so the chances of coming face to face with one, albeit unknowingly, is pretty high. The remainder represent native or indigenous species that may exist somewhere else, but got to St Helena by themselves, and non-native species that were brought to the island accidentally or on purpose by man.

It's not unreasonable, here, to make a comparison with the Galápagos archipelago. While the Galápagos hold approximately 1,183 endemic terrestrial invertebrate species compared with St Helena's 455, they are spread over a much larger area: 3,090 square miles (8,010km²) against St Helena's 45 (122km²). Thus the average density of endemic invertebrates on St Helena is 25 times that on the Galápagos: 10.11 invertebrates per square mile (3.73 per km²), against just 0.38 (0.15 per km²).

Nevertheless, the figures hide some sobering facts. Among them is the demise of the **giant earwig** (*Labidura herculeana*). At up to a whopping 3in (8cm) long, it was probably the world's largest earwig and was endemic to St Helena. It was last known from the Horse Point area, but having not been seen in over 40 years, it was declared extinct in 2015. It's by no means a one-off story, with other invertebrate losses including the **giant ground beetle** (*Aplothorax burchellii*), which once occupied the drier scrubland, and the **St Helena darter dragonfly** (*Sympetrum dilatatum*).

Still hanging in there, however, is the **spiky yellow woodlouse** (*Pseudolaureola atlantica*) which, along with related species from places as far apart as South America, Madagascar, Australia and South Africa, is a relic of creatures from millions of years ago. Today it is found only on the endemic black scale fern (*Diplazium filamentosum*) in The Peaks National Park. And while most of the endemic snails are extinct, the richly pink **blushing snail** (*Succinea sanctaehelenae*) remains common and can be seen after rain across the island.

Spiders present a broader mix, with the **golden sail spider** (*Argyrodes excelsa*) just one of 45 or 46 endemic spiders on St Helena. It has long fragile legs and hangs upside down on the endemic ferns. Some 285 species of **beetle** are to be found here, more than half of them unique to the island. One of the most important groups of beetles are the weevils, with 82 endemic species, all thought to have evolved from just a few early ancestors that landed here millions of years ago. Not all the bugs are benign, though, so look but don't touch – and in particular give a wide berth to the 4in (10cm) **red-headed centipede** (*Scolopendra morsitans*), which has a healthy and exceptionally painful bite.

## MARINE LIFE
**Marine mammals** St Helenian waters are home year-round to three species of **dolphin**, which frequent the northwestern, leeward side of the island. Most commonly seen in James Bay is the pan-tropical spotted dolphin (*Stenella attenuata*), which despite the name is not obviously spotted – at least from a distance. Locally known as porpoises, they tend to congregate in the mornings in pods of up to 300, often swimming in the bow waves of boats and enthralling spectators with their acrobatic displays. The larger bottlenose dolphin (*Tursiops truncates*) is more commonly seen in the winter months, between July and September, usually in groups of up to 40. Then there's also the rough-toothed dolphin (*Steno bredanensis*), which is sometimes spotted among the bottlenose dolphins.

During the second half of the year, between about June and December, St Helena plays host to **humpback whales** (*Megaptera novaeangliae*), which come to the island to give birth. At up to 50ft (15m) in length, they're unmistakable from a boat or on shore, whether displaying their spectacular lobtailing techniques or simply cruising past, perhaps with a calf in tow.

**Sea turtles** Of the two species of sea turtle in these waters, the smaller **hawksbill turtle** (*Eretmochelys imbricata*) is present all year. Its exquisite shell is the source of the traditional 'tortoiseshell', long coveted for ornamental purposes, but now firmly outlawed under the CITES convention as well by local ordinance. Small specimens of the **green sea turtle** (*Chelonia mydas; see page 127*) can also be seen at any time, but during the early months of the year they are occasionally joined by mating females who – like their counterparts on Ascension – are likely to have undertaken the long journey from Brazil to lay their eggs on these shores. Sadly, sandy beaches are not a feature of St Helena, though occasionally a few turtles are known to make their way ashore in Sandy Bay.

**Fish** Rare is the visitor who would not be thrilled to see a **whale shark** (*Rhincodon typus*). These giants of the fish world, measuring up to 41ft (12.6m) in length, are present from about November to May, but are rarely seen in aggregations outside January and February. Despite their huge mouths, these sharks are filter-feeders, sifting mostly plankton from the sea water, and unless you're stupid enough to swim close to their tails (which is strictly forbidden), they are considered entirely benign. Also drawn to these shores in the summer months are the **Chilean devil ray** (*Mobula tarapacana*).

**Endemic fish** Of the wide variety of fish off the shores of St Helena, it is estimated that eight are endemic, and a further 18 inhabit the waters only around here and Ascension. The good news is that, unlike the endemic plants, many of these unique creatures are exceptionally easy to see. Almost any snorkeller on St Helena is likely to find themselves surrounded by clouds of tiny St Helena butterflyfish (*Chaetodon sanctahelenae*), known locally as cunningfish. These local names can be useful, such as the greenfish, which is readily seen and refers to the St Helena wrasse (*Thalassoma sanctahelenae*), but are occasionally misleading. The hogfish (*Acanthostracion notacanthus*) is actually a cowfish; the bastard hogfish is the St Helena pufferfish (*Canthigaster sanctaehelenae*); and the reddish-orange fish that the islanders refer to as a parrotfish is in fact a hogfish (*Bodianus insularis*).

Among the real rarities is the **silver eel** (*Ariosoma mellissii*), discovered in 1870, and known only on St Helena. It has pectoral combined dorsal fins that are continuous around the tail, and powerful jaws with small teeth at the front and one or two rows of teeth at the back. Silver eels can often be seen in the sand during night dives at Egg Island.

# CONSERVATION

In 1996, Diana's Peak was proclaimed St Helena's first national park, covering 158 acres (64ha) of tree-fern thicket on the three main peaks along the central ridge. Since then, the park has been extended and renamed The Peaks National Park (page 112), and in 2015 a further two parks were created: Sandy Bay National Park and the East Coast Scenic Reserve National Park (page 107). These three form part of a National Conservation Area Network that also includes six nature reserves, five 'important wirebird areas', and nine heritage conservation areas – this last incorporating the newly proclaimed Heritage Coast, between Ladder Hill Fort and Banks' Battery.

As part of the St Helena government's commitment to conservation, they have established dedicated terrestrial and marine conservation teams. The former maintain an endemic plant nursery at Scotland and work to clear invasive species, planting endemic ones in their place. They are joined by the independent St Helena Nature Conservation Group, which works to help preserve and promote St Helena's unique species. On the marine side, the team is committed to preserving the island's unique species and to ensuring sustainable management of marine resources.

**FLORA** Disappearance of the native flora has long been a concern, and over the years, rare endemics have been propagated and grown in attempts by a few individuals to save them, but it was only in the 1950s, upon the initiative of N R Kerr, St Helena's then superintendent of education, that real conservation work began. Since the 1970s, co-operation between the St Helenian authorities and various bodies that include the Fauna and Flora Preservation Society, the Worldwide Fund for Nature and the Royal Botanic Gardens, Kew, has seen further attempts to propagate many endemic species. Species have been retrieved from the brink of extinction, in at least one case literally from the very last surviving plant, while others have been down to the last handful; some have become extinct in the wild and only survived as rare specimens in gardens. Certain species have proved exceedingly difficult to propagate or intractable in cultivation. Mercifully, others have been very successful and sufficient numbers have been built up to allow planting in public places and in some cases even experimental planting on a larger scale.

There is also an ongoing programme to clear away invasive exotic plants from the peaks, both to encourage natural regeneration and to restock populations with nursery-raised seedlings and cuttings. Progress is slow, but gradually newly planted areas of cabbage trees, tree ferns and the like are filling in the gaps left by the invaders, a sight readily observed in several places, including on Diana's Peak Postbox walk.

The millennium was marked with a project to plant a gumwood forest on wasteland around Horse Point. Today, the Millennium Forest (page 110) is in the hands of the St Helena National Trust, where as one of three 'community forests' (the others are at Blue Point and High Peak) it continues to grow and expand. Numerous gumwood trees have been planted by islanders and visitors alike, with further trees – now including ebonies – being continuously added. In addition, a nursery has been established in order to nurture and study other endemic plants, which are being used to underplant the trees and shrubs.

**FAUNA** The St Helena National Trust has a team dedicated to conservation of the wirebird. Aside from monitoring the population, and producing an annual census, they take responsibility for trapping feral cats, the birds' major predator,

On a micro level, the Trust employs an entomologist who is involved with its 'bugs on the brink' project. This aims to coordinate information on the island's endemic bugs with a view to creating identification resources, Red Listing the endemic species, creating a reference collection and raising public awareness.

# Practical Information

St Helena is in a state of flux. After centuries of access exclusively by sea, the imminent opening of an airport has introduced an underlying current of expectation and concern that infiltrates almost every aspect of island life.

Until the airport opens in 2016, tourism will continue to depend on the arrival of the RMS *St Helena*, along with the odd cruise ship or yacht. For most St Helenians, the RMS is far more than a passenger/cargo ship: it's an extension of the island that creates a buffer zone with the outside world, a little bit of St Helena that in itself is an introduction to the island. While locals may have mixed feelings about the airport, almost all bemoan the loss of their ship. Its arrival from Cape Town every three weeks or so signals the arrival of friends and family, as well as tourists; of long-awaited parcels and letters; of supplies from food to building materials.

For the visitor, too, the introduction of air traffic will be a mixed blessing. The five-day journey by sea from Cape Town is a leisurely and very pleasant introduction to the island, but it remains the preserve of those lucky enough to have at least three weeks to spare. Conversely, seaborne passengers rarely stay on the island for longer than eight days. The airport, however, will open up the island to those with a window of only a week or two, but with the flexibility of staying for longer.

On St Helena itself, the likelihood is that change will be gradual. The island pace of life is slow and measured. The people are genuinely welcoming, liberal with a friendly wave or an impromptu chat, with visitors as well as neighbours. If that means a longer queue than you would like, or a short traffic delay, so be it. This is not a mass-market destination. Supplies will continue to be brought in by sea, and tourist numbers – at least initially – will remain low enough to retain an air of exclusivity. For the most part, pre-booking – of places to stay, car hire, tours and even dinner venues – will still be essential; food will be pricy and shops erratically stocked; and internet access both patchy and expensive. Yet for an island with spectacular contrasts of scenery, an astonishing variety of wildlife, plants and history, some interesting buildings and of course Napoleon's final home, a laid-back atmosphere and an unusually friendly and unpretentious population, it is hard to think of anywhere better.

## WHEN TO GO AND HIGHLIGHTS

The main tourist season on St Helena is from November to March, when it is summer in the southern hemisphere and the days are predominantly sunny and hot. You can expect some rainfall, especially out of Jamestown in March (page 4), but rarely does it last long at this time of year. Between April and October there are fewer tourists, but it is noticeably cooler than in the summer months, and generally wetter too.

### HIGHLIGHTS

**Wildlife** One of St Helena's biggest draws is the appearance of **whale sharks** (pages 46 and 79) around the island. They are usually present between November and May, but visitors in January will have the greatest chance of seeing and perhaps swimming with these truly gentle giants. The other big marine attraction, **humpback whales** (page 46), arrive during the winter months, between July and December, with calves being present from August. Pods of **dolphins** (page 45), especially the pan-tropical spotted species, are regularly seen off the northwest coast throughout the year.

For birders, the must-see is the **wirebird** (page 42), St Helena's only surviving endemic bird, which is surprisingly easy to spot year round. Even for the least-interested visitor, the knowledge that you are in the only place in the world where you can see this little plover is pretty humbling.

**Botany** St Helena's unique flora is a botanist's dream: some 45 endemic plants, many on the brink of extinction. Trees on the peaks flower in succession, so there's no best time to see them, but if you'd like to spot species like babies' toes and ice plant in flower, you'll need to be here around November to January. See also pages 30–41.

**History** Military history and its related sites abound, from the garrisons established by the East India Company through the whole story of Napoleon's exile and on to the Boer War. While there's no 'best' time to visit such places, there will be considerable extra interest in the Napoleonic sites between October 2015 and May 2021, which mark the bicentenary of the former emperor's time on the island.

**Walking** Dramatic seascapes, scenic grandeur and postbox walks attract and challenge hikers. Walking in the summer months, with a fierce overhead sun and little shade, can be difficult, but there's usually a breeze outside Jamestown, and the rewards are significant. It's often more pleasant later in the year, although rainfall tends to be higher between July and September. See also pages 74–6.

**Diving** Clear water with good visibility, interesting marine life – including some easily spotted endemic fish – and numerous wrecks make diving a very attractive option on St Helena. Water temperatures are warmest between about October and April, but diving is possible year-round. That said, there are occasions when the rollers are up and the sea too rough; typically this is in the early part of the year, and can last about a week. See also pages 77–8.

**Fishing** With limited boats in unpolluted waters, sportfishing is one of St Helena's best-kept secrets. Fishing is possible all year round, but arguably at its best between October and May. See also pages 79–80.

**Photography** For landscape photographers, the sheer variety to be found in such a small area justifies the long journey to St Helena. There's plenty at the macro level, too, from one-off insects and extraordinary spiders to plant life that's seen nowhere else on earth. Clear skies are more prevalent in the summer months, but sunlight is less harsh in the spring and autumn.

**PUBLIC HOLIDAYS AND FESTIVALS** St Helena is good at festivals. Colourful street parades draw big crowds, whether at Christmas or for one-off carnival occasions. If you're on the island, keep an eye on the local paper for forthcoming events: perhaps a pancake race on Shrove Tuesday, or something wacky like Gravity Rush, or simply the Guides and Scouts marching to church on Mothering Sunday.

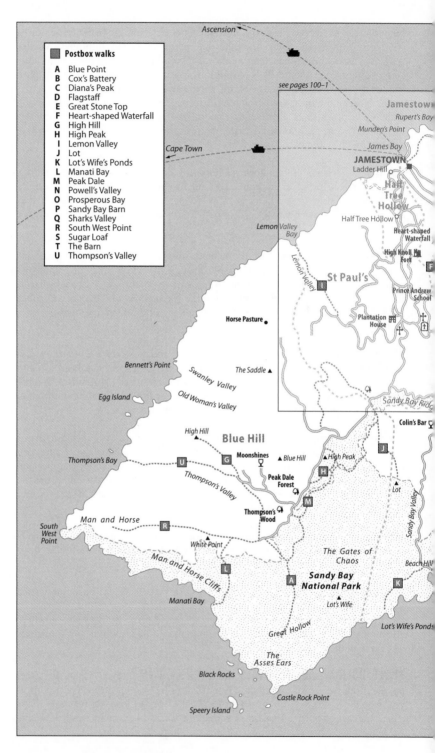

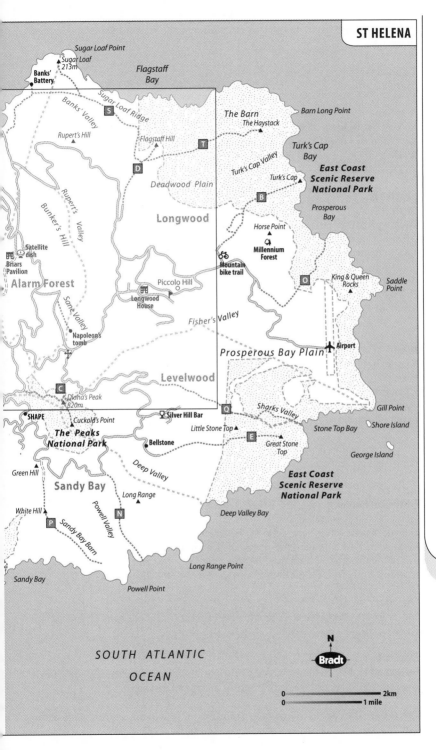

Sugar Loaf Point

Sugar Loaf
213m

Banks'
Battery

Flagstaff
Bay

Banks' Valley

Sugar Loaf Ridge

The Barn

The Haystack

Barn Long Point

Rupert's Hill

Flagstaff Hill

Turk's Cap Valley

Turk's Cap
Bay

Turk's Cap

East Coast
Scenic Reserve
National Park

Deadwood Plain

Longwood

Prosperous
Bay

Rupert's Valley

Bunker's Hill

Horse Point

Millennium
Forest

Satellite
dish

Briars
Pavilion

Alarm Forest

Sane Valley

Mountain
bike trail

King & Queen
Rocks

Saddle
Point

O

Piccolo Hill

Longwood
House

Fisher's Valley

Napoleon's
tomb

Prosperous Bay Plain

Airport

Levelwood

C

Diana's Peak
820m

Silver Hill Bar

Sharks Valley

Gill Point

SHAPE

Cuckold's Point

Q

Little Stone Top

Stone Top Bay

Shore Island

The Peaks
National Park

Bellstone

E

Great Stone
Top

George Island

Green Hill

Sandy Bay

Long Range

Deep Valley

East Coast
Scenic Reserve
National Park

White Hill

P

Sandy Bay Barn

N

Powell Valley

Deep Valley Bay

Sandy Bay

Powell Point

Long Range Point

SOUTH ATLANTIC

OCEAN

N

Bradt

0        2km
0        1 mile

**Public holidays** With one or two exceptions, public holidays are similar to those in the UK.

| | |
|---|---|
| **1 January** | New Year's Day |
| **March/April** | Good Friday and Easter Monday |
| **21 May** | St Helena Day |
| **May/June** | Whit Monday (day after Whitsuntide) |
| **Second Sat in June** | Queen's Birthday |
| **Last Mon in August** | August Bank Holiday |
| **25 December** | Christmas Day |
| **26 December** | Boxing Day |

## Festivals
### March
**Walking Festival** (*Details available from the tourist office*) This annual two-week event was moved from July to March in 2015, and is anticipated to retain this new slot. Inaugurated in 2009, it involves a number of specialised walks, including a guided historical walk of Jamestown, a coastal walk to Lot's Wife's Ponds, a walk through The Peaks National Park and a couple of sponsored events in aid of local charities. In 2015, these took the form of a challenging coast-to-coast walk from Sandy Bay to Jamestown, organised by the St Helena Nature Conservation Group (SNCG), and a shorter, more manageable stroll through Plantation Forest.

### May
**Miss St Helena** This pageant, sponsored by local businesses and organisations, takes place every second May. The next one is in 2016.

### June
**Gravity Rush** (*SHAPE;* ✆ *24690;* e *shape@helanta.co.sh; entry £30 approx*) One of the island's more wacky events involves non-motorised go-karts racing downhill from Upper Jamestown through to the market. 'Gravity' just about sums it up – these karts go fast!

### July
**Festival of Running** (✆ *22820;* e *nasas@helanta.co.sh; entry £2 per event*) This week-long occasion, organised by the National Amateur Sports Association (NASAS) and the tourist office, lays claim to the title of the most remote running festival in the world. By summer 2015, it had evolved to incorporate seven events: a 3km fun run/walk, a 10km road race, a 15km trail run, a half and full marathon, a new triathlon, and of course the obligatory ascent of the 699-step Jacob's Ladder.

### October
**Cancer Awareness Carnival** A programme of events in aid of cancer charities takes place every other year. The next one is in 2016.

### December
**Festival of Lights** Held just before Christmas, this colourful street parade attracts large crowds to Jamestown, with plenty of music and dancing.

**Sports Day** The day after Christmas, a sports day is held in the centre of Jamestown, with Market Street closed to traffic in the afternoon.

# TOURIST INFORMATION AND TOUR OPERATORS

**TOURIST INFORMATION**  St Helena Tourism (*The Canister, Main St, Jamestown;* \ 22158; e *enquiries@sthelena.co.sh; www.sthelenatourism.com*) is the mainstay of any trip to St Helena, both before you go in order to plan accommodation, car hire and activities, and on the island.

**TOUR OPERATORS**  Only a handful of specialist tour operators currently offer St Helena, though with the introduction of flights to the island, it's likely that others will wake up to the island's attractions. For cruise operators, see page 58.

## UK

**AW Ship Management**  9 Alie St, London E1 8DE; \020 7575 6000; e reservations@awsml.co.uk; www. rms-st-helena.com. Formerly known as Andrew Weir Shipping, the agents for the RMS *St Helena* also handle flights, transfers & accommodation for St Helena, Ascension & Cape Town.

**Discover the World**  Arctic Hse, 8 Bolters Lane, Banstead, Surrey SM7 2AR; \01737 214291; e travel@discover-the-world.co.uk; www.discover-the-world.co.uk; see ad, 2nd colour section. Tailor-made holidays to St Helena.

**Halcyon Collections**  207 Regent St, London W1B 3HH; \020 7193 2363; e reservations@halcyon-collections.com; www.halcyon-collections.com. Upmarket operator offering bespoke trips to St Helena, with the potential to include Tristan & Ascension.

**Island Holidays**  PO Box 26317, Comrie, Crieff PH6 2YL; \01764 670107; e enquiries@islandholidays. co.uk; www.islandholidays.co.uk. Specialists in the South Atlantic islands, including St Helena, Ascension & Tristan, offering both independent travel & escorted small groups. See ad, page 118.

**Voyages Jules Verne**  21 Dorset Sq, London NW1 6QE; \0845 166 7003, 020 7616 1000; e sales@vjv. co.uk; www.vjv.com. All-inclusive escorted tours.

## Europe

**Rejseselskabet Jesper Hannibal**  Fredensgade 36B, 8000 Aarhus C, Denmark; \+45 70 270370; www.jesperhannibal.dk

**Marketcruise**  Vaartweg 23-G, PO Box 1067, 1400 BB Bussum, Netherlands; \+31 35 69 55125; e info@marketcruise.nl; www. marketcruise.nl

**Il Viaggio Journeys & Voyages**  Via Schiaparelli 18, 20125 Milano, Italy; \+39 02 67 390 001, +39 02 66 982 915; e info@ilviaggio.biz; www. ilviaggio.biz

## South Africa

**Andrew Weir Shipping**  24th Floor, 1 Thibault Sq, Cape Town 8000; \+27 21 425 1165; e sthelenaline@mweb.co.za; www.rms-st-helena. com. The representatives of the RMS *St Helena* also book flights, transfers & accommodation on St Helena & Ascension.

## Canada

**Great Canadian Travel Company**  164 Marin St, Winnipeg, Manitoba R2H 0T4; \+1 204 949 3847; www.greatcanadiantravel.com. See ad, 2nd colour section.

## RED TAPE

All visitors over the age of 12 years disembarking at St Helena must pay a landing fee of £17, which allows a stay of up to 183 days on the island. You must have a valid passport with at least six months to run, adequate medical insurance (see below), proof of confirmed accommodation and adequate funds for the duration of your stay, and an onward ticket from St Helena.

Your **travel insurance** policy must cover you for all medical and repatriation expenses. Cancellation insurance is also strongly advised.

**IMMIGRATION**  Visitors are normally granted a stay of up to 183 days. Those wishing to stay longer may apply for an extension for up to a year from the police

St Helena: Practical Information   RED TAPE

3

station. Given that almost all visitors will be coming to the island via South Africa, do also check whether or not you will need a South African visa, as these cannot be issued on St Helena.

**CUSTOMS** As in the UK, visitors under the age of 18 years are not permitted to take in alcoholic products, while cigarettes and other tobacco products are limited to those over 16.

Duty-free allowances are:

| | |
|---|---|
| 1 litre spirits or alcohol over 22% volume | 250ml perfume *or* toilet water |
| 2 litres wine *or* 12 x 340ml bottles/cans of beer | 200 cigarettes *or* 250g other tobacco goods |

No fresh produce or honey – even something as seemingly innocuous as an apple – may be taken on to the island unless accompanied by both an import permit and export inspection certificates from the country of origin. This is a precaution against potential pests and diseases unwittingly being introduced to the island. Bags are routinely inspected by customs officers and biosecurity is tight. Indeed, legislation is already in place to empower the rejection of any container that is found to be harbouring insects, spiders or other bugs.

For passengers of cruise ships/exploration vessels, who are only on the island for a very limited time, there are usually special immigration and customs arrangements, which will be explained on board. For those arriving by yacht, see box, page 58.

**EMBASSIES AND CONSULATES** As a British Overseas Territory, the islands of St Helena, Ascension and Tristan da Cunha are represented overseas by embassies of the United Kingdom. In the UK, the St Helena Government representative is Mrs Kedell Worboys MBE (*Alliance Hse, 12 Caxton St, London SW1H 0QS;* ✆ *020 3818 7610;* e *shgukrep@sthelenagov.com*). On St Helena, requests for consular assistance are dealt with by the police.

## GETTING THERE AND AWAY

Until the airport is open, the time that visitors spend on the island – whether they come via Ascension or Cape Town – is limited by the schedule of the RMS *St Helena*. As a result, most have traditionally come for eight days – during which time the ship has continued its voyage to Ascension and is on the return trip to Cape Town. A few just drop in for a couple of days when the ship is in harbour *en route* to Ascension, while some stay longer by flying to Ascension and transferring onto the ship, then returning (after two weeks) on the same route, or (after three) via Cape Town. Although the introduction of weekly flights will add a degree of flexibility, the loss of the RMS will create its own difficulties, not least of access to Ascension from St Helena.

During peak season, and particularly at Christmas, it makes sense to reserve tickets and accommodation as far in advance as possible as space fills up quickly with Saints returning from abroad for the holidays.

**BY AIR** The long-awaited airport is expected to open in mid 2016, just four years after work started on Prosperous Bay Plain. Initially, there will be weekly flights to the island from Johannesburg, operated by **Comair** (*www.comair.co.za*), a subsidiary of British Airways that is linked to the budget airline, kulala.com. The brand-new Boeing 737 that will ply the route has a capacity of 150 passengers, but is likely to carry no more than 120 passengers in order to allow additional space for fuel and cargo on the five-hour journey to St Helena. Flights are scheduled to depart from Johannesburg at 09.00 every Saturday, returning from St Helena early the same afternoon. Visitors from outside South Africa, therefore, will almost certainly need to spend a night in or near Johannesburg at the beginning and end of their trip.

At the end of May 2015, charter company **Atlantic Star Airlines** (*www. atlanticstarairlines.com*) announced that they would be launching a second service between London and St Helena, with direct flights once a fortnight in each direction from March 2016. The flight time will be around 12 hours, including a refuelling stop in west Africa. Outbound flights will leave London in the evening, arriving first thing in the morning, with return flights departing early the following morning. In the longer term, Atlantic Star is also planning a regular connnection between St Helena and Ascension.

For the first time, visitors to the island will be greeted not by the cliffs of James Bay that tower over Jamestown, but by the no-less dramatic volcanic landscape of Prosperous Bay Plain, with the plane landing beneath the sheer drop of Great Stone Top as it looms over the sea. It would be hard to imagine a more scenic location for an airport.

**Getting to Jamestown** Such is the isolation of Prosperous Bay Plain that a new road – currently known as the Haul Road – had to be constructed from Rupert's Valley before work on the airport could begin. For those arriving by air, this 8½-mile (13.7km), two-lane road will be an unusually straightforward introduction to St Helena's normally tortuous road network. From Rupert's, it is anticipated that access to Jamestown will continue down Side Path, the whole journey taking about half an hour. It's reasonable to assume that most places of accommodation will arrange collection of their guests from the airport.

**BY SEA** *(For details on getting to Cape Town, see page 183)*
**RMS *St Helena*** For close on 40 years, nearly all visitors to St Helena have arrived on the RMS *St Helena* (✆ *020 7575 6480; Cape Town* ✆ *+27 (0)21 425 1165; http://rms-st-helena.com*), one of the world's last two operating Royal Mail ships and the island's only source of supplies. Sadly, the ship's days are numbered, and she is scheduled to be withdrawn in July 2016.

The present ship, which is operated by AW Ship Management (page 53), was launched by Prince Andrew at Aberdeen in 1989, and refitted in 2012. Some 344ft (105m) long and 63ft (19.2m) wide, she can now carry up to 158 passengers in 57 cabins. Although the RMS used to cover the route between the UK and St Helena, for the last few years she has largely been limited to a shuttle service between Cape Town, St Helena and Ascension Island.

For her final three trips, however, the RMS will return to the glory days. In April 2016, instead of visiting Ascension, she will make a last call at Tristan da Cunha. The next trip will see her sail to the UK, arriving on 5 June, ready for her farewell voyage: from the UK to St Helena via Tenerife and Ascension. Following a further brief call at Ascension, she will be back on St Helena on 6 July 2016, before setting sail for Cape Town on 10 July. Truly the end of an extraordinary maritime era.

***Schedules*** Round-trip voyages from Cape Town will continue to operate as normal until April 2016. It's a five-night journey from Cape Town to St Helena, typically departing at around 16.00 (depending on cargo), with passenger embarkation at 14.00. All being well, the ship arrives at St Helena on the morning of the sixth day. For the return trip, there is no fixed schedule, but passengers are notified of embarkation times at least a day ahead. Inevitably, inclement weather can cause delays, as can occasional mechanical problems. Bad weather is more

Staffed largely by Saints, the RMS *St Helena* is relaxed and informal in atmosphere, with comfortable accommodation, a big sheltered sundeck, and enough space for you to chat or to while away the hours in peace.

The day starts with an early-morning cup of tea or coffee, brought to your cabin by the steward at around 07.00, along with the day's copy of the *Ocean Mail*. The ship's newsletter contains a list of the day's planned activities, any practical information, and the suggested dress code for dinner (though not one that's rigorously enforced). Then every day, at 12.30 prompt, the officer of the watch announces the latest news from the bridge, from the ship's latest position and distance from land, to the state of the sea and the ocean depth, to the current speed in nautical miles and the estimated time of arrival. From a small vessel surrounded by endless miles of water, news of progress is somehow both interesting and surprisingly comforting.

Aside from films and videos shown through the day, there are organised games of bridge and Scrabble, as well as shuttleboard, quoits, cricket and darts. The main lounge has a surprisingly good library of novels and non-fiction books, and you'll also find board games, crossword puzzles, jigsaws and sudokus on board. In the evening, you can expect plenty of light-hearted brain games, including a highly competitive quiz. And on the Cape Town leg of the journey, the captain's cocktail party is considered a highlight, an opportunity to dress up for those who wish.

Like many a cruise ship, the RMS takes food seriously; be warned! You can take breakfast and lunch in the dining room, where the menu is extensive, or in the sun lounge, which offers a lighter alternative and the option to eat on deck. Afternoon tea, with sandwiches and cake, fills any gap before dinner, a more formal meal served exclusively in the dining room. There are usually two sittings – which you select at the time of booking – and seating is often at designated tables. The service is excellent, and the menu – which changes daily and has plenty of vegetarian options – includes starters, soups, main courses, desserts and cheese or a savoury, so you're unlikely to go hungry.

To counteract all that food, opportunities for exercise are limited. Those working out in the small gym are rewarded by what must be one of the best sea views to be had from a cycle machine. There's a refreshing saltwater pool on deck, though you'd struggle to swim anywhere. And you could always run up and down the stairs…

Retail therapy is confined to a small shop, which combines souvenirs and presents with practical items such as sunscreen and toothpaste. There are a couple of bars on board, for which you can open a tab at the beginning of the voyage, and where you can buy duty-free goods before disembarking. There's on-board internet access, with Wi-Fi in the two lounges, but prices are high, and blogging, for example, can clock up the pounds terrifyingly fast.

Out at sea, seals and whales may pass alongside, especially near Cape Town, while schools of dolphins are relatively common close to St Helena. Once out of sight of land, however, the most likely sighting is that of flying fish speeding away from the ship's wake. Occasionally you'll be accompanied by an ocean-going bird, and an unexpected splash towards the horizon may be all that alerts you to the presence of a whale, but these are a bonus. Otherwise it's just you, the ship and up to 4,000m of water down to the sea bed.

likely in the winter months, from around June to August, but can occur at any time, so it's important to build in at least one night in Cape Town (pages 183–6) at the end of your holiday in order not to miss your return flight.

The voyage between St Helena and Ascension takes approximately 52 hours, and the return journey 48 hours, but timings depend on cargo and passenger numbers. Sometimes the voyage will depart in the evening and will spend three nights at sea, to avoid disembarkation after dark.

**Accommodation** Somewhat confusingly the best cabins are on B deck, with mid-range cabins on the deck above. Both have en-suite facilities, whereas the cheapest – on C deck – have a basin but share toilets and showers. All cabins are air conditioned, but those on C deck – only some of which have a porthole – can get quite hot in the height of summer.

**Fares** One-way fares per person in a two-berth cabin are as follows.

|                       | A & B decks    | C deck     |
|-----------------------|----------------|------------|
| **Cape Town–St Helena** | £1,114–2,069 | £462–535   |
| **Ascension–St Helena** | £629–1,381   | £373–444   |
| **Ascension–Cape Town** | £1,743–3,452 | £834–980   |

The fare for a round trip is simply double the one-way fare.

**On-board practicalities** The RMS accepts both British and St Helenian currency. Payments on board may also be made by credit card, at a 3% surcharge. On the clothing front, the ship is largely informal, with smart casual dress suitable most evenings. For the occasional dinner when formal attire is suggested, a jacket and tie would be appropriate for men, if not compulsory.

**Arrival and departure** Embarkation and disembarkation from the *St Helena* is via motorboat, sometimes in choppy seas. Sensible shoes are a requirement – no flip-flops or high heels – as the transfer can be quite tricky. For those who may have difficulty, a rudimentary 'air taxi' is in operation, hoisted onto a pontoon boat by crane and thence onto the wharf.

**The future** So what next for St Helena's maritime links when the RMS finally enters dry dock? A new cargo ship is being commissioned to bring supplies to the island, although whether or not it will take passengers remains to be seen. Either way, the ship will almost certainly dock at the new wharf in Rupert's Bay rather than off Jamestown. Otherwise, it looks likely that the fishing fleet and pleasure boats in James Bay will in future be joined only by the occasional trans-Atlantic yacht.

**Cruise ship** A few cruise ships make a brief stop at St Helena, usually between October and April; they've even had a visit from the *Queen Mary 2*. A list of forthcoming vessels is posted on the tourist board website, and is available on St Helena from Solomon & Co ( 22523; e *shipping.manager@solomons.co.sh; www. solomons-sthelena.com*).

All ships have to drop anchor in James Bay, from where – weather permitting – passengers are transferred to the landing steps in Jamestown by the ship's crew, but it's important to note that sometimes the decision is taken that it is too rough to

**RADIO CONTACT** Call ahead on Channel 16, or the harbourmaster on Channel 14 during working hours.

**ANCHORAGE** Visiting yachts will be allocated a mooring just west of the main settlement of Jamestown (✪ 15°55.400'S, 05°43.500'W), where 25 numbered red and yellow buoys have been installed parallel to the cliffs.

A ferry service (summoned by calling 'ferry services' on Channel 16) operates 04.00–20.00 during the week, and 04.00–19.00 at weekends, at £1.50 per person. Do note that landing on the slippery quay can be quite hazardous if a swell is running, and occasionally impossible.

**FORMALITIES** Port fees (£35 plus £2–3 per night mooring fee) are payable at the port office, and a landing fee (from £12pp for those staying longer than 72 hours) at the immigration office. You'll also need to provide proof of **medical insurance**, or to purchase suitable cover locally, and to pass through customs. See also pages 53–4.

**HARBOUR FACILITIES** Fresh water is available on the wharf, and there are toilets and showers close by.

**OTHER PRACTICALITIES** Diesel, petrol and bottled gas can be obtained from Solomon's Fuel Station (*Back Way;* ☎ *22259*). For sail repairs, contact Wanda at Abiwan's (*Foresters Bldg; Market St;* ☎ *22082;* ⊕ *08.30–16.00 Mon, Tue, Thu, Fri, 09.00–13.00 1st & 2nd Sat of mth, or by appointment*).

allow passengers ashore. Representatives from St Helena Tourism will sometimes embark to welcome passengers.

### Cruise ship operators

**Birdquest** Two Jays, Kemple End, Stonyhurst, Clitheroe, Lancs BB7 9QY; ☎ 01254 826317; e birders@birdquest-tours.com; www.birdquest-tours.com. Specialist birding operator featuring guided trips on the *Atlantic Odyssey* to St Helena, Ascension & Tristan da Cunha.

**Cruise & Maritime Voyages** Gateway Hse, Stonehouse Lane, Purfleet, Essex RM19 1NS; ☎ 0844 998 3795; e sales@cruiseandmaritime.com; www. cruiseandmaritime.com. St Helena & Ascension.

**Cunard Line** Carnival Hse, 100 Harbour Parade, Southampton SO15 1ST; ☎ 0843 374 2224; www.

cunard.co.uk. Several cruises take in St Helena.

**Oceanwide Expeditions** Bellamypark 9, 4381 CG Vlissingen, Netherlands; ☎ +31 118 410410; e info@oceanwide-expeditions.com; www. oceanwide-expeditions.com. Specialist polar operator with stopovers at St Helena, Ascension & Tristan. From €6,350pp sharing, exc flights.

**Regent Seven Seas Cruises** Beresford House, Town Quay, Southampton SO14 2AQ; ☎ 02380 682280; www.rssc.com. St Helena stops on cruises out of Cape Town. From £4,229pp, inc flights from London.

**Private yacht** Around 200 yachts call at St Helena each year, most between December and April. Some are *en route* between South Africa and South America; others visit as part of a round-the-world voyage. For practical information, see box, above.

The Governor's Cup (see box, page 79) has significantly raised the credentials of St Helena as a yachting venue since its inauguration in 1996, and while the format is set to change post-airport, the race remains firmly on the yachting calendar. Yachts also stop at St Helena as part of the annual World ARC rally.

## BEFORE YOU GO
**Insurance**   All visitors to St Helena are required to have valid **medical insurance**, proof of which must be shown on arrival. This must include coverage for the cost of evacuation in the event of a medical emergency.

## Immunisations and recommended precautions
*Legal requirements*   Although yellow fever does not occur on St Helena, visitors coming from a yellow fever endemic area must have proof of vaccination against yellow fever. Consult your doctor or a travel clinic at least ten days before your departure. If the vaccine is not deemed suitable for you then obtain an exemption certificate instead.

*Recommended precautions*   It is wise to be up to date with **tetanus**, **diphtheria** and **polio** (now given as an all-in-one vaccine, Revaxis, which lasts for ten years). Other vaccines may be recommended, such as **hepatitis B** for health-care workers, so if in doubt check with your GP or a travel clinic at least four weeks before you go.

### TRAVEL CLINICS AND HEALTH INFORMATION   A full list of current travel clinic websites worldwide is available on www.istm.org. For other journey preparation information, consult www.nathnac.org/ds/map_world.aspx (UK) or http://wwwnc. cdc.gov/travel/ (US). Information about various medications may be found on www.netdoctor.co.uk/travel. All advice found online should be used in conjunction with expert advice received prior to or during travel.

### ON ST HELENA
**Water**   The water on the island is safe to drink but outside Jamestown it may neither look nor taste particularly appetising. Bottled water is freely available, but recycling facilities are still limited, so do bear this in mind and refill where you can. As with many isolated places, St Helena has its share of water shortages, though the implications usually go no further than a hosepipe ban.

**Sunburn and sunstroke**   The sun is strong on the coast and it is very easy to get burned, especially out on the water, or on some of the coastal walks where shade is at a premium. A hat and suncream are essentials, as is plenty of water, and it's a good idea to wear a T-shirt when snorkelling.

**Insect bites**   There are plenty of mosquitoes on St Helena, but the good news is that they do not carry malaria. Nevertheless, it makes sense to use a good insect repellent, especially after dark.

**Health care**   St Helena's general hospital, in upper Jamestown (☏ 22500), has 54 beds, and was earmarked in 2015 for significant refurbishment. The hospital is also the base for the island's general practitioners, dentist and pharmacy.

Occasionally, visiting specialists from the UK or South Africa hold clinics for those requiring treatment, but for further treatment, or in more complicated cases, patients are referred overseas. Concerns over medical care, especially in an

## LONG-HAUL FLIGHTS, CLOTS AND DVT

Any prolonged immobility, including travel by land or air, can result in deep-vein thrombosis (DVT), with the risk of embolus to the lungs. Certain factors can increase the risk, including:

- Previous clot or a close relative with a history
- Being over 40, with increased risk over 80 years old
- Recent major operation or varicose-veins surgery
- Cancer
- Stroke
- Heart disease
- Obesity
- Pregnancy
- Hormone therapy
- Heavy smoking
- Severe varicose veins
- Being very tall (over 6ft/1.8m) or short (under 5ft/1.5m)

A deep-vein thrombosis causes painful swelling and redness of the calf or sometimes the thigh. It is only dangerous if a clot travels to the lungs (pulmonary embolus). Symptoms of a pulmonary embolus (PE) – which commonly start three to ten days after a long flight – include chest pain, shortness of breath, and sometimes coughing up small amounts of blood. Anyone who thinks that they might have a DVT needs to see a doctor immediately.

### PREVENTION OF DVT
- Keep mobile before and during the flight; move around every couple of hours
- Drink plenty of fluids during the flight
- Avoid taking sleeping pills and excessive tea, coffee and alcohol
- Consider wearing flight socks or support stockings (see www.legshealth.com)

If you think you are at increased risk of a clot, ask your doctor if it is safe to travel.

---

emergency, were a major consideration in the construction of an airport, something that was underlined when, in March 2015, a seven-year-old girl was taken seriously ill. A request to shipping in the area resulted in the diversion of a Dutch container ship, which rushed her to Ascension, where an RAF plane took her to the UK for treatment at Great Ormond Street Hospital.

Health care is not free of charge, with visitors paying more than local residents. As a visitor, you can expect to pay £80.60 for an initial outpatient's consultation.

British passport holders in need of medical and dental services pay approximately double the rate for locals, on presentation of a UK passport, driving licence or NHS medical card. Non-British passport holders pay about three times the local rate.

**Pharmacies**   Over-the-counter remedies such as mild painkillers can be found in the shops in Jamestown, but other pharmaceutical supplies may be obtained only from the hospital. Although the hospital is relatively well supplied, there may be certain things that are not available. Visitors requiring prescription drugs should bring more than an adequate supply with them.

**Medical kit**  Consider taking a small personal medical kit, to include the following:

- alcohol-based hand gel
- antihistamine tablets (also useful for seasickness)
- blister plasters (if you plan any serious walking)
- insect repellent
- lipsalve (ideally containing a sunscreen)
- Micropore tape (for closing small cuts – and invaluable for blisters)
- sunscreen
- sufficient quantities of prescription medication
- spare glasses and/or contact lenses

## SAFETY

St Helena is generally considered to be pretty safe. Anything more than petty theft, public drunkenness and traffic violations is rare, and the only nuisance that you're likely to encounter is a noisy stereo or the boom of music from the bars in Jamestown on a Friday and Saturday night. Only in very rare cases has a violent crime been committed, and even then, the parties concerned have generally had a dispute with each other.

On an island where doors are left open, and cars unlocked, it's easy to get lazy about personal possessions, but it still makes sense to take normal precautions. Keep valuables somewhere sensible (though there's no such thing as a room safe yet), and don't flash the cash.

It is generally considered safe to wander around Jamestown after dark, but if you're walking along country roads at night, watch out for passing cars as the roads are narrow and for the most part unlit.

Recreational drugs of any description are illegal. Although the occasional person has been caught trying to smuggle marijuana on the ship, hard drugs have to date not been a problem.

**Women travellers** can expect to be treated with respect, and are at no greater risk on St Helena than anyone else.

### ESCAPE!

As Napoleon's captors were only too aware, one of the advantages of being on an isolated island in the middle of the South Atlantic is that, if a prisoner escapes, he has a very high chance of being caught. In 1990, however, a Dutch sailor called Merk was arrested off St Helena when his boat was discovered to be carrying considerable quantities of marijuana. He spent two years in Jamestown prison but somehow he managed to escape, stole a yacht and made his way to Brazil. (A *Mail on Sunday* article at the time claimed, probably falsely, that he had got someone on the island to make him a dinghy, using bamboo as a mast and a tarpaulin as a sail, and named it *Napoleon's Revenge*.) The Dutch Embassy managed to get him sent back to the Netherlands where – as possession of marijuana is not considered a serious offence – he was immediately set free.

## TRAVELLING WITH CHILDREN

A warm welcome is pretty well guaranteed for families, but on the practical side, you're unlikely to find child safety seats in cars, or highchairs in restaurants, or dedicated baby-changing areas (though one such has just been installed in the toilets by the wharf in Jamestown). Be aware, too, that St Helena has narrow roads, high cliffs and dangerous ocean currents, so you'll need to keep a watchful eye on younger members of your group. The same, of course, goes for those voyaging on the RMS *St Helena*, although the ship does have a small play area that is relatively secure.

## WHAT TO TAKE

**CLOTHING** Dress is very casual although you might want some smarter clothes for eating out or if you get invited to a function on the island – as well as for the RMS *St Helena*.

In the summer months, between about October and April, loose, comfortable clothes are best, with a sunhat to protect yourself from the worst of the sun's rays, and some form of waterproof for the occasional downpour. That said, while it can be very hot and humid in Jamestown, it is noticeably cooler inland, so a light fleece

---

### NOTES FOR TRAVELLERS WITH LIMITED MOBILITY           *Gordon Rattray*

If you can get on to dry land, the rest will be easy (comparatively)! The RMS *St Helena* has one officially 'accessible' cabin, while for getting ashore there's a so-called 'air taxi': essentially a container with seats which is winched onto a pontoon boat and then onto shore – thus making it more or less accessible for those with limited mobility. Certainly we have seen it work successfully for one wheelchair user. Cruise-ship passengers are likely to find landing more difficult, but they tend to be exceptionally careful, so it sometimes happens that no passengers at all are permitted to land. Those arriving at the new airport should have no such problems, provided that they can cope with transport by car or minibus, though a decision on the availability of an aisle chair has not yet been taken.

**GETTING AROUND** The only public vehicles are normal taxi cars or minibuses; there is not yet any public transport fitted with wheelchair lifts.

**WHERE TO STAY** There are several ground-floor rooms in hotels and guesthouses, but there is no establishment with completely accessible lodgings.

**PUBLIC BUILDINGS AND ATTRACTIONS** Planning for new public buildings now incorporates access for people with disabilities, but aside from the Museum of St Helena, which has a lift and access ramp, none of the island's buildings, historical or civil, display any special features.

**TRAVEL INSURANCE** Although most insurance companies will insure disabled travellers, it is essential that they are made aware of your disability. Recommendations for travel insurance purchased in the UK include Age UK (℡ 0800 389 4852; www.ageuk.org.uk), who have no upper age limit, and Free Spirit (℡ 0845 230 5000; www.free-spirit.com), who cater for people with pre-existing medical conditions.

or sweatshirt is useful, especially when the wind gets up. Between June and August, temperatures can fall to as low as 50°F (10°C) and the days can be wet, so layers come into their own.

For much of the year, sandals are generally fine for wandering around Jamestown, but do take something more substantial if you plan on exploring; even the walk down to Napoleon's tomb can get very wet and slippery. Sturdy walking shoes or boots are essential if you plan to do any hiking, and especially on the postbox walks. The terrain is frequently steep, and many of the paths are narrow with significant patches of loose stones.

Walkers may find hiking poles a useful extra, while for underwater enthusiasts, a mask and snorkel are absolute musts. If you're planning to dive, don't forget your certification and log book.

**ELECTRICAL EQUIPMENT** St Helena's electricity supply is 240V, 50Hz, and the plugs, with three square pins, are the same as those in the UK.

**PHOTOGRAPHIC EQUIPMENT** Do bring anything that you might need with you, including spare batteries and memory cards. Moonbeams in Jamestown offer some basic photographic services, and will burn images to CD, but that's about it. Binoculars are a bonus if you have even the faintest interest in the birds, as well as for watching ships and wildlife from a vantage point on land.

## MONEY AND BANKING

**CURRENCY** The currency in St Helena and Ascension (and on the RMS *St Helena*) is the St Helena pound (SHP) which is linked 1:1 with the British pound (GBP). The notes and coins are similar to their British equivalents, and British money is accepted on both islands, though change will be given in St Helena pounds. United States dollars and even euros may be accepted in a few places, especially on cruise-ship days, but this is by no means the norm.

**HOW TO TAKE YOUR MONEY** For most purposes it is advisable to have a supply of cash in UK sterling. Guests at the Consulate Hotel may arrange to send their spending money in advance, which is then handed to them on arrival. Travellers' cheques may be cashed at the bank, but are not usable elsewhere.

**Credit and debit cards** There are as yet no ATMs on the island, but this is likely to change before long. For now, you can normally obtain cash against a Visa or MasterCard credit or debit card at the only bank, the Bank of St Helena (page 90), on presentation of suitable photo identification, such as a passport. Expect to pay a fee of around 5% on cash withdrawals. Cards are rarely accepted for payment, except for telecommunications services at Sure.

**Currency exchange** The bank will exchange GB pounds, South African rand, US dollars and euros, and will cash travellers' cheques. It is advisable to change back any surplus St Helenian currency before leaving as it can be difficult to exchange outside St Helena and Ascension (but note that it is valid on the RMS *St Helena*).

**BUDGETING** Since all accommodation on St Helena and Ascension must be pre-booked, the key costs of a holiday will be paid in advance – which certainly makes day-to-day budgeting easier. For details of accommodation costs, see pages 67–8.

3

On-island spending broadly comes down to three key costs: food and drink, transport, and tours. Although food is relatively expensive, eating out is surprisingly affordable – around £18 per head for a three-course evening meal without drinks, or perhaps £5 per person at lunchtime. If you're staying in a hotel or guesthouse on a B&B basis, and thus eating out at lunch and dinner, it would be reasonable to allow around £30 a day for meals. Self-catering travellers can save substantially on this, even if they dine out on several occasions.

With car hire from £12 a day, and fuel roughly on a par with that in the UK, a reasonable cost for a week would be around £125. Then there are guided tours, boat trips and other excursion costs – which, based on one such option per day, might total around £150 for a week. Based on these figures, a generous budget would be £500 a head for a week, and less if you're sharing the cost of car hire. At the other end of the spectrum, allowing for eating in at least some of the time and just one or two excursions, you could reasonably bring this down to about £250. And if you're happy to walk everywhere and eat in most of the time, then a budget of £100 would be entirely reasonable.

## OPENING HOURS

Opening hours on St Helena are not so much erratic as old-fashioned. With only a few exceptions, you cannot just walk into a restaurant or hotel and expect a meal, and there's no such thing as 24-hour shopping.

Most shops, especially grocery stores, open at 09.00, and close at around 17.00, Monday to Friday, although some still close at lunchtime, and several are shut on Wednesday afternoons – early-closing day. On Saturdays, you can expect shops to close at midday, but in Jamestown at least many are open again in the evening for late-night shopping from about 18.30 until 20.30. Then a few shops, including Thorpe's in Jamestown, also open on a Sunday morning. Of course there are variations in this. Some shops, especially those in the tourist sector, may concentrate on the busier days of the week, and others may open outside normal hours if the RMS *St Helena* or a cruise ship is in port.

Government offices – and this includes the tourist board and the National Trust – are open Monday–Friday, 08.30–16.00. Island tours, boat trips and activities such as fishing and diving must normally be arranged ahead and may not be available every day. They may also operate only with a minimum number of participants, or at a minimum charge. And while the Napoleonic sites are anticipated to open longer hours in future, they are unlikely to be as accessible as a similar institution in, say, Paris.

## GETTING AROUND

There is a skeletal scheduled bus service and a reasonable number of taxis, but most St Helenians get around by car. For those staying in Jamestown, a combination of walking, taxis and buses can work well, especially if you are into water-based activities, which all start from Jamestown. For those staying 'in the country', or interested in hiking, having your own transport is almost essential. If you don't have a vehicle and start walking along the road, you may well be offered a lift – but don't bank on it.

There are as yet no bicycles for hire, and cycling is currently illegal on some roads, including both of those leading out of Jamestown. Although this restriction may be lifted in the near future, once you've seen the terrain, you'll understand why it was imposed in the first place!

**CAR HIRE** Rental cars are often in short supply, so it is essential that you book one well ahead of your visit – possibly even months in advance, especially in peak season. Many are the visitors who fail to do this and find themselves struggling without independent transport.

Despite the bus service and the option of guided tours, hiring a car for a few days is arguably the best way in which to get a feel for the interior of the island. Even if you are staying in Jamestown, a car is very useful, and it is vital if you are staying out in the country.

Cars may be hired either through your tour operator, your hotel, the tourist office (page 53), or direct with one of the following:

🚗 **Brendan's Motors** 🔧23726, 23737;
e brendans.motors@helanta.co.sh. Fleet of 10 cars.
🚗 **Colin Williams** 🔧22742; e colinsgarage@
helanta.co.sh
🚗 **Fox Motors** 🔧24404; e foxmotors@helanta.
co.sh

🚗 **Joshua's Hire Drive** 🔧23648; e lynnie.d@
helanta.co.sh
🚗 **Reg Yon Enterprises** 🔧23459; e keith.
michielle@helanta.co.sh
🚗 **Rex Lawrence** 🔧22617
🚗 **Russell Thomas** 🔧23169

Generally you're looking at some pretty old cars, most with manual transmission, so don't come with expectations of a shiny new Avis-style motor. Most have been driven on island roads over many years, with the inevitable impact on brakes, clutches and tyres. If the windows don't open properly, that's relatively minor!

Rates vary slightly, but you can expect to pay upwards of £12 per day, including fully comprehensive insurance, plus a drop-off/collection fee of around £10. You'll need a valid driving licence from your own country, and when completing the paperwork, you must make sure that you are the named driver on the insurance policy. The minimum age for hiring a car is 21. Some operators make it a condition of hire that you do not go off road, so if you choose to ignore that, you can expect to pay for any damage, including punctures, that may be incurred as a result.

The island has just three **fuel stations**, in Jamestown, Half Tree Hollow and Longwood. In spring 2015, petrol cost £1.29 a litre, and diesel £1.11, so roughly on a par with prices in the UK. It's reasonable to assume that your car will be delivered with at least some fuel, and it should be returned with a similar amount.

**Driving on St Helena** There are about 60 miles (97km) of surfaced road on the island, most of them single track, with steep gradients and hairpin bends common. Driving out of Jamestown in particular is quite a challenge, especially on Ladder Hill Road, which leads to the western side of the island: a steep, single-track road with several blind corners. Island etiquette dictates that the driver coming downhill should make way for traffic coming up, so you need to allow time to find a passing place. Driving is on the left, as in the UK and South Africa.

With most businesses centred on Jamestown, there are noticeable rush hours around the town – between 08.00 and 09.00 in the morning coming downhill, and uphill at 16.00–17.15 in the evening, as offices and then shops close. Unless you're going in the same direction, you'd be well advised to avoid driving at these times.

The speed limit in Jamestown is 20mph (32km/h). Elsewhere, normal speed limits are 30mph (48km/h), unless otherwise posted, but for the most part you'd be hard pushed to come anywhere near that. Road signs are shown in miles rather than kilometres.

Drink-drive laws are slightly less strict than in the UK, with a maximum allowance of 50 micrograms of alcohol per 100ml (compared with the UK's 35 micrograms) and are strictly enforced. Seatbelts are not compulsory.

**BY TAXI** Taxi services as such are relatively limited, but there is considerable overlap with those offering excursions (pages 97–9), so do check them out, too. Dedicated taxi drivers include:

| | |
|---|---|
| **Cecil George (Simba)** ✆23520 | **Joshua's Taxis** ✆23648 |
| **Fox's Motors** ✆24404 | **Patrick Young** ✆24031 |
| **Francis Raymond** ✆23525 | |

Taxis are designated by a special licence plate, whereby there is a space after the normal number followed by an extra digit (eg: 432 4). This additional number signifies the maximum number of paying passengers permitted in the vehicle.

Taxis are not metered and fares are negotiable. As a guide, based on fuel prices in 2015, the short journey from Jamestown to Half Tree Hollow (near the top of Jacob's Ladder), should cost around £4–6 one way, while from Jamestown to Farm Lodge Country House Hotel on Rosemary Plain you can expect to pay around £12–15.

Most taxi drivers also offer various tours, including one of about three hours, taking in the major sights: Briars Pavilion, Napoleon's burial site, Longwood House and Plantation House. For details, see pages 97–9.

**BY BUS** St Helena has a very limited public bus service, more geared to the needs of locals than those of visitors. Although it is possible, with some planning, to use the bus service to reach some of the island's attractions and walking opportunities, it will limit your options.

Timetables are displayed outside the post office in Jamestown, and are also available at the tourist office. Do check these carefully and allow sufficient time to catch the return bus – otherwise you may face a long walk back to Jamestown.

**Routes** Of the four routes, A, B, C and G, note that C and G are one way only; there is no return service to Jamestown. Routes A and B both start in the country, but the first buses out of Jamestown are at 08.35 and 08.30 respectively, and the service runs through the day.

**Route A** (*Daily from Jamestown 08.35, 15.05, 21.00; Tue, Thu, Fri also 13.00; Sat also 13.00, midnight*) Bottom Woods, Hutt's Gate, Alarm Forest, Gordon's Post, Briars Village, Jamestown (tourist office)

**Route B** (*Daily from Jamestown 08.30, 15.00, 21.00*) White Gate, Thompson's Hill, Rosemary Plain, New Ground, Jamestown (Grand Parade)

**Route C** (*Mon, Tue, Fri, Sat noon, Thu 12.30*) Jamestown (Grand Parade), Ladder Hill, New Ground, Rosemary Plain, Thompson's Hill, White Gate. One-way service only.

**Route G** (*Thu, Fri & Sat 13.00*) Jamestown, Briars Village, Alarm Forest, Hutt's Gate, Levelwood. One-way service only.

Highlights of some of the stops along routes A and B are:

- **Bottom Woods** Longwood House, Millennium Forest
- **Briars Village** The Briars Pavilion, Heart-shaped Waterfall
- **Gordon's Post** Distillery

- **Hutt's Gate** Diana's Peak, Halley's Mount
- **Rosemary Plain** Coffee plantation, Farm Lodge, Lemon Valley Postbox walk
- **White Gate** Plantation House, St Paul's Cathedral, Boer Cemetery

**Fares** Single fares are based on distance, from 75p for up to three miles, £1.25 for three to six miles and £2 for over six miles. Children under ten travel half price. Although there are occasional bus shelters, there are no bus stop signs, so it's not always obvious where to wait for a bus. That said, you may also flag down buses or ask to be dropped off between official stops.

**GUIDED TOURS** See pages 97–9.

**MAPS AND CHARTS** The 1:25,000 Ordnance Survey map, known as 'the tourist map', used to be the best for visitors and is still available from the post office and other outlets in Jamestown (£5), but it is woefully out of date. The good news is that by February 2016, a fully revised version should be available, both on the island and online, to include indications of roads that are particularly steep, or single track with passing places, features that are not found on a standard OS map.

Widely available overseas, the Gizi map covers St Helena at 1:35,000, with a small inset of Jamestown at 1:6,000 and coverage of Ascension, Tristan da Cunha, Inaccessible and Gough at 1:75,000 – though Nightingale Island is a slightly bizarre omission. With relief colouring, it's a fairly good map, though not entirely accurate.

Navigation charts covering St Helena, Ascension and Tristan da Cunha are available at various scales from specialist outlets.

## ACCOMMODATION

It's a condition of entry to St Helena that all visitors have confirmed accommodation prior to their arrival, as options are limited. During high season, which is winter in Europe, demand for accommodation is high, so it's important to make reservations well in advance, and to be flexible; the opening of the airport is likely to exacerbate the situation in the short term.

Tour operators will of course make accommodation arrangements for you with one of their preferred hotels or guesthouses. If you choose to book for yourself, do remember that you must do so before you set sail. Few places to stay have their own website, but the tourist office website (*www.sthelenatourism.com/accommodation*) features pretty comprehensive details of all types of accommodation, and reservations may be made through them.

Jamestown itself (pages 85–8) is certainly the most convenient place to stay, especially if you're not planning to hire a car, and/or if you're planning to spend time on the water. Those who would prefer to get away from it all might prefer to look

| ACCOMMODATION PRICE CODES | |
|---|---|
| Based on a double room per night, with breakfast | |
| £££££ | > £220 |
| ££££ | £180–220 |
| £££ | £140–180 |
| ££ | £100–140 |
| £ | < £100 |

inland at St Paul's, Longwood and Alarm Forest (pages 103–4), where tranquillity and sea views are the norm, while Half Tree Hollow (page 99) is something of a halfway option, relatively close to Jamestown but often with a good vantage point out to sea. Although Jamestown is normally no more than a 20-minute drive from any of these, it's best to hire a car if you're staying out of town. It's also worth noting that rain and fog are more prevalent inland than in Jamestown or Half Tree Hollow, and that the temperatures in outlying districts tend to be cooler.

## CATERED ACCOMMODATION

This is pretty expensive everywhere, even by European standards: around £200 per night for a double room en suite in a hotel with breakfast, or from around £120 in a guesthouse or B&B – though here rates are more variable. Behind these prices are the long-term legacy of low occupancy rates, with tourists on the RMS *St Helena* arriving just one week in three, as well as the exceptionally high cost of electricity.

### Hotels

The island currently boasts just two hotels, one of them in Jamestown (page 87), with a second, more personal, out at Rosemary Plain in St Paul's (page 103). A third hotel, also in Jamestown, is scheduled for completion in mid-to-late 2016.

### Guesthouses and B&Bs

These form the backbone of catered accommodation on the island, and offer a great opportunity to get to know some of the St Helenian people. Some offer en-suite rooms, while in others you'll be sharing facilities, and styles vary from stylish and modern to the truly homely. Pretty well everywhere, you'll find yourself hosted by people who are only too happy to tell you about the island and the local traditions.

## SELF-CATERING

This is St Helena's trump card in terms of accommodation, offering exceptional value for money in simple flats or houses where you'll feel almost part of the community. Given the importance of such accommodation to long-stay visitors as well as tourists, it's beyond the scope of this book to detail them all, since options vary at any given time, but the tourist board lists a comprehensive selection on their website and will book a place for you. (Don't be surprised if you don't get your first choice; these places can get booked up months or even years in advance.) We have, though, attempted to give a flavour of each location, so that you can select the best area for you (see pages 87, 99, 103 and 104).

Self-catering rates vary, with prices in Jamestown generally higher than in the country, but typically you're looking at around £25–40 a night for two or even more people, to include electricity and (usually) local telephone calls, with a discount for stays of a month or longer. Many hosts also include a starter pack, typically including milk, butter or margarine, cheese, fruit juice, bread and – if you're lucky – eggs (which are often in short supply). You'll usually find staples such as tea and coffee, salt and pepper, too, as well as basic cleaning equipment. Standards are generally good and many are in great locations, ideal for walks or just for lingering on a veranda looking out to sea.

Most places are fully equipped with standard appliances: cookers, microwaves, kettles, toasters and washing machines are pretty standard, and many will also have a radio and/or television. Furniture, however, is likely to be pretty basic – more 1950s than minimalist – and bedding and décor likewise, so be realistic about your expectations.

## CAMPING

Although St Helenians have a tradition of camping at Christmas and Easter, the campsites are rudimentary, and are not set up for visitors – yet.

**FOOD** Key to the traditional St Helenian diet – and relatively inexpensive – is fish, and especially tuna, though wahoo and dorado make a regular appearance. Popularly made into fishcakes – which may be served with tomato and onion 'gravy' or perhaps pumpkin stew – tuna also surfaces stuffed, grilled and in the other island favourite, pilau. Pronounced 'ploe', this local version of the Indian staple combines rice with pretty well any meat or fish and vegetables in a spicy curry sauce.

Indeed, curry is a regular at island dinner tables, but rather more unusually it appears on Sundays and at special occasions such as birthdays and weddings alongside a full English roast with all the trimmings – with both eaten at the same time.

Other island specialities are black pudding, coconut fingers, boiled pudding and bread 'n' dance – a simple sandwich with a filling of thickened tomato sauce that is so named because it used to be served at island dances, along with coffee and homemade fruit syrup.

For availability of food, see page 90; food shopping in St Helena can be quite a challenge!

**DRINK** The local **spirit**, Tungi, is distilled on the island from the prickly pear, and is very much an acquired taste. The distillery (page 109) also produces a spiced rum – marketed as White Lion, and sometimes drunk as a shipwreck, with Sprite and a dash of lime – as well as a delicious coffee liqueur, Midnight Mist, based on locally grown coffee. These and other spirits are sold in a particularly attractive bottle, somewhat evocative of Jacob's Ladder, but they're cheaper in the standard bottles.

A couple of fairly basic **wines**, Mount Actaeon and Diana's Peak, are produced at the distillery, too, but most other drinks – soft and alcoholic – are imported from South Africa. Wines marketed under the Bell Stone brand are simply South African wines that have been labelled in St Helena.

A bottle of red or white wine costs around £5–10 in the shops, or from about £10 in a restaurant, depending on the quality and venue, but don't expect much in the way of choice. Spirits are relatively expensive. For a canned soft drink, such as Sprite, you can expect to pay £1 or so in a café, while bottled beer will set you back around £1.40, and a 1.5-litre bottle of water from a shop some £1.05.

As in the UK, the minimum age to drink alcohol on licensed premises is 18, but note that in Jamestown, it is against the law to drink alcohol in public.

St Helenian **coffee** is almost as hard to come by on St Helena as overseas – but it's good! It's served – and sold by the bag – at the Coffee Shop in Jamestown, who grow their own, as does the Farm Lodge Country House Hotel. Known as green-tipped Bourbon Arabica coffee, the local coffee was introduced from the Yemen in 1732,

St Helena: Practical Information **FOOD AND DRINK**

**3**

## RESTAURANT PRICE CODES

Based on the average price of a main course, or equivalent. Where the only option is a two- or three-course meal, this has been averaged out.

| | |
|---|---|
| £££££ | > £15 |
| ££££ | £10–15 |
| £££ | £7.50–10 |
| ££ | £5–7.50 |
| £ | < £5 |

and thrives in the St Helenian environment. If you want to find out more, make time for a visit to the coffee plantation on Rosemary Plain (page 107).

**RESTAURANTS** There are few restaurants to choose from, largely because of an erratic flow of tourists: depending on the RMS *St Helena*'s schedule, there can sometimes be only a handful of visitors on the island at any one time. With average wages of £75–100 a week, eating out is not a viable option for many locals and despite the ever-flowing stream of government consultants and visiting engineers, etc, there simply isn't the through traffic to stimulate a vibrant restaurant scene.

For **lunch**, there is the choice between cafeteria-style food, take-away or a sit-down menu, and reservations are not normally required. Outside Jamestown, there are very few places to eat so it is best to take a packed lunch if you are going into the country. Almost all hotels and B&Bs will provide these for their guests on request, or you can pick up the makings of a picnic from cafés in Jamestown or one of the supermarkets.

For **dinner** at most restaurants, you'll need to book at least a day ahead although there are exceptions. In some places, you'll also need to agree the menu in advance, which is at least a bonus for those with special dietary requirements. Prices vary but fish is generally cheaper than meat, from £6 or so for a main course. For a set menu, however, you can expect to pay upwards of around £14 a head for two courses, or £16 plus for three.

## ENTERTAINMENT AND NIGHTLIFE

Pretty well all nightlife is centred on a handful of pubs and bars, most in Jamestown, but one or two out in the country. Several have a DJ on a Friday or Saturday night, and in some that's alternated with live music. Check for the latest in one of the weekly papers, or at the tourist office.

Legally, pubs may open between 11.00 and 23.00 every day, but most choose to keep shorter hours, at least from Monday to Thursday. Some of the bars, including Donny's in Jamestown, Pub Paradise at Longwood, and Colin's in Sandy Bay, open later at weekends.

## SHOPPING

Do make time to explore the various shops around St Helena, particularly in Jamestown (page 90). Despite the presence of a few small supermarkets, some are still reminiscent of general stores that used to be found in every town and village in the UK, and are well worth a rummage. With perseverance, you'll find most of what you want, providing you are not in a hurry.

Just a few names dominate most of the shops and indeed much of the business life of St Helena. Solomon's (partly government owned) is the major player, owner not just of several grocery shops but also a large bakery and two of the three fuel stations (see also box, page 71). Also significant in the retail sector are the privately owned Thorpe's, and Larry and Lyn Thomas's Rose & Crown.

Pretty well all basic foodstuffs, and much of the fresh food, is imported from South Africa, though don't be surprised to find some British brand names in the mix. The likes of both Tesco and Asda products surface in some very surprising places!

Agricultural land on the island isn't as scarce as you might think, but although various fruits and vegetables are grown, including bananas, mangoes, tomatoes, cabbage and herbs, they tend to be grown, traded and bartered among islanders. A little bit of local knowledge can be very useful in this respect. In particular, it's

## SOLOMON & COMPANY

No book about St Helena would be complete without reference to Solomon & Co, which has run, and indeed dominated, the trade of the island since Saul Solomon founded it in 1780.

Initially a general store and boarding house, it has evolved to become a significant stakeholder in the island's business dealings.

The early history of the company seems shrouded in mystery, although we know that Saul Solomon, who became known as the Merchant King, introduced the first press on the island in 1806, and that, later, the company was heavily involved in the flax industry until its collapse. It was known at various times as Solomon Dickson & Taylor, Solomon Moss Gideon & Co and Solomon Hogg & Co, before taking on today's name. In the 1960s, when the business changed hands, the St Helena government bought a 32% share and by 1980 had bought the entire shareholding. Nevertheless, it is still run as an independent plc with local island shareholders. There is hardly an aspect of the island's economy in which Solomon's doesn't have an interest – from wholesaling, retailing and chandlery to bulk fuel, petrol supplies, bakeries, insurance, overseas procurement, building, financial services, butchery and livestock. It is the handling agent for the RMS *St Helena* and incoming cruise ships and is also a substantial landholder.

worth knowing that most growers take their produce to market – or realistically to the shops – on a Thursday morning, so to make the most of that week's bounty you need to get there early and queue up. Come 11.00, the shelves are likely to be as bare as the evening before.

Shortages of imported produce in the shops are a fact of life. One visitor tells of a week without potatoes; another of almost no fruit, and apples are regularly sold out almost as soon as they arrive on the island. The truth is not so much that there is an overall lack of such things, but that canny shopping means that they are bought almost as soon as they're released from the customs shed and carefully hoarded until the next shipment is due.

Meat, too, is often imported, especially beef, but both pork and lamb are farmed on the island, and the pork in particular is excellent. Bread, which until recently had to be ordered in advance, is now in regular supply from Solomon's bakery at Half Tree Hollow.

For **opening hours**, which are normally posted on shop doors, see page 64.

## MEDIA AND COMMUNICATIONS

**TELEVISION** It wasn't until 1995 that television came to St Helena, brought to the island via satellite. Today, the 17 available channels include BBC World News and a wide range of sports and entertainment options – so diehard sports fans, or even addicts of British soap operas, should be able to get their regular fix, albeit sometimes at rather anti-social hours. In 2015, South Atlantic Media Services (SAMS) were trialling a local news broadcast service in partnership with Vision Media, to be shown on television on Friday and Saturday evenings and on YouTube.

**RADIO** Radio is particularly important to St Helenians, a source of local news as well as entertainment. Of the two local radio stations, one is the government-owned but independently run SAMS (South Atlantic Media Services) Radio 1, broadcast on 102.7MHz, 90.5MHz, 105.1MHz and 105.3MHz). Its rival, the entirely independent Saint FM Community Radio (*www.saint.fm*), was launched in 2013 when the original Saint FM closed in protest against what it considered to be unfair competition. Featuring a similar mix of news, music, interviews, live discussions and daily features, it broadcasts from 07.00 to 21.30 daily on 93.1, 95.1 and 106.7FM.

**NEWSPAPERS** Each of the radio stations owns a local weekly newspaper – respectively *The Sentinel* (*www.sams.sh/L2_sentinel.html*) and the rather more acerbic *St Helena Independent* (*www.saint.fm/the-independent*) – though neither is immune to controversy. Both are produced in fairly basic monochrome format, at £1 and 90p respectively, but are also available in colour online.

Content is almost entirely local, even parochial, but together the two papers offer an interesting insight into life on the island, together with details of events, information about who is currently visiting, and opinions from all sectors of the St Helenian community – both at home and overseas.

**POST** St Helena's main post office, in Jamestown (pages 90–1), is also home to the Philatelic Bureau, with stamps from St Helena, Ascension Island and Tristan da Cunha, as well as first-day covers. Such items may also be bought online (see box, below). All districts on the island have a sub-post office operating in a general store or grocery shop, where you can buy stamps, etc.

## STAMPS FOR SOUVENIRS    *John Moody*

From the late 16th century, ships that called in at St Helena would leave letters under large stones placed in prominent landing places, ready for collection by passing ships. One such stone, now carrying an inscription as to its previous use, can be seen close to the entrance to the Castle. Later it was arranged that post could be left at the government secretary's office in the Castle to await the next ship, although no one had any idea when that next ship would call.

It wasn't until 23 February 1815, when the first post office on the island was established by the governor, that letters carried any indication of having come from St Helena. Thereafter, all letters and parcels had to have an official post office postmark or stamps.

The first stamp of St Helena was issued on 1 January 1856. A 6d (six penny) blue imperforate stamp, it featured an engraved portrait of Queen Victoria. From 1863 to 1880, this stamp was issued in various colours, perforated and overprinted for values from 1d (one penny) to 5s (five shillings). The design continued in use until 1884, when a new set was issued for the colony, and the tradition continues today.

With modern satellite communications, however, the necessity of producing stamps for letters and parcels has considerably decreased. Yet philatelists love stamps from isolated outposts such as St Helena, and for cruise-ship passengers, the local stamps provide an attractive souvenir, so they are a good source of revenue for the island. As a consequence, St Helena issues regular sets of stamps featuring local views, events, organisations, flora, fauna, ships etc. The island also joins with other members of the Commonwealth to produce omnibus issues, mainly celebrating Royal occasions.

There is no door-to-door delivery service; indeed, the island has just a single postcode (STHL 1ZZ) and street addresses are rare. Instead, most people have a PO box number. After the mail arrives on the ship, post for the outlying districts is sent out to the sub post offices, but letters for Jamestown are held at the main post office, ready for collection. Post for tourists should be addressed Poste Restante.

Inevitably, all mail will – until the airport opens – continue to go by sea, but 'airmail' is best posted just before the RMS *St Helena* sets sail for Ascension, from where it is flown on by the RAF. The deadline for posting letters before the ship sails is usually announced on the door of the main office. Mail sent via Cape Town can take many weeks to reach its destination.

The cost of stamps is relatively modest:

|              | Surface | Airmail |
|--------------|---------|---------|
| Postcard     | 40p     | 50p     |
| Letter (10g) | 60p     | 60p     |

**TELEPHONE** In 1899, the Eastern Telegraph Company employed almost 40 people on the island, but direct-dial connections were a long time coming. It was not until December 1989 that St Helena acquired international direct dialling, plus fax and data transmission worldwide. Today, all telecommunications are handled exclusively by Sure (*www.sure.co.sh*), the latest rebranding of Cable and Wireless.

The island's telephone network was overhauled in 2013, since when all the old four-digit numbers have been prefixed by the number 2. The international telephone code for St Helena is +290. To call overseas from St Helena, dial 00 followed by the usual international codes (for example, +44 for the UK; +1 for the USA and Canada), but there is often a ten-second delay before you are connected so don't hang up if you do not get an immediate ringing tone.

Local calls cost 3p a minute, but overseas calls are extremely expensive: 86p a minute to the UK, and 99p to the USA.

Public phone booths are liberally dotted around in Jamestown and elsewhere on the island, an important facility in a place where there are no mobile phones. Phonecards for £5 and £10 may be bought in Jamestown from Sure (*Main St; ☎22900*), as well as from the post office, Anne's Place, the Consulate Hotel and various grocery shops. Note, however, that some payphones do not accept phonecards, so make sure that you have coins available too. Reverse-charge (collect) calls cannot be made to St Helena numbers, though you can do so to Ascension.

### Emergency telephone numbers
**Police or fire** ☎999
**Hospital or ambulance** ☎911

**Mobile phones** St Helena must be one of the last bastions in the world without mobile-phone coverage, but not for much longer. It is anticipated that coverage will be unrolled on the island at some point during 2015, a change that many foresee will have a greater impact on island culture than the opening of the airport.

**INTERNET** Internet service was brought to the island in 1998 through Ascension Island, with broadband following in 2008. Now St Helena has its own server but access is still very expensive and fairly slow. Wi-Fi is available in several designated places, including the Consulate Hotel and Anne's Place, at a rate fixed by Sure, of £3.30 for half an hour.

# BUSINESS AND PROPERTY

A business interest in St Helena has never been more timely. As the airport is set to open up the island to a greater number of visitors, so Enterprise St Helena (*ESH; ESH Business Park, Lower Half Tree Hollow;* \ *22920;* e *info@esh.co; www. investinsthelena.com*) has been tasked with active promotion of inward investment. In addition to tourism, areas targeted for consideration include construction, agriculture and fishing.

Property development, too, falls within the ESH remit, regulated by a Land Development Control Plan that outlines the St Helena government's policy of sustainable development over a ten-year period until 2022. Following considerable relaxation of the regulations in recent years, non-residents are now permitted to purchase freehold land of up to two acres (0.8ha). There are restrictions on the sale of larger areas of land, and listed buildings, but in both cases non-resident buyers are still eligible.

# CULTURAL ETIQUETTE

St Helenians are a friendly lot, and visitors are genuinely welcomed; pretty well anywhere on the island you'll be greeted or stopped for a chat. Underlying this is a tolerance borne of years of integration, yet society is still deeply conservative. In relationships, as in other aspects of life, discretion is valued; St Helena is not a place for public displays of affection, no matter who you are with.

Do remember, as well, that the island has an air of small-town life. Everyone knows about everyone else's business, and word travels fast, so when talking to Saints, be aware that they could well know, or be related to, anyone you are talking about.

# ACTIVITIES

**WALKING/HIKING** With its varying and rugged terrain, St Helena is an experienced walker's paradise. Much of the island is inaccessible by car and the only way to explore the diversity of the landscape is on foot.

Walks can vary from gentle strolls along country roads to strenuous hikes along the coast or ridges, with spectacular scenery and often unique flora. Paths are often steep, if not necessarily difficult, and drop offs can in places be sheer. Appropriate hiking shoes or boots are essential, and a walking pole useful for some of the postbox walks. There's little shade, too, so a hat and sunscreen are important, as is plenty of water. Ideally, consult a local walker before setting off, and always make sure that someone knows where you are going.

## Organised and guided walks
Guided walks are run once a month by the St Helena Nature Conservation Group (*SNCG; www.shncg.org*), usually starting at 10.00. Details are available on their website or from the tourist office in Jamestown. There's also a two-week Walking Festival in March, with a series of guided and self-guided walks of varying levels of difficulty (page 52).

If you'd rather walk independently, but would like to have a guide, ask at the tourist office, or contact one of the following:

**Aaron Legg**  See Aaron's Adventure Tours, page 98
**Valerie Joshua**  \ 22235

**Postbox walks** The SNCG has developed a series of 21 'postbox' walks which, between them, effectively take you on a round-the-island walking tour, visiting almost every area of coastline, and showcasing the very best of St Helena's scenic beauty. From the verdant central ridge to the volcanic drama of the northeast and Sandy Bay, from rolling pastureland to fragrant pine woods and stupendous views down to the sea: it would be hard to imagine greater variety in such a small area.

Absolutely essential for anyone planning one of these walks is the companion book, *A description of the Post Box walks on St Helena* (page 191). Written by members of the SNCG, it is available from the tourist office and other outlets in Jamestown.

Based upon a similar concept on Dartmoor, each of the walks is linear, with a postbox at the end concealing a log book and a rubber stamp for you to keep a record of your achievement. If any of the stamps are missing, you can get your walk authenticated at the tourist office.

The walks are graded 1–9 for both difficulty and terrain, 1 being the easiest – though note that there are no walks at grade 1. All the gradings were reassessed for the second edition of the book, with some curious anomalies ironed out, but do bear in mind that they were set by experienced walkers who are familiar with the terrain, so don't underestimate their interpretation of 'moderate'. Even those graded at 2 or 3 may involve some quite steep paths and not a few feature vertiginous drop offs. None of them could be classified as a walk in the park.

Few of the postbox walks are waymarked, and on some the route may not always be obvious, though stone cairns do help in places. Even so, with sheer drops not uncommon it's advisable at least to consider a local guide, especially for any walk graded 5 or above.

The walks below are listed in order of grading, starting with the least challenging. Alongside each is the district and/or national park. Sadly, two of the original walks – to Gill Point and King and Queen Rocks – have been affected by the airport, and are now closed, but two others – Blue Point and the Heart-shaped Waterfall – have been added in their place. If you've only time for two, then Diana's Peak and Lot's Wife's Ponds makes a pretty unbeatable combination, but every walk is different. Details of each are to be found in the corresponding sections in *Chapter 6*.

**Flagstaff**  (2/2; 1hr 15mins) Longwood/East Coast Scenic Reserve National Park; page 111.

**Cox's Battery**  (3/2; 1hr 45mins) Longwood/East Coast Scenic Reserve National Park; pages 111–12.

**Peak Dale**  (3/2; 1hr 45mins) Peaks National Park; page 117.

**Blue Point**  (3/3; 1hr 20mins) Sandy Bay/Sandy Bay National Park; page 117.

**Heart-shaped Waterfall**  (3/3; 1hr 30mins) Alarm Forest, accessed from Jamestown (or Briars Village); pages 95–6.

**High Peak**  (3/3; 1hr 15mins, or 3/2; 30mins) Peaks National Park; page 114.

**High Hill**  (3/4; 1hr 15mins) Blue Hill; page 117.

**South West Point**  (4/3; 2hrs 30mins) Blue Hill/Sandy Bay National Park; page 117.

**Diana's Peak**  (5/5; 2hrs) Peaks National Park; pages 112–13.

**Great Stone Top**  (5/5; 2hrs 30mins) Levelwood/East Coast Scenic Reserve National Park; page 115.

**Sandy Bay Barn**  (5/6; 2hrs 15mins) Sandy Bay; page 116.

**Sugar Loaf**  (5/6 or 6/6 depending on route; both 3hrs 30mins) Jamestown, but best accessed from Longwood; page 111.

**Lemon Valley**  (6/6; 2hrs 45mins) St Paul's; page 107.

**Lot's Wife's Ponds**  (6/8; 2hrs 30mins) Sandy Bay/Sandy Bay National Park; page 116.

**Shark's Valley**  (6/8; 3hrs 30mins) Levelwood/East Coast Scenic Reserve National Park; page 115.

**Prosperous Bay**  (7/8; 3hrs 30mins) Longwood/East Coast Scenic Reserve National Park; page 112.

**Lot**  (7/9; 3hrs) Sandy Bay/Sandy Bay National Park; page 117.

**Manati Bay** (8/7; 3hrs) Blue Hill/Sandy Bay National Park; page 117.
**Thompson's Valley** (8/7; 3hrs 15mins) Blue Hill; page 117.

**The Barn** (8/9; 4hrs 15mins) Longwood/East Coast Scenic Reserve National Park; page 111.
**Powell's Valley** (9/9; 2hrs 30mins) Sandy Bay; page 116.

**Other walks** While the postbox walks are a real highlight, there are others that have plenty of merit. If time is short, the George Benjamin Arboretum nature trail (page 113) has much to offer, or if you've a little longer, you could consider the circular Ridges Roads walk (page 106). For those staying in Jamestown without transport, Munden's Battery is worth consideration (page 96). And if you're after a long walk that is perhaps a little less challenging than some of the postbox walks, the Mackintosh Trail might fit the bill (page 114).

## OTHER LAND-BASED ACTIVITIES

**Mountain biking** A tough scramble through the volcanic ups and downs of the northeast of the island, below The Barn – that's St Helena's first mountain-bike trail. The inaugural competition, in 2015, was a great success; now they just need an operator who can offer mountain biking for visitors. The trail is clearly waymarked from the start of Cox's Battery Postbox walk (pages 111–12).

**Golf** St Helena Golf Club (✆ 24421; bar ⊕ 15.50–20.00 Wed, Sat & Sun), formed in 1903, hosts one of the most remote and challenging courses in the world – despite being just 4,783 yards (4,374m) long. Located close to Napoleon's former residence at Longwood, its magnificent scenic surroundings also attract wirebirds, as well as the occasional roaming donkey.

The nine-hole course, usually played twice with different tee boxes to give 18 holes, has a par of 68. Competitions are held every Saturday and Sunday from midday. Visitors are welcome, either on a one-off basis, in which case they pay just green fees (£7.50 for nine holes) or as temporary members (£30/3mths). Clubs can be hired for £3 including the bag.

**Stargazing** The lack of light pollution on St Helena puts her skies up there with the best for stargazing. They're at their clearest during the relatively dry summer months, between October and February. At present there is no specialist on hand to guide you through the heavens, but that doesn't detract from the magic.

**ON THE WATER** Almost all water activity on St Helena takes place from Jamestown, which – with its location on the leeward coast of the island – offers the most protected waters. That said, even here the seas can get rough, so do check the forecast, especially if you're swimming or kayaking.

As most boats operate only with minimum numbers, or for a minimum rate, they don't go out every day, but that's a situation that's likely to change as visitor numbers rise. All watersports can be booked direct, or through the tourist office (✆ 22158).

**Swimming** Despite some 38 miles (60km) of coastline, the opportunities for swimming in the sea on St Helena are limited by both access and by strong currents and undertows.

Access to the coast is possible by car in just three places: Jamestown and Rupert's Bay in the northwest of the island, and Sandy Bay to the south. Of these, most people stick to swimming from Jamestown and – further southeast – Lemon Valley.

Despite its name, Sandy Bay is characterised by a rather uninviting volcanic black sand, and strong undercurrents make swimming here extremely dangerous – never mind the Portuguese man o' wars (*Physalia physalis*). There are no golden sandy beaches. Indeed, the only place you're likely to come across patches of soft golden sand is high above the ocean, along the postbox walk to Lot's Wife's Ponds.

On the sheltered, northwestern side of the island, swimming is possible from most coastal areas when the sea is calm, including Rupert's Valley and Banks' Battery, but don't attempt to jump in off the rocks unless you've first checked that you can get out without difficulty. More sheltered, and safer, is to swim off the wharf in Jamestown, where there's also a good swimming pool (page 95). Continuing along the coast, Lemon Valley is an ideal spot to swim or snorkel, with steps up to a simple deck, and makes a popular excursion from Jamestown (page 107).

Swimming is also possible in a number of natural pools, sheltered from the sea by the rocks. The most popular is Lot's Wife's Ponds to the south (accessed along Lot's Wife's Ponds Postbox walk, page 116), and there's also Shark's Valley to the east (page 115), but again, don't be tempted to swim in the sea in these places.

**Diving and snorkelling** Diving in St Helena is extraordinary on many counts – not least the remote location and clear, unpolluted waters. Visibility regularly tops out at around 60ft (20m) and not far offshore, the rocks plunge almost straight down into the abyss, so that only 15m or so from the coast you'll be diving in water that's up to 3,280ft (1,000m) deep. In the summer months, between about November and March, water temperatures of around 79°F (26°C) are not unusual, falling to around 66°F (19°C) later in the year, so diving is possible all year round. Typically you'll be going out in a rigid inflatable boat (RIB), with a back-roll entry, but occasionally one of the operators will take a larger boat instead.

There is no shortage of marine life to be seen in these waters (pages 45–6), including butterflyfish, parrotfish, damselfish, trumpetfish, scorpionfish, jacks, puffers and morays, several of them not seen anywhere else in the world. And the good news is that many of these rarities are very easily enjoyed by snorkellers, as well as divers. Slip into the water off the wharf in Jamestown, or at Lemon Valley, and you'll be instantly surrounded by clouds of tiny endemic butterflyfish, their white bodies neatly outlined with bright yellow piping. Look down and you may spot the distinct glimmer of a greenfish, or a lone cowfish, locally known as a hogfish. More widespread is the ghostly trantran, or pipefish, and you can't miss the ocean surgeonfish – eloquently known as the shitty trooper – which tends to feed in shoals.

Devil rays are a real draw in the summer months, while in January, or sometimes February, you may be lucky enough to see a whale shark. Turtles – both hawksbill and green – are present all year. And a fair few wrecks added to the mix make for plenty of variety.

**Dive sites** Most of the dive sites are within a relatively small area of inshore waters, just a very short boat ride east or west of Jamestown. Sites such as Long Ledge and Cat Island typify the sort of diving you can expect. Boulders encrusted with red algae (*Wrangelia pencillata*) that look vivid scarlet in the sunshine, dulling to a deep rust on cloudier days. Inviting shallow swim-throughs, their roofs painted brilliant yellow by orange cup coral (*Balanophyllia helenae*). And fish aplenty, from the pretty St Helena butterflyfish to shoals of jacks and the occasional moray eel or spiny lobster.

3

**Wreck dives** Countless ships have foundered in St Helena's treacherous seas, some in sufficiently shallow waters as to make excellent wreck dives. Easiest to access is the SS *Papanui*, a steam passenger ship which caught fire and sank in James Bay in 1911, fortunately with no loss of life. The wreck, its rudder clearly visible above the surface in the centre of the bay, is in no more than 42ft (13m) of water, and is only about 400 yards (365m) offshore, so is well within reach of stronger swimmers, too.

Close by lies the rather dull wreck of the *Spangereid*, a coal ship that also caught fire and sank, in 1920, but far more interesting is the *Bedgellet*, which was engaged by the owner to salvage the *Papanui*, but was deliberately scuttled near Long Ledge in 2001 when the money ran out.

Of the remaining five wreck dives, two – both in relatively deep water – stand out: the *Witte Leeuw*, at 35m off Munden's Point, and the RFA *Darkdale*, at 45m in James Bay. The **Witte Leeuw** (**White Lion**), a Dutch cargo ship carrying porcelain, diamonds and spices, went down in 1613. While the ribs of the vessel and some of her cannons are still visible, her treasure was long ago spirited away to the Rijksmuseum in Amsterdam. The story of the *Darkdale* is both more recent and more sobering. A British Royal Fleet Auxiliary tanker, she was torpedoed in October 1941 by a German submarine, with the loss of 41 lives. All are commemorated on the cenotaph, close to the seafront. It's long been known that oil was still on board, and in 2015, measures were in hand to pump this out in order to protect the island's pristine marine environment.

**Practicalities** If you're planning to dive, don't forget to bring your certification and log book. Although most equipment can be hired, it's always good to have your own mask and fins, and a dive computer is a big plus. Both dive operators rent out excellent diving kit at reasonable cost, including wetsuits suitable for summer and winter temperatures. Masks, snorkels, fins and a range of scuba gear can be bought on the island from Sub Tropic Adventures, The Hive in Jamestown, and George Young at Chubb's Spring (✆ *22141*).

At present, between the two local dive operators, there are regular dives every Thursday at 16.30, and on Saturday and Sunday mornings, with others on request for a minimum of six – either divers or snorkellers. Into the Blue also runs a ladies' dive at 16.30 on Tuesday. To make a reservation, either phone direct, or book through the tourist office.

Do note that there are no decompression facilities on St Helena, so it is particularly important to follow sensible diving practice.

**Dive operators** Both dive operators on St Helena are certified PADI instructors. As well as taking out recreational divers, they run a series of courses. For a one-off opportunity to try diving, perhaps for the first time, there's Discover Scuba, while more in-depth options range from the entry-level Open Water to Divemaster. Children aged eight or over can have a go with the Bubble Maker course, while ten year olds can tackle the Open Water qualification. Both can also handle Open Water referrals.

ᵻ✓ **Into the Blue** ✆23459, 23978; e craigiyon@ helanta.co.sh. Dive instructor Craig Yon qualified in South Africa. Once the airport is open, he is planning a 2-dive option, with a stop at Lemon Valley, perhaps for a picnic lunch. *£14.50/dive, exc equipment (av £20 total)*

ᵻ✓ **Sub Tropic Adventures** ✆22758; e sub-tropic.scuba@helanta.co.sh; www.stsa.co.sh. Anthony Thomas, who also trained in South Africa, set up his business in 2000. Along with the standard dives are a 2-dive option, & a 5-day package with 3 dives a day. *£15/dive, £25 inc equipment*

Although plenty of yachts find their way to St Helena from all over the world, the island is best known in sailing circles for the Governor's Cup. The brainchild of a former master of the RMS *St Helena*, Captain David Roberts, the biannual race between Cape Town and St Helena was inaugurated in 1996.

Although there had been a race before on this route, the southeasterly trade winds present a peculiar challenge: a speedy passage to St Helena followed by a beat all the way back to Cape Town against the wind, a long, arduous and drawn-out affair. What makes the Governor's Cup different is that it's a one-way race. Once participating yachts reach St Helena, those that are not proceeding onto a longer voyage are hoisted out of the water and onto the deck of the RMS *St Helena*, which then sails back to Cape Town with the yachts and crew on board.

The last race, held in 2014, attracted 18 entrants, from ocean-going racing vessels to monohull cruisers, some of them taking part as part of a longer voyage. Over the years, several St Helenians have been selected to crew for various yachts, and two fully owned and crewed St Helenian boats have taken part, the latest – *Diddakoi* – in 2008. The 2014 race was the last in its current format, since with the decommissioning of the RMS *St Helena*, probably in 2016, the logistics will inevitably need a rethink.

In the meantime, the likelihood is that St Helena will gain in popularity among the yachting fraternity, not least for those wishing to avoid the increasingly dangerous waters south of the Suez Canal. And here, the advent of the airport could well pay dividends, making it realistic to change crew at St Helena, or – with the possibility of getting parts reasonably quickly – to undertake even major repairs.

**Boat trips** As with other water-based activities, boat trips depart from Jamestown, and – with only one or two exceptions – stick to the sheltered northwest of the island. It's a great way to observe the cliffs from the seaward side, their improbably narrow ledges occupied by pure white fairy terns, and the occasional dangling rope hinting at the lengths a fisherman has gone to secure his catch. You'll usually see plenty of dolphin acrobatics, especially in the mornings, and get up close to the bird colonies on Speery and Egg islands. If you're lucky, you may spot a whale shark at the beginning of the year, while in winter, between around July and September, you may be rewarded by the sighting of a visiting humpback whale. On a practical note, all boats are fitted with suitable lifejackets, which must be worn.

***Swimming with whale sharks*** In season, roughly between January and early March (though the best time to see them is in January), most boat trips offer the opportunity to swim with whale sharks – so even if you're on a fishing trip, do take your swimming things (including a mask and snorkel), just in case. To protect both swimmers and sharks, swimmers must remain at least 3m from any whale shark, and 4m from its tail, and no flash photography is allowed.

***Fishing*** James Bay offers good sportfishing by any standards, with wahoo, yellow-fin tuna and dorado regularly caught inshore, and larger specimens, as well as marlin and the very occasional sailfish, further out. Smaller fish such as grouper and bullseye can be caught from the rocks, though do be careful as the seas around

St Helena: Practical Information  ACTIVITIES

3

here can be pretty volatile and the terrain slippery. Fishing tackle may be found in Jamestown at Solomon's DIY shop on Main Street.

While it's perfectly possible to team up with one of the local fishermen, there are two outfits with full public liability insurance that offer dedicated sportfishing for visitors: Into the Blue and Sub Tropic Adventures.

**Boat operators** Bookings with most of the following can be made direct or through the tourist office ( 22158).

**Crystal Klear Tours** 24675; e david.linda@ helanta.co.sh. Inshore boat tours in a shaded, glass-bottomed boat offer a dry-footed view of the underwater world, with commentary on sea life & wrecks by Graham Sim. The trip from Rupert's to Lemon Valley take around 1½hrs. Up to 18 passengers. *£18pp/min £150*

**Enchanted Isle** 23339; e enchantedisle@ helanta.co.sh, mvenchantedisle@gmail.com; www.enchantedisleltd.co.sh. New to the island in Oct 2014, Johnny Herne's 42ft (13m) boat, *Enchanted Isle*, offers 3hr nature tours along the leeward side of the island, from Jamestown to Speery Island. On board is natural history expert Graham Sim, whose knowledge of the birds & marine life, as well as island history, is a real bonus. Also possible is a 4hr round-the-island tour for up to 25 passengers, & there are plans for game-fishing trips (max 10 passengers). Excellent, non-bulky lifejackets are an added bonus. *3hrs £20pp/min £150; 4hrs £25pp/min £200*

**Gannet III** 23133; e bedwell.shanade@ helanta.co.sh, gannet3@helanta.co.sh. Natural history, round-the-island, sunset & booze cruises are available in this 35-seater part-covered launch. *2–4hrs; £140–200/boat*

**Into the Blue** 23459, 23677, 23978; e keith. michelle@helanta.co.sh. Keith & Craig Yon have a fleet of boats that can be chartered for scenic boat trips or excursions to Lemon Valley. Keith also organises excellent fishing trips, from family days out to serious game fishing, currently in his open boat, *Starlite* – which takes up to 20 passengers, but no more than 6 if they're all fishing. Typically you'll leave around 07.00, returning at 13.00 or slightly later. A larger boat to permit overnight fishing trips was expected to arrive in mid 2015. *Boat trips £100–150; fishing £200/boat; rates for overnight fishing on application*

**Pink Lady Boat Tours** 22699; e mia@ helanta.co.sh. Local couple Mia Henry & Leeroy Caswell offer dolphin- & birdwatching tours (2hrs), coastal sightseeing, sunset champagne cruises, swimming & watersports aboard their small motorboat, *Pink Lady. 2hrs £180/max 9 passengers; tailor-made trips on request*

**Sub Tropic Adventures** See page 78. Dive operator Anthony Thomas has 2 boats, *Sea Horse* & *Sea Hawk*, giving him the flexibility to run dolphin- & whale-watching tours, sportfishing trips & tailor-made cruises. *Boat trips £15pp/max 14 passengers; sportfishing £200/boat*

**Kayaking** Sea kayaking is certainly the most peaceful means of exploring the coastline of James Bay, and an ideal way to get to Lemon Valley (page 107) for a picnic and a swim. Good-quality single and double kayaks can be rented from New Horizons, the community youth group in Jamestown ( 22034; *£2/4 sgl/dbl per day, inc lifejackets*).

You'll need to carry your kayak to the sea, where you can launch off the rocks below Donny's Bar, but it isn't the easiest place to access, or the most pristine spot, and shoes are a must. When kayaking, keep inshore to avoid the strong offshore currents, and note that it's generally easier paddling towards Lemon Valley than coming back, so allow an hour or so for the return trip.

**Other watersports** More extreme watersports were introduced to James Bay only in 2015. For safety reasons, there is talk of creating a 25m offshore 'swim zone' in the harbour, with watersports falling outside of this area.

**Oceano Xtreme**   ESH Unit 12, Half Tree Hollow; 23850; e oceanoxtremesthelena@gmail.com. Local watersports enthusiast Paul Scipio offers jetskiing, flyboarding, wakeboarding, waterskiing, tubing, kneeboarding – all with buoyancy aids & full public liability insurance. He's planning to introduce an inflatable platform with a slide in the harbour, too, & perhaps an ice-cream van alongside a ticket office on the harbour wall. *Tubing £3/10mins (no unaccompanied children under 8); jet ski £30/hr; boat hire with choice of activity £50/hr (max 8 passengers)*

## CULTURAL VISITS

It's all very well to read about local culture, but all too often this is experienced secondhand. St Helena, however, has long offered the opportunity to spend time in an island home, perhaps for tea or coffee, or for Sunday lunch cooked by your host – giving visitors the chance to ask questions or simply just to enjoy being in a Saint home. Costs vary but guests at Patsy Flagg's home (*Harlyn, Half Tree Hollow;* 23727) can expect to pay around £10 per person for a family lunch, or £15 for a three-course dinner, and for afternoon tea or coffee with sandwiches and cake you'll be looking at around £4 a head.

In a development of home hosting, Linda and Derek Richards ( 24620, 22666; e office@islandimages.co.sh; www.islandimages.co.sh) have opened the doors of their modern home-cum-B&B in St Paul's (Richards Travel Lodge, page 103), not just for meals, but also to visitors who would like to learn to cook local specialities (*£15–25pp, depending on numbers*). Along with favourites such as fishcakes, pilau and stuffed tuna (delicious!) are slightly more esoteric options such as goat meat curry and potjie meals, cooked in a cast-iron pot. It's all very relaxed, and if you'd prefer to watch over a glass of wine, that's fine, too. Either way, you get to feast on the results. There's also the option of informal barbecues, with great views from their garden out to sea. All such visits must be pre-booked, either direct or through the tourist office.

## TRAVELLING POSITIVELY

Many visitors would like to give something back to the people of St Helena on returning home. Donating books that you have finished will help keep the library supplied, and a small donation to the Guides or Scouts would never go amiss on an island where young people benefit so much from the opportunities they provide. Even if you'll be on St Helena for only a relatively short period of time, you could consider volunteering, too. There are numerous opportunities to get involved, either in person or financially, and it would add a new dimension to your stay. These are just some of them.

**Friends of St Helena**   See page 193.

**St Helena National Trust (SHNT)**   Broadway Hse, Jamestown; 22190; e sth.nattrust@helanta.sh; www.nationaltrust.org.sh. An umbrella conservation organisation established in 2002, the SHNT is dedicated to the preservation of the island's heritage, from historic buildings through to a broad conservation remit. Included in its portfolio are the Millennium Forest (page 110) & the Heart-shaped Waterfall (pages 95–6), & the Trust is also setting up forest schools to encourage youngsters to 'learn in a local woodland'. Membership – more of a supporters' network – is £50 a year, but for £10, visitors can adopt a wirebird, or plant a tree in the Millennium Forest (either in person or remotely). Volunteers can just turn up to help, even for just half a day, or longer-term placements can be organised.

**SHAPE**   (See also page 115) SHAPE aims to provide training & work-related experience for people of working age with disabilities, with the intention of them leading independent and fulfilling lives. The group is entirely self-funding, so welcomes both donations & volunteers, as well as visitors.

# 4

# Jamestown

For more than 500 years, Jamestown – indeed, St Helena as a whole – has been approached exclusively from the sea, a sight that has variously instilled awe, inspiration and a deep sense of foreboding. Such is the unique nature of the island that it has been submitted for consideration as a UNESCO World Heritage Site, largely because of its extraordinary biodiversity, landscape and geological features.

## ST HELENA FROM THE SEA

From the deck of a ship, St Helena looks dauntingly bleak, the buildings of Jamestown scattered like so many flimsy boxes at the foot of dramatic cliffs. Yet while the key first impression is of barren rocks, it's **Jamestown** itself that draws the eye, its scale more manageable to the human psyche than the surrounding grandeur. From the harbour, the cluster of houses that define the little town draws the eye along the valley to hint at the hilly, green interior of the island. About halfway up, the group of houses on the hill make up

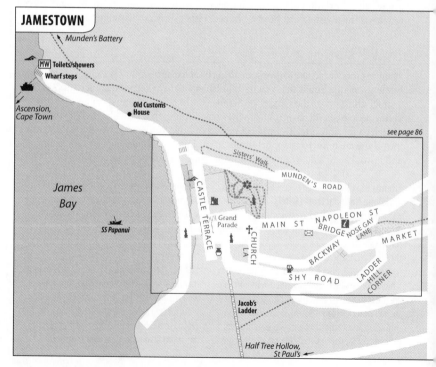

see page 86

**The Briars**, where Napoleon spent his happiest time on St Helena, at the Briars Pavilion.

Look beyond Jamestown and – especially with a pair of binoculars – you can spot many of the island's key features, with glimpses into the almost hidden valleys that dissect those towering cliffs. First, take your gaze to the far left (northeast) of the island, where the prominent **Sugar Loaf** rises up 700ft (213m), part of the ridge of a volcano that was extinguished 11 million years ago. In the days of sail, the prevailing southeast trade winds meant that ships could reach James Bay only by rounding Sugar Loaf Point, which was used as a signalling station by the British until 1877.

About halfway down from the top of Sugar Loaf towards the ocean, some 160ft (49m) above sea level, you'll spot the military fortification **Middle Point** and, a little further to the right, **Half Moon Battery**. Both were erected by the British at the beginning of the 18th century. The oldest defences, however, at the lower right along the bay, were already standing by 1678. Named **Banks' Platform** in honour of the commanding officer who oversaw its construction, the original fortifications here were eventually destroyed by the continuous battering of heavy breakers, but they were rebuilt to further secure the island during Napoleon's exile. Towards the left of the valley, the fortification wall with an outlet of water is one of several similar ruins that can still be seen around the coast.

Continuing to the right in the direction of Jamestown, you'll come to **Rupert's Bay**, which was probably named in honour of Prince Rupert, a leading Royalist cavalry commander in the English Civil War. The old fortress wall to the left of the valley is the remainder of the British defence installations that were built and improved during the 18th century.

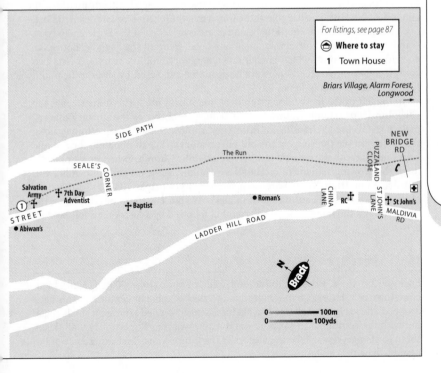

For listings, see page 87

🛏 **Where to stay**

1    Town House

Long the industrial centre of St Helena, with the island's only fish-processing plant, **Rupert's Valley** is the site of a new wharf, which will in future be the docking point for cargo and cruise ships. The chimney between the two white fuel tanks is a part of a desalinisation plant that was built in the early 20th century to provide potable water for Boer War prisoners, but was never fully utilised. Between 1840 and 1847, Rupert's was also 'home' to the 9,000 slaves who were freed from passing ships by Her Majesty's Navy, and has recently been the site of a major archaeological investigation. In 2015, the future of the human remains excavated was the subject of considerable discussion, but no decision has yet been taken.

Between Rupert's Valley and Jamestown is **Munden's Hill**, named after Sir Richard Munden, under whose command the British won back St Helena from the Dutch in 1673, and who subsequently built the first fortresses along the rock ledges.

Well visible are the connecting paths from Jamestown to Banks' Battery and up to the fortification of Upper Munden, where prickly-pear cacti line the ridge. Once well-developed roads, these are now suitable only for walkers, who are protected from falling rocks by heavy metal meshing installed across the cliffs. Lower down, the buildings that can be seen from the ship are defence installations, used during World War II, while between 1957 and 1961, the **dilapidated buildings** above provided housing for three princes from Bahrain, the last people to be exiled to St Helena. To the right, there is a sign stating that east of this point is where the **first telegraph cable** between England and Cape Town came onshore in 1899. Then in the centre of the hill, close to sea level, you can make out old cannons on the rocks.

Moving now to the right (southwest) of Jamestown, you can clearly see **Jacob's Ladder** (pages 94–5), its progression of 699 steps marching relentlessly up the steep cliff to **Ladder Hill**. The flagpole at the top marks the location of **Ladder Hill Fort**, one of numerous fortifications that stand guard over much of the St Helenian coast – and now earmarked for development as a hotel. Beneath the flagpole, notice the ancient layers of lava, which cooled down some ten million years ago. The two conspicuous white triangles here are navigational aids, used by ships to help find their anchor position in James Bay.

To the left of the ladder, the prominent house with the white stone steps is the **Cliff Top House**. Built in the late 19th century, probably as the military officers' mess, it is now used as housing for British government employees. Continuing along the ridge, you see the ruins of the **old observatory**, while dominating the top, the large building with the red roof is the **New Apostolic Church**. Other, smaller houses mark the growing settlement of **Half Tree Hollow**, while on the hill behind, you can make out **High Knoll Fort**, completed in 1894 (pages 104–5). To the right of the houses are two guns, installed in 2003. As your eye continues on round, the island follows the same pattern: a barren hill followed by a lush valley, followed by a barren hill…

## JAMESTOWN

Enclosed on three sides by forbidding walls of rock some 500ft (150m) high, Jamestown is St Helena's first – indeed only – port of call. For centuries, ships have dropped anchor in its sheltered bay, their passengers ferried ashore on small boats. But with the coming of the airport – and a new wharf in Rupert's Bay – all this is about to change; few will be the visitors of the future whose first experience of the island will be the capital.

Founded in 1659, but largely built in the 18th century, Jamestown could almost have been plucked from a Jane Austen novel. The little town stretches up a narrow valley, accessible only along two improbably narrow roads that slope down the hillside from on high. Its wide central street that once reverberated to the march of soldiers is lined with graceful houses. Its people are used to a slow, measured way of life, where it's normal to greet a passing stranger. Some visitors spend just a few hours here; others a week or more. However long you have, you're likely to discover that Jamestown is central to a real understanding of St Helena.

## TOURIST INFORMATION AND TRAVEL AGENTS
### Tourist information

**St Helena Tourism** [86 B5] The Canister, Main St; 22158; e enquiries@tourism.co.sh; www.sthelenatourism.com; ☺ 08.30–16.00 Mon–Fri, 09.00–13.00 Sat. The tourist office on St Helena plays a considerably more important role than most. As well as being a source of information on all things visitor-orientated, it acts as a central booking office for accommodation, restaurants & activities – a particularly vital role on an island where advance reservations for almost everything are essential. A small selection of leaflets, books & postcards is a useful adjunct.

**Travel agents** For details of individual tour operators on St Helena, see pages 97–9.

**Saint Travel** Halfway Hse, St Paul's; 25091; e enquiries@saint-travel.com; www.saint-travel.com. Established by Merrill Joshua in 2015, this new one-stop shop offers flight bookings, accommodation, vehicle hire, tours & corporate services.

**Solomon & Co** [86 B5] Main St; 22523; www.solomons-sthelena.com; ☺ 00.30–15.00 Mon– Fri, 09.00–13.00 Sat when RMS in port. As well as handling ticket sales for the RMS *St Helena* & onward flights, Solomon's act as agents for cruise ships, & handles a series of on-island trips from the wharf, including a historical tour of Jamestown, a trip to High Knoll Fort, & a tour round the island. Private tours can be arranged on request.

**GETTING AROUND** Jamestown is exceptionally compact, and it's possible to walk everywhere. Indeed, car parking is so limited that it's easier to go without on the days when you're planning to stay in town, or take an excursion of some sort. If you're looking for a space, do be careful if you park on the harbour. Those Atlantic rollers can be sizeable, with potential detrimental impact on any car on the seaward side.

The official taxi stand is located in the centre of Jamestown, behind the tourist office, where taxis are usually parked in front of the phone booths. When a passenger ship is in James Bay, however, you can also find taxis parked at the harbour. With cars in short supply, it's a good idea to pre-book a taxi, either direct or through the tourist office. For details of taxis, as well as buses and car hire, see pages 64–7.

 **WHERE TO STAY** *Map, page 86, unless otherwise stated*
Most of St Helena's accommodation is in Jamestown, with good reason. The small capital is a vibrant microcosm of urban life, with restaurants, cafés and shops, and all water-orientated activities on your doorstep, and the starting point for all guided tours. On the down side, Lower Jamestown – where most places to stay are located – can get pretty noisy at weekends, so if that's likely to be a problem, think carefully about the location of your room, or consider somewhere out of town.

For many years, St Helena has had just two hotels – the Consulate in Jamestown, and the Farm Lodge Country House Hotel (page 103) in the St Paul's area, for which a car is essential. Plans are in hand, however, for a significant new hotel in the centre of Jamestown, which is expected to open in 2016.

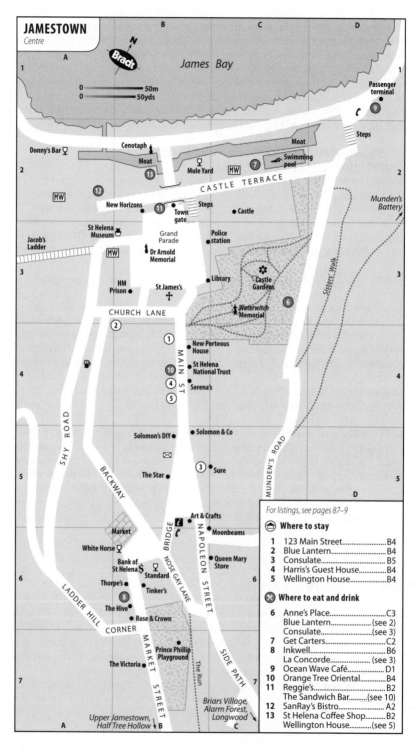

# JAMESTOWN
*Centre*

N

*Bradt*

James Bay

A    B    C    D

0 ———————— 50m
0 ———————— 50yds

1

Passenger
terminal
**9**

Donny's Bar ♀          Cenotaph          Moat                              Steps

Moat          **13**          Mule Yard     MW     **7**          Swimming
pool

2

MW     **12**          New Horizons          Steps          Munden's
Battery

CASTLE TERRACE

**11**     Town
gate          ● Castle

Jacob's
Ladder          St Helena
Museum          Grand
Parade          Police
station

MW

Dr Arnold
Memorial

3

HM
Prison          St James's          ● Library          Castle
Gardens          **6**

Sisters' Walk

CHURCH LANE          Waterwitch
Memorial

**2**

**1**     New Porteous
House

MAIN ST

**10**     St Helena
National Trust

**4**          Serena's

**5**

4

Solomon's DIY ●     ● Solomon & Co

✉

**3** ● Sure

The Star ●

5

SHY ROAD

BACKWAY

Art & Crafts
ℹ
Moonbeams

Market

White Horse ♀

Bank of
St Helena $     Standard          Queen Mary
Store

Thorpe's ●          Tinker's

**8**

The Hive ●

Rose & Crown ●

The Victoria ●          Prince Phillip
Playground

NAPOLEON STREET

BRIDGE

NOSE GAY LANE

MARKET STREET

SIDE PATH

The Run

6

LADDER HILL CORNER

7

Upper Jamestown,
Half Tree Hollow ↓          Briars Village,
Alarm Forest,
Longwood

# Discover
# St Helena
## with the experts

Remote and unspoilt, this is an island with a fascinating history, spectacular scenery and endemic wildlife. Enjoy an independent self-drive and discover Napoleon's legacy, the 699-step Jacob's Ladder, a 182 year old tortoise, the Post Box Walks and so much more. Take a wildlife cruise or a guided 4WD tour and really get off the beaten track.

As tailor made experts since 1984, we're pretty good at putting together holidays that exceed expectations.

See our full collection at
**discover-the-world.co.uk**

Images © iStock.com/StHelena

*top*    The she cabbage (*Lachanodes arborea*; left) and babies' toes (*Hydrodea cryptantha*; right), two of at least 45 endemic plants on St Helena (pages 35 and 33) (TH)

*above left*    The distinctive masked booby (*Sula dactylatra*) nests on cliff tops on both St Helena and Ascension (page 44) (AIG)

*above right*    The Madagascar fody (*Foudia madagascaniensis*), or cardinal, adds a splash of colour to St Helena's birdlife (pages 42–3) (JPG)

*below*    Thousands of sooty terns (*Onychoprion fuscata*) congregate on Ascension's Wideawake Fairs to hatch their eggs (page 151) (TH)

*top*     Ascension's land crabs (*Johngarthia lagostoma*) often surprise visitors to Green Mountain (pages 126–7) (TH)

*above*     Female green turtle (*Chelonia mydas*) returning to the sea on Long Beach, Ascension (page 127) (TH)

*below*     Whale sharks (*Rhincodon typus*) are one of St Helena's best-loved visitors early in the year (page 46) (MS/EMD)

Once barren rock, Green Mountain today offers
superb walking through dense vegetation
(pages 146–9) (TH)

# Ascension in colour

*above left*   Relaxed bars and clubs are a part of life on Ascension (page 143) (TH)

*above right*   Heavy artillery hints at Ascension's strategic role on the world stage (AIG)

*below*   St Mary's Church stands out against Cross Hill in Georgetown (page 145) (TH)

*bottom*   Comfortless Cove, a scenic spot for swimming or snorkelling (page 150) (TH)

# Tristan da Cunha in colour

*top left & top right*   Tristan's signposts bear witness to the island's remoteness (AT)

*above left*   Nightingale's population of subantarctic fur seals (*Arctocephalus tropicalis*) haul up to breed and moult on all the Tristan islands (page 182) (AT)

*below*   St Joseph's Church in The Settlement is dwarfed by the volcanic backdrop (page 175) (AT)

*top* Northern rockhopper penguins (*Eudyptes moseleyi*) enliven the landscape of all the islands in the Tristan group, and knitted ones make a great souvenir (page 180) (AT)

*above* The endemic Tristan albatross (*Diomedia dabbenena*) has a wingspan of up to 118in (3m) (page 157) (AT)

*right* View of Edinburgh of the Seven Seas from the volcano (page 173) (SS)

*below* Breathtaking landscapes are the hallmark of Gough, one of the world's most important seabird islands (pages 180–2) (CS)

# EXILE, BUT ONLY FOR AWHILE

PHOTO CREDIT: PAUL TYSON

## EXPERIENCE THE REAL SAINT HELENA

Up until 2016, the only way to get to Saint Helena, an island in the South Atlantic Ocean is by boat, usually a five-day journey from Cape Town.

But that will change in March 2016, when a weekly flight service from Johannesburg commences to the island. What was a five-day trip will soon become a four-and-a-half-hour flight.

A new airport means an increase in tourism, and easier access to the island where fallen French emperor Bonaparte died in exile. With a population of 700, Jamestown is the only port, framed by craggy volcanic cliffs.

**YOUR JOURNEY:** For now, The RMS Saint Helena – the last commercially operating Royal Mail Ship in operation today – remains as the only passenger ship serving the British island. And beginning March 2016, a weekly flight service from Johannesburg.

**YOUR STAY:** The mid-18th Century Consulate Hotel offers relaxing accommodation in the centre of Jamestown. The hotel was recently renovated for guests' comfort, while maintaining its historical charm.

### Call us today for your custom quote to see this remarkable island.

**Phone: 1+ (204) 949 0199**
**Email: sthelena@gctravel.ca**

The **Great Canadian Travel** Company Ltd.

**164 Marion Street • Winnipeg, Manitoba Canada • R2H 0T4**

*Interesting travel experiences for interested people.*

Guesthouses and B&Bs are only slightly more numerous, but represent a range of styles, from the homely and traditional to the more contemporary.

## Self-catering

As elsewhere on St Helena, self-catering in Jamestown is very affordable compared with other accommodation. In **Lower Jamestown**, near the shops and the harbour, you'll be in the hub of things, with all that goes with that in terms of noise – especially at weekends. Here, options range from traditional flats above the shops and more modern conversions with their own veranda, to semi-detached houses and – most basic of all – Coles Bunker, owned by the National Trust. Effectively a hostel, it offers a couple of rooms with shared bathroom, whereas other options are entirely self-contained, with their own bathroom, kitchen and living area, and up to four bedrooms. Prices start from around £40 a night for two people sharing.

**Upper Jamestown** is generally quieter, with bungalows and houses with a veranda or shared garden, as well as flats – some of them in the attractive Cambrian House. There are a couple of small shops in the area, but for the most part you'll need to make the 15-minute walk down hill to the town centre for supplies. Many landlords will collect visitors from the seafront on arrival, so you don't have to worry about your luggage, but once the airport opens it would be as well to check arrangements at the time of booking. For details of what to expect, and how to book, see page 68.

## Hotels

🏠 **123 Main Street** (32 rooms) Main St; e reservations@mantiscollection.com; www.mantiscollection.com. By mid 2016, the 3 historic Georgian houses that front Main St will be restored & transformed into a new boutique hotel, complete with bar & restaurant open to the public. Some of the rooms will look over Main St; others will be at the back in a new extension, so almost certainly quieter. **£££££**

🏠 **Consulate Hotel** (18 rooms) Main St; ✆ 22962; e consulathotel@gmail.com, con.hotel@helanta.co.sh; see ad, 2nd colour section. The biggest hotel on the island, the Consulate occupies adjoining properties that date to the mid 18th century. Since it was bought by Hazel Wilmot in 2008, it has been refurbished with an eclectic range of pictures, tapestries & period furniture that adds a strong sense of place. En-suite rooms, some very spacious, have twin or dbl beds kitted out with crisp white linen, & will be getting a further facelift before the airport opens. A fan, phone & coffee/tea-making facilities are standard. Plans are in hand for another 24 rooms at the back, including 8 in the peaceful & private terrace gardens.

Central to the hotel is a welcoming courtyard bar (⊕ *up to 11.00–23.00 daily, depending on demand*), while at the front is a popular coffee shop (page 88). Both are open to non-residents, but upstairs the colonial wrought-iron balcony overlooking the centre of Jamestown, & 2 comfortable lounges with an extensive library, are exclusive to guests. Gift shop & off licence. Wi-Fi. **££££**

## Guesthouses & B&Bs

🏠 **Town House** [map, page 82] (5 rooms) Market St; ✆ 23030; e colin.marlene.yon@helanta.co.sh. Colin & Marlene Yon's home is a comfortable, relaxed & very welcoming B&B with no ceremony. Rooms – 2 dbls & 3 twins – are nicely decorated in St Helenian style, 4 with en-suite shower & 1 with a private bathroom. Guests are welcome to share the lounge with TV, to help themselves to tea, coffee & cake, & to use the honesty bar – with money going to charity. Packed lunches & evening meals on request. Wi-Fi. **££–£££**

🏠 **Blue Lantern** (8 rooms) Narrabacks; ✆ 25555; e keith.michielle@helanta.co.sh. Opened in Mar 2015, Keith Yon's refreshingly modern venture is more akin to a pension than a B&B. Upstairs, relatively small en-suite rooms (6 dbls, 2 twins) with tea/coffee facilities lead off a spacious lounge area with comfortable sofas & wall-mounted TV. Décor is contemporary, with pine furniture & bright splashes of colour from fabrics, lamps & artwork. A small veranda makes a nice spot for an evening drink with a view of Jacob's Ladder, & while it's not a pretty location, it's also potentially quieter than Main St. Beneath is a large restaurant (page 88). **££**

🏠 **Harris's Guest House** (3 rooms) Main St; ☎22729. A classic motherly landlady & a very good cook, Irene Harris runs an old-fashioned B&B in the heart of town, its spacious lounge groaning with family memorabilia. Upstairs, a large family room with 2 dbl beds is en suite, while another family room & a twin share a bathroom, separate shower & separate toilet off the laundry room, with washing machine. Each room has a fan, & there's a TV with DVD & video. Lunch & dinner in the cosy dining room are available on request (£££). A taxi service & car hire (£12.50/day) are offered to guests. **££**

🏠 **Wellington House** (6 rooms) Main St; ☎22529; e wellingtonhouse@helanta.co.sh. The grand name, high ceilings & beautifully polished wooden floors of this 18th-century building belie a friendly guesthouse that has been in Ivy Robinson's family for more than 50 years. Rooms – 5 twins & a dbl – are a bit old-fashioned, though spacious & comfortably furnished. None are en suite – yet – & the quirky bathroom facilities in the attic above are rather spartan. Downstairs, there's a formal dining room & a TV & video in the rather smart lounge, where tea/coffee are available on request. **£**

🍴 **WHERE TO EAT AND DRINK** *Map, page 86*

As well as the following, all within Jamestown, it's worth considering **Tasty Bites** in Half Tree Hollow (page 102), whose manager will collect diners from Jamestown, or driving out to **Farm Lodge** (page 103) or **Sunflower Café** (page 104). With the notable exception of Anne's Place, you'll usually need to make a reservation for dinner.

There are also two mobile **take-away** food bars by the Castle, usually open on a Saturday from about 10.00. One sells burgers and hotdogs, the other fried chicken and various rice dishes (£).

## Restaurants

🍴 **Consulate Hotel** Main St; ☎22962; café ⏲ 08.30–17.00 daily, restaurant ⏲ 19.00. The Consulate's 1st-floor restaurant, reopened in late 2015, is an attraction in itself, decked out with heavy wooden furniture, ship's timbers & pulleys, & traditional blue-&-white crockery. The 3-course menu will feature island-grown vegetables, salads & herbs. Reservations essential. On the ground floor, La Concorde Coffee Shop offers light but innovative breakfasts & lunches & a good selection of cakes & pastries in Parisian-style splendour: intricate cast-iron light fixtures, a grand piano & a hefty collection of Napoleonic memorabilia. *Café £–££, restaurant ££££*

🍴 **Blue Lantern** Narrabacks; ☎25555; ⏲ from 18.30 Tue–Sat, lunch Sun. The large but pleasantly uncluttered restaurant at the Blue Lantern opened in May 2015. The à la carte menu has a distinct South African slant, majoring on steaks, surf 'n' turf etc, something of a first for St Helena, & there's also a set 2- & 3-course option. Large-screen TV is a plus or a minus, depending on your tastes. **££££**

🍴 **Orange Tree Oriental Restaurant** Association Hall, Main St; ☎22126, 23370; ⏲ 12.00–14.00 & 17.00–21.30 Mon–Sat. St Helena's first oriental restaurant, the Orange Tree offers a relatively small menu of Chinese & Thai dishes, from the standard sweet & sour pork to some – such as Thai tuna curry – with a local twist. Portions are huge, & service friendly, but space is limited so you may need to book. **££££**

🍴 **Wellington House** Main St; ☎22529; ⏲ 19.00, reservations only. The Wellington has the feel of a hotel dining room, albeit with pretty lace tablecloths, but service is friendly & owner Ivy Robinson serves up home-cooked 3-course meals, based on family recipes, in gargantuan portions. Tea or coffee are available from 10.00, but like the restaurant, must be booked a day ahead. **£££–££££**

🍴 **Anne's Place** Castle Gardens; ☎22797; ⏲ around 10.00–14.30 & 18.00–20.00 daily, but flexible depending on custom. A favourite with the yachting fraternity since 1979, Anne's might have seen better days but it's exceptionally laid back & the setting – on a cool terrace in the Castle Gardens – takes a lot of beating. There's no need to book, either. Anne's daughter-in-law majors on simple grills & light meals, with local specialities to order. Freshly caught fish with chips & salad is good value, & keep a space for homemade lemon meringue pie if it's on the menu. Help yourself to tea & (usually) fresh coffee. Wi-Fi. **£–££**

## Cafés

**Inkwell** 22887; ⏰ 09.30–15.00 Mon, Tue, Thu & Fri. This simple café, convenient for local shops, is also linked to the bookshop of the same name. Alongside rolls, sandwiches & coffee are daily specials such as soups & homemade fish burgers with salad. £

**La Concorde Coffee Shop** See page 88.

**Ocean Wave Café** Harbour front; ⏰ 10.00–14.00 Mon–Fri, 10.00–13.00 Sat. Under new management since May 2015, this modern café has a gem of a location on the harbour. The menu focuses on salads, sandwiches, wraps, cakes & pastries. £

**St Helena Coffee Shop** New Horizons Leisure Park; ⏰ 08.00–15.00 Wed–Sat & when RMS *St Helena* in harbour. Specialising in coffee from their own plantation, this umbrella-shaded open-air café near the seafront serves b/fasts, toasted sandwiches, hot sausage rolls & daily specials such as homemade quiche & salad. Popular with both visitors & local office workers. £

**The Sandwich Bar** Association Hall, Main St; 22666; ⏰ 07.30–14.00 Mon–Fri. B/fasts, sandwiches, salads, homemade soups & baked potatoes: The Sandwich Bar does what it says, & more. Local specialities include fish cakes daily, plus bread 'n' dance (on Mon) & pilau (on Wed). Packed lunches can be made up, too. Wi-Fi. £

**SanRay's Bistro** ⏰ 10.00–14.00 Mon–Fri, 17.00–late Fri, 18.00–late Sat. More of a take-away than a bistro in feel, SanRay's nevertheless has a covered wooden seating area behind Donny's which is a relaxed place to enjoy tuna, chips & salad or a steaming (polystyrene) plate of traditional pilau. Particularly busy on Fri nights. £

## Take-aways

**Get Carters** The Mule Yard; 22277; e getcarters@helanta.co.sh; ⏰ 18.00–21.00 Fri, 12.00–21.00 Sat. Jamestown's take-away pizza place does a roaring trade, with small, regular & mega options. You can have paninis, too, & waffles to finish. On Fri nights the menu is augmented by Mexican, Moroccan & other more cosmopolitan offerings. ££

**Reggie's** Arch Gate Corner; 22353; ⏰ 10.00–14.00 Mon, Wed, Thu & Fri, 17.00–21.00 Sat. Take-away pasta, burgers & even steak from a small window just inside the Arch. £

**The Star** Main St; 22683. The Star's take-away counter offers a range of hot food, from pies & pastries to pilau & soup. £

**PUBS AND NIGHTLIFE** Generally very quiet during the week, Main Street in Jamestown can get pretty rowdy on Friday and Saturday nights, when carousing can go on into the early hours of the morning.

The two pubs, **The Standard** and **The White Horse** [86 B6], are definitely for drinking only – gastropubs have not yet arrived in the South Atlantic. Both are licensed to open 11.00–01.00 daily, but unless it's busy, the White Horse in particular may be firmly shut until 17.00, and lack of customers will cause either or both to close much earlier. There's sports TV at The Standard, and live music on a Saturday night.

Relatively new to Jamestown is the concept of pop-up bars. At weekends, keep an eye out on the harbour front for the open-air Amphibian. On a warm evening, it's a great place to chill with a cool beer after a swim or dive. For pubs and bars outside Jamestown, see pages 102, 104 and 114.

**Donny's Bar** [86 A2] ⏰ 16.00–12.00 Thu & Sun, 11.00–02.00 Fri/Sat, & when ships are in harbour. Arguably the best permanent location on the seafront, Donny's is *the* place to come on a Fri & Sat night, with a large open-air terrace, a disco with occasional live music & a friendly vibe. It's currently the only cocktail place on the island, too; for a local take on an old favourite, try a Tungi margarita. When the airport goes live, opening hours are likely to be longer, & Donny plans to open a restaurant above the bar – with guaranteed sea views.

**The Mule Yard** [86 B2] ⏰ 14.00–late Mon–Wed, 11.00–late Thu–Sat, varies Sun. It's about as casual as it gets; this open-air bar, with a few bench seats and a sports TV vying for attention with the stereo system. Join the throng on a Fri after work & you'll be seeing in the weekend, St Helena-style.

**SHOPPING** If you search long enough, you'll find most things in Jamestown. It's not without reason that locals sometimes refer to shopping as an adventure!

**Food** Jamestown boasts a reasonable range of food shops, and while supplies – particularly of fresh produce – are limited, you can usually find something that will approximate to what you're after – or serve as a replacement.

For **fruit and vegetables**, start at St Helena Growers' Cooperative in the Market, The Star or Thorpe's (*also* ⊕ *10.00–13.00 Sun*). The best time is Thursday morning, when local produce such as bananas, onions, carrots, potatoes, tomatoes and cabbage is brought into town from farms in the country. Ideally join the queue early; by 11.00 much of it will be gone. After that, and particularly as the week progresses, the shelves can look very thin, though shopping around can turn up a hidden handful of beans, or even a lettuce.

Good **bread** is usually available from The Star, which – like the bakery at Half Tree Hollow – is owned by Solomon's. Their range includes baguettes and croissants, as well as cakes and quiches.

For **fresh fish**, unless you're in a position to catch your own, pop into KGT Williams in the Market, though note that it closes earlier than most shops. Frozen **meat** is freely available, but for fresh pork or beef, try one of the two butchers: Steven's, again in the Market, and Tinker's [86 B4], which is part of and opposite Thorpe's. The Star often has a decent selection of fresh meat, too, especially pork.

Other food shops worth knowing about are the small grocery shop in the basement of the **Wellington House** (entrance at the side), which has quite a good range of spices, and two other splendidly eclectic stores: **The Victoria** on Market Street [86 B7] and the unmissable **Queen Mary Store** on Napoleon Street [86 C6].

**Gifts and souvenirs** Many of the shops sell gifts in some shape or form, but it pays to shop around for something more interesting.

**Art & Crafts**  [86 B5] The Canister, Main St;
☏ 22101; ⊕ 10.00–15.00 Mon, Tue, Thu & Fri,
10.00–13.00 Sat, & when RMS/cruise ships in
harbour. Run by volunteers, the shop next to
the tourist office aims to support local artists &
craftsmen, including the charity, SHAPE (page 115).
As well as paintings of or inspired by St Helena, there
are unusual items such as 'seedwork' mats, bags &
jewellery, woven plastic baskets & heavy wooden
photo frames, plus a small selection of books.
**G-Unique Designs**  [86 B6] The Market, Market
St. Handmade beaded & silver jewellery. See page
102 for details.
**The Hive**  [86 B6] Market St; ☏ 22427. Alongside
the gifts & stationery are swimwear, children's
sunsuits & snorkel gear.

**Inkwell**  [86 B6] Market St; ☏ 22887;
e theinkwell@helanta.co.sh; ⊕ 09.30–15.00
Mon, Tue, Thu, Fri, 10.00–13.00 Sat. The island's
only dedicated bookshop has a small range with a
particular focus on novels & children's books. Ask
at the café if it appears to be closed.
**Moonbeams**  [86 B5] Napoleon St; ☏ 22944;
www.moonbeamsforall.com. As well as a good
selection of cards & gifts, including personalised
items, & locally made souvenirs, Moonbeams offers
photographic services, & can burn images to CD.
**Roman's**  Market St, Upper Jamestown; ☏ 22757.
Souvenirs inc St Helena-themed tea towels & bags.
**Serena's**  [86 B4] Main St; ☏ 22792. A selection of
gifts & souvenirs, from T-shirts & sticks of rock to St
Helena key rings & egg cups.

## OTHER PRACTICALITIES
**Bank of St Helena**  [86 B6] Market St;
☏ 22390; e jamestown@sthelenabank.com; www.
sainthelenabank.com; ⊕ 08.45–15.00 Mon–Fri,
09.00–12.00 Sat

**DHL**  Customs Hse, The Wharf; ☏ 22643;
⊕ 08.00–16.00 Mon–Fri
**Post office**  [86 B5] Main St; ☏ 22629;
⊕ 08.30–15.45 Mon–Fri, 08.30–12.00 Sat.

As well as offering standard postal services, the main post office is home to the Philatelic Bureau (*www.postoffice.gov.sh*). It also sells the old Ordnance Survey maps of the island at 1:25,000 & – in 6 sheets – at 1:10,000.

**Sure** [86 B5] Bishop's Rooms, Main St; ☎22900; www.sure.co.sh; ⏰ 09.00–15.30 Mon, Tue, Thu & Fri, 09.00–13.00 Wed. The island's sole telecommunications provider also sells phonecards (£5 & £10).

## WHAT TO SEE AND DO
### A walking tour of Jamestown
You can walk around Jamestown on your own easily enough, but to get the most out of it, do consider Basil George's historical town walk (*Magma Way;* ☎ *24525;* e *busy.bee@helanta.co.sh; 2hrs; min 5 people*). Along with historical background, he takes in visits to the Castle, St James's Church, Jacob's Ladder, the Court House and Castle Gardens, and ends for a chat with tea and cake at somewhere central like the Consulate Hotel.

For a self-guided walk, start at the steps leading from the water up to the wharf, which have been the official entrance to Jamestown, and indeed St Helena, for centuries. Sailors in the 1700s came onshore in more or less the same way as passengers from the RMS *St Helena*, or any other passenger ship or boat – and will continue to do so until the new wharf opens. Then, for the first time, visitors by sea will disembark in Rupert's Bay, leaving the old wharf to visiting yachtsmen, along with the likes of fishing boats, pleasure craft and watersports' enthusiasts.

About 50 yards (45m) from the wharf steps, you will come upon a two-storey **pink house**, built in the late 18th century. The closest dwelling to the ocean on St Helena, it was last inhabited by a fisherman, but today is used by St Helena Yacht Club.

A little further on is the old, blue-painted **Customs House**, constructed in the middle of the 18th century but now replaced with an attractive new building a little further down the quayside. The slightly raised building behind it, with the arched roof, was built in the early 19th century and was once used as a mortuary.

Continuing along the waterfront you'll be following the bastion of the **outer town wall**. This defence installation was built as early as the 17th century. The **old moat**, parallel to the bastion, used to demarcate the sea wall; the harbour front that you see today is on reclaimed land. Further on is the **cenotaph** [86 B2], a memorial to the men of St Helena who fought and died in the two World Wars, including the crew of the RFA *Darkdale* (page 20). Glance to the right over James Bay, where you can just make out a piece of steel jutting out of the water. This is part of the rudder of the **SS *Papanui***, which sank in James Bay in 1911 after a fire on board. Coal, which had been loaded in Las Palmas, caught fire during the journey to Cape Town and within three hours of arriving at St Helena, it is said that the vessel was engulfed in flames that lit up the entire valley.

Now direct your attention towards the **town gate** or **arch** [86 B2], and the town's inner wall. These walls are made from basalt, which is in plentiful supply due to the volcanic nature of the island. Until 1935, the moat was crossed using a drawbridge. Just before the arch, spare a glance into the **Mule Yard** on your left, whose venerable peepul trees were brought from India in 1750. On the arch itself, look up: above is the coat of arms of the last governor of the East India Company, Charles Dallas, who held the office from 1828 until 1836. The other side of the gate is topped by a picture of the wirebird, the island's national bird, flanked on each gatepost by depictions of the arum lily, which was until recently the national flower.

The town gate opens onto the **Grand Parade** [86 B3], today guarded by sedentary parked cars, but used in earlier years as the drill ground for the British garrison. To your left are the gates to the **Castle** [86 C2], also topped with the Dallas coat of arms. Once used as the winter residence of the governor, and now home to the government offices, the building is a castle in name only. The original two structures on this site, dating to 1659 and 1708, are commemorated by a stone tablet built into the wall to the left of the entrance. By the 1860s, the second building was so badly damaged by termites that a third – the present castle – was erected in 1867.

To the right of the castle gates is a **post stone**, dating to 1643, which was moved here some years ago. Before the island was settled, ships would often leave letters and messages for other ships behind basalt rocks such as the. Immediately adjacent is the entrance to the **former barracks**, the top of the arch emblazoned with the letters VR. Standing for Victoria Regina, they were probably put in place to mark the golden or diamond jubilee of Britain's Queen Victoria, so in 1887 or 1897. The complex to the right, next to the gardens, was built at the beginning of the 19th century and incorporates the **police headquarters**, the **court building** and the **public library** (page 94).

On the other side of the parade ground, between an ecru-coloured warehouse (formerly Lawler's Hotel) and the Public Works Department (PWD) store, is the **St Helena Museum** (pages 93–4), and rising right in front of you is **Jacob's Ladder**, completed by the military in 1829 (pages 94–5).

Back in the centre of the parade ground you'll find a **memorial pillar** [86 B3] erected in honour of Dr W J J Arnold, a colonial surgeon and three-times acting governor of St Helena during the early 20th century. Dominating the area behind it is **St James's Church** (page 93), the oldest Anglican church south of the Equator, which lies close to where the Portuguese erected the first chapel on the island, in the 16th century. Right at the back of the parade ground is the rather quaint **prison** [86 B3], built in the first half of the 19th century and still functioning as a jail, despite the slightly Toytown appearance.

From the Grand Parade, follow Main Street towards the centre of town. On the left are the **Castle Gardens** [86 C3], originally the garden of the East India Company. Colourful and tranquil, they lie in the cool shade of several gloriously gnarled old banyan trees, some of which are said to have been here in 1815 when Napoleon arrived on the island. In the middle of the gardens is a memorial to the Brig of War **Waterwitch** [86 C3] and her Royal Navy crew, who helped fight the slave trade in the middle of the 19th century, and on the grass lies a hefty anchor, found in the bay during construction work. The gardens are a lovely place for a picnic – or head across to Anne's Place at the back for a cool beer or bite to eat.

Next to the gardens, **New Porteous House** [86 B4] was built to replace the original Porteous House, where Napoleon and his entourage spent their first night on St Helena. That house burned down in 1865, although the neighbouring houses still date back to the first half of the 18th century.

Across the street from the Castle Gardens are three similar-looking houses: numbers 1, 2 and 3 on Main Street. They were built in the 18th century, serving as the headquarters of the **East India Company** and the dwellings of government employees. The three houses have now been requisitioned for a new hotel, scheduled to open in 2016.

Continuing uphill you'll come to a blue-painted building, **Wellington House** [86 B4], also dating from the 18th century and now a guesthouse. Legend has it that the Duke of Wellington stayed here in 1805 on his way home from India, but in truth it is believed that he, like Napoleon, stayed at Porteous House.

Further up is the **post office** [86 B5], built in the Victorian style with verandas. A post office since 1907, the building was originally used as the officers' mess for the British garrison, until the troops left the island.

The cream-coloured buildings with the blue balustrades, on the other side of the street, were for the most part built in the second half of the 19th century; only the

**Consulate Hotel** [86 C5] dates to the 18th, although the iron railway girders that support the veranda were installed after termites destroyed the original wooden posts. During the whaling period in the 1850s, the hotel was the residence of the American vice-consul.

At the end of Main Street, two large peepul trees mark the spot where the slave market was held before the abolition of slavery in 1832. The trees, which are sacred in India, are all that remains of an entire avenue planted the length of Main Street. The long building behind them, known as The Canister, today houses the **tourist office** [86 B5].

To the right of The Canister (mind the cars!), the road widens to form a dog leg, called the **Bridge**. The cast-iron and wrought-iron building that dominates the right-hand side of the street is the **Market** [86 B6] (⊕ *08.30–16.00 Mon–Fri, 08.30– 13.00 Sat*), which was earmarked for refurbishment during 2015. Prefabricated in England in 1865, the structure was shipped to St Helena in individual pieces, ready for assembly on the island. The materials were chosen to protect the building from termites, which wrought significant damage on many of the island's buildings during the 1860s. The clock tower in front was constructed in 1930.

## St James's Church [86 B3]

[86 B3] The oldest Anglican church south of the Equator, St James's stands on or around the site of the first chapel on the island, which was built by the Portuguese at the beginning of the 16th century. Indeed, it is said that the small wooden door behind the rows of pews came from the original chapel, though there is no evidence to prove it.

The present church was completed in 1774, around a century after its predecessor, which by all accounts was rather badly built. Since its inauguration, it appears that there have been significant alterations to the structure. There are marks on the walls inside, for instance, which suggest that the roof height has been raised and that the church once had a gallery. Outside, the original tower at the west end of the church was dismantled in 1843 for safety reasons and replaced with a new one, with a spire, by the north door. In turn, this spire, too, was deemed unsafe, and was removed in 1980, though in 2015 it was being replaced with a fibreglass replica.

Taking pride of place in the entrance porch is a large black marble slab, erected 'by the people of St Helena' in 2002 to commemorate the year in which full British citizenship was returned to the Saints. Engraved with the salient words from the Royal Charter of 1673, their citizenship rights would appear to be unequivocal, granted by King Charles II as if 'they had been abideing and borne within this Our kingdome of England'.

The interior of the church feels larger than you might expect in such a small town, and quite stark, until you remember that it served a significant military garrison as well as the civilian population. As if to underline this, several of the pews are marked 'military'. Above the altar, there is a simple stained-glass window of the Good Shepherd, which was installed in 1874, but aside from the windows to either side of this, adornment is relatively modest. There are, though, many sombre plaques and tombstones that commemorate soldiers and East India Company employees, and travellers to England from India who stopped at St Helena to recover from what proved to be fatal diseases.

## St Helena Museum [86 B3]

[86 B3] (*Foot of Jacob's Ladder;* ✆ *22845;* e *museum@helanta. co.sh; www.museumofsainthelena.org;* ⊕ *10.00–16.00 Tue, Thu & Fri, 10.00–12.00 Sat, & when cruise ship or RMS in port; free, but donations welcome*) The independent St Helena Heritage Society maintains a fascinating little museum, which was opened in 2002 to coincide with the quincentenary of the discovery of St Helena. Laid out on two levels, it has a lift to the upper storey, and downstairs is a small shop.

First port of call for visitors should be the three-dimensional map of St Helena, a great way to get an understanding of the island's terrain. Other key exhibits include a classic 1960s' Humber Super Snipe, once the governor's car, and the original Casson organ from St Paul's Cathedral, still in working order. Then there are items recovered from the shipwrecked *Witte Leeuw* and *Papanui*, those made by Boer War prisoners, and plenty on the island's military history and maritime tradition.

Upstairs, much of the gallery is given over to social history, including several objects once in daily use, such as musical and scientific instruments, and dressing-up clothes for children's role play. There are also special exhibitions, including one covering the English angle on Napoleon's exile, to run during the bicentenary of his time on the island.

Plans are in hand to extend the museum into a neighbouring building, which will also incorporate the library and archives.

**St Helena National Trust Flax Mill Museum** The St Helena National Trust is working towards the establishment of a new museum in the Pipe Building, close to the main museum, dedicated to a vital era of the island's industrial history, the flax industry. Work has yet to start, so watch this space.

**St Helena Archives** (*The Castle;* ✆ *22470;* e *archives@sainthelena.gov.sh;* ⊕ *08.30–15.30 Mon–Fri*) Established in 1962, the archives holds records dating back to the earliest days of the East India Company, from 1673 to 1876, and on to the Crown Administration from 1836. The first include letters to and from England, as well as judicial, military, maritime and other administrative records, not to mention registers of wills (1682–1839), and leases and deeds (1682–1849). Among others, the Crown Administration papers comprise council records, correspondence between the governor and the Secretary of State for the Colonies, and the island's Blue Books.

The archives also hold copies of many of the island's newspapers and publications, dating back to 1851 – though the first newspaper was published in 1806 – and the Anglican parish registers, which date back to 1680. The helpful staff are always willing to assist with personal research.

For those interested in their family roots on St Helena, the archives provide a tracing service by email (*£32/7hrs, then £4.50/hr*).

**Library** [86 B3] (*Grand Parade;* ✆ *22580;* ⊕ *10.00–17.00 Mon, Tue, Thu & Fri, 10.00–13.00 &18.00–20.00 Sat*) Supposedly the oldest in the southern hemisphere, the library holds an extensive collection of reference books on St Helena, Ascension and Tristan da Cunha, and Napoleonic history. It is also a reasonable if somewhat old-fashioned lending library with a good children's section. Visitors may take out temporary membership for £5, plus a refundable deposit of £20 for borrowing up to four books. And if you have spare books of your own, the library is happy to add them to its collection or put them on sale.

**Jacob's Ladder** [86 A1] Completed in 1829, Jacob's Ladder was built by the military to transport manure to the countryside from the stables in Jamestown, and to move ammunition and supplies between the capital and the various fortifications around the island. Once there were tramways at the side of the 699 steps, operated by mules at the top, to haul goods up the 602ft (183m) to Ladder Hill, at an incline of

39–44°. Over the years the ladder has been used by countless schoolchildren, many of whom devised a way of descending that makes sliding down the banisters look very tame by comparison. Today, it's still used by a few locals to access Half Tree Hollow from Jamestown, and by others as part of a fitness regime, but for many tourists it's a challenge in its own right. It's a tough climb, but the views from the top are worth it, though do note that coming down is equally challenging! And talking of challenges, the record ascent time stands at five minutes, 11 seconds. Certificates stating that you've conquered the ladder are available from the museum for £2.50 each.

**Watersports and boat trips** All boat trips and watersports on St Helena, including diving and fishing, operate out of Jamestown. For details, see pages 76–81.

*Swimming* Jamestown's 33m open-air freshwater **swimming pool** [86 C2] (✆ 22650; ☼ *school hols 10.00–17.45 daily, term time 12.00–13.00 Mon–Wed & Fri, 15.00–17.45 Thu; £1/50p/25p adult/under 16/under 5*), just behind the Mule Yard, is exceptionally inviting on a hot summer's day. Originally built by the Royal Engineers for military exercises, it's now open to all comers and includes a small children's paddling pool. Drinks are available.

It is also possible to swim from the wharf, either from the landing steps, where the snorkelling is unexpectedly good, or further along. In calm weather (but do check the forecast) strong swimmers could also consider checking out the wreck of the SS *Papanui* that lies in the bay (page 91). Further afield, a boat trip to swim at Lemon Valley is well worth consideration (page 107).

**WALKS FROM JAMESTOWN** As well as Jacob's Ladder (pages 94–5), a few other walks from Jamestown variously offer a sense of history and more than a hint of the interior of the island. Whether or not you have time to explore further afield, they're worthy of consideration.

**The Run** (*1hr; moderate*) The name refers to a channel built in 1857 to carry water from the Heart-shaped Waterfall, and sewage from the houses, through Jamestown and out to sea. Today, some of it flows beneath various buildings in the centre of town, emerging near the Blue Lantern and exiting below Donny's Bar. What's left may not be the prettiest of walks, but it does provide an interesting glimpse behind the scenes of urban life. Access is along Nose Gay Lane, behind the Standard Tavern, which leads you down to the edge of the run itself (not above it, as you might think). The path is narrow in places, and can get overgrown, so you'll need to be careful. Following the channel away from Jamestown will eventually bring you out by the sluice gate, beyond the hospital. If you return down the road, rather than retracing your steps, you'll pass the Anglican St John's Church. Rather more intimate than St James's, its yellow slit windows fill the church with a feeling of sunlight. Spare a glance for the massive gravestones propped up against the outside walls, before returning to Jamestown along Market Street.

**Heart-shaped Waterfall Postbox walk** (*3/3; 1hr 30mins, plus access from Jamestown or Briars Village; see page 75 for explanation of grading*) The classic heart shape of the rock formation that is part of the backdrop to Upper Jamestown is clearly visible from Side Path. While the waterfall that bears its name is sometimes not even a trickle, the surrounding area is exceptionally verdant, and makes the focus of a very attractive walk. To see the falls in flood, though, you'll need to be here immediately after the winter rains, around September/October time.

Jamestown JAMESTOWN

4

To reach the start of the path, follow Market Street from Jamestown, pass the hospital, and continue until you reach a road that climbs up the hill. Follow this road until it takes a sharp left-hand turn, from where the path is marked straight ahead. The postbox walk itself is steep but not difficult; a series of wooden steps and woodland paths that take you past a newly planted copse of endemic plants and on through dense woodland to the base of the waterfall. For much of the year, water gives way to a cascade of grass and ferns that tumble down the cliff, culminating in a grove of wild ginger whose scent is intoxicating. There's a large platform at the end where you can sit and watch the fairy terns in the surrounding thorn trees before returning along the same route. The walk can also be accessed from the top of Side Path, or – best of all – from Briars Village, along a pleasant track just below the Sure communication satellite.

**Munden's Battery** (*1½hrs; moderate*) Just east of Jamestown, Munden's Battery occupies a strategic location overlooking James Bay. The fortifications here date back to 1673, when Sir Richard Munden helped the British to regain possession of the island from the Dutch. Between then and World War II, the defences were sporadically developed, both on top of the hill – Upper Munden – and lower down. Between 1957 and 1961, the now-derelict buildings on this lower level housed St Helena's last political prisoners – three Bahraini princes. Having been sentenced to 14 years' imprisonment for offences against the state, they were exiled here at the request of the ruler of Bahrain, but were released following a writ of habeas corpus.

At both levels, it's a fascinating spot, littered with rusting cannons (and, sadly, rather a lot of rubbish), and with plenty to explore in its old bunkers and gun emplacements. If the various vantage points today reveal no more than colourful boats bobbing in the harbour, the top of the ridge is a great spot for birdwatching. Look in particular for red-billed tropicbirds, and in the summer months, for migrating skuas.

From Jamestown, the most straightforward path is to walk up behind the Castle Gardens onto Sisters' Walk, built by Governor Patton for his daughters in the early 19th century. When the path divides, the routes are obvious – one to Lower Munden's Battery, the second to Upper Munden's. A third path is clearly closed off as it is no longer safe. Return by the same route, or follow the ridge towards Rupert's Valley and back down Side Path; the National Trust publishes a leaflet giving details.

Note that Rupert's Valley is also an alternative starting point for the **Sugar Loaf Postbox walk**; for details, see page 111.

# ST HELENA ISLAND TOURS

Magma Way specialises in scheduled group tours and deals with organisations that would like to bring a group to experience the island 'The Magma Way'. In order to deliver tours of quality and give personal attention, numbers in a group tour will be a minimum of 5 and a maximum of 12. **e** busy.bee@helanta.co.sh

MAGMA WAY
ST HELENA

# 5

# Beyond Jamestown

It's an oft-repeated comment that everywhere on St Helena is within a half-hour drive of Jamestown, but within that half hour (or so!) you can find yourself variously absorbing Napoleonic culture, ogling at stupendous scenery, staring in wonder at the last surviving specimens of an endemic plant, or tackling one of the challenging postbox walks. And that's just for starters.

For the purposes of this guide, we have divided the island broadly into its component districts around the island from Jamestown: Half Tree Hollow just above Jamestown; the northern districts of St Paul's, Alarm Forest and Longwood, which incorporate the three major Napoleonic sites; the central Peaks National Park; and finally the southern districts of Levelwood, Sandy Bay and Blue Hill.

Despite the small distances, crossing the guts and the gulleys, the ridges and the valleys is deceptive. The constant hills and switchback roads outside Jamestown make it surprisingly easy to get lost, so a map is essential for orientation purposes. See page 67 for the best options.

## GUIDED TOURS AND SUGGESTED ITINERARIES

With careful planning, it is possible to pack a lot of sightseeing into just a few hours and make the most of even a short stay. Several companies offer guided tours of the island, but their styles are very different. Alternatively you can hire a taxi (page 66) and ask for their advice, or come up with your own itinerary.

For cruise-ship passengers, organised group tours can be arranged on the ship before you arrive. It's also possible to book tours on the RMS *St Helena* before disembarking, though the available options change from trip to trip. All tours start in Jamestown and – where relevant – are scheduled to fit in with the time that the cruise ship is in harbour.

**TOUR OPERATORS** Many of St Helena's tour operators are characters in their own right, people who have in-depth knowledge of the island and are very happy to share it with visitors. Others may simply comment on the sites as you pass them. Although each of the tours that they offer is different, pretty well all have at least one option that includes the three main Napoleonic sites – Longwood House, Sane Valley and The Briars Pavilion – and returns to Jamestown via Plantation House, the governor's residence and home to an ancient giant tortoise known as Jonathan. Some outfits charge per person, others for the trip, but almost all have a minimum charge.

Although all tours can be booked direct, it's often easier for those staying on the island to make reservations through the tourist office, which can then consolidate requests. On most of the longer tours, you'll need to take your own packed lunch, although this can sometimes be arranged at the time of booking. For suggested self-drive or taxi-based itineraries, see below. For details of the various attractions, see pages 102, 104–11, 113–14 and 115–17.

**Aaron's Adventure Tours** ☎23987; e aat@
helanta.co.sh; For in-depth exploration of the
island, don't miss Aaron Legg's 4x4 tour, which as
well as covering all the standard sights, takes you
on a roller-coaster of a ride to some truly out-of-
the-way places, with exceptional scenery. Aaron
was an assistant purser on the RMS *St Helena* for
5yrs, & is a friendly, personable guide. He also
offers customised tours, specialising in Sandy Bay,
& is a very good walking guide. *7hrs; £30pp/3–6
passengers*

**Charabanc Tours** Chad's, Main St, Jamestown;
☎22735/2518; e corkerstouristservice@helanta.
co.sh. These extremely popular tours are conducted
by knowledgeable & informative owners Tracey
& Colin Corker in their 18-seater 1929 Chevrolet,
with the hood down in good weather. Their most
popular itinerary incorporates the Napoleonic
sites (⊙ *09.30–14.00 approx; £18pp*). A longer
2-in-1 tour (⊙ *09.30– 16.00 approx; £30pp*)
combines the Napoleonic sites with sightseeing
around the island, including the distillery. For both
tours, meet outside Chad's (almost next to the
Consulate Hotel). *4–7hrs per trip; £18–30pp; max
18 passengers*

**Contours** ☎22822; e audrey.constantine@
helanta.co.sh. Operating with a 7-seater Toyota,
owner Bert Constantine has devised 6 individual
itineraries, from the historical Napoleonic & Boer
War trails, to the more general Millennium Forest
& scenic tour & his most offbeat option, 'out west'.

**Harry Legg Tours** ☎24240; e wendy.lucky@
helanta.co.sh, oxie.iceman@helanta.co.sh.
The Napoleonic sites feature heavily on these
tours, some alone, & some in combination with
particularly scenic areas of the island. *Island tour
5–6hrs; £60 per trip/up to 4 passengers*

**Hensel Peters** ☎22701; e hensel.caroline@
helanta.co.sh. From a series of 5 varied tours, 3
are based on the Napoleonic sites with various
add ons, with the others taking in the spectacular
scenery of Sandy Bay or going right round the
island. *2–5hrs depending on trip; £30–80 per trip/
up to 4 passengers*

**History on Wheels** ☎23346; e dorob@helanta.
co.sh; http://robertpeterstours.blog.com. One of St
Helena's best-known characters, Robert Peters is a
favourite with visiting yachtsmen, who crowd into
his battered open-sided vehicle (or a more sedate
8-seater minibus) to explore the island – & listen
to his stories. His 3 tours cover different areas but

the real draw is Robert himself. For similar rates,
he'll also take walkers to the start of their trail
& collect them later in the day. *4–5hrs per trip;
£12pp/min £40; 8/10 passengers*

**Home James** ☎22158 (tourist office); e home_
james_sh@yahoo.com. British residents James
Kellett & Nigel McMichael offer comfortable tailor-
made island tours in smart 4x4 vehicles, complete
with posh picnic. *3–5hrs per trip; from £25pp, max
8 passengers*

**Horizons Tours** ☎22887, 24031; e puddles@
helanta.co.sh. Day trips in a Land Rover Freelander,
including a picnic lunch with tea, coffee or fruit
juice, make these tours quite different. Choose from
the eastern side of the island, with the Napoleonic
sites, the Millennium Forest & the dramatic scenery
around The Barn, or the exceptional natural beauty
of Blue Hill & Sandy Bay beach. *4hrs per trip; £30pp/
min £60; max 4 passengers*

**Larry's Island Tours** ☎24187. Larry Johnson
offers 2 separate tours. One takes in the Napoleonic
sites & the eastern side of the island, returning
across the Ridges via Plantation Hse. The 2nd is
more westerly, from Prince's Lodge & St Paul's
Cathedral through Sandy Bay to Blue Hill. *5–6hrs
per trip; £50/up to 3 passengers*

**Magma Way** ☎24525; e busy.bee@helanta.
co.sh. If you do only one tour on St Helena, make
sure it's with Basil George, who runs this family
company. One of the most knowledgeable people
on the island, he has a delightful wry sense of
humour & an indefatigable interest in people &
places. As well as an excellent historical town walk
of Jamestown (page 91), Basil offers a series of
tours 'to give the best of the island': a package
of a full week's holiday with an exceptionally
sympathetic & perceptive host. Itineraries can also
be tailor made. See ad, page 96.

**No Limits Travels & Tours** St Paul's; ☎24620,
22666; e office@islandimages.co.sh; www.
islandimages.co.sh. Derek & Linda Richards set
this up in 2015 to offer personalised tours based
on the principles of conservation & responsible
tourism. Tours, both day & evening, include
collection in an air-conditioned vehicle, BBQ lunch/
dinner or a packed lunch with drinks, & return to
your accommodation. *3–6hrs depending on trip,
£25–40pp; max 6 passengers*

**St Helena National Trust** Broadway Hse,
Main St, Jamestown; ☎22190; www.nationaltrust.
org.sh. The National Trust offers a range of Land

Rover tours that reflect its role in heritage & environmental conservation. These include wirebird tours (*3hrs*), perhaps combined with planting a tree at the Millennium Forest; High Peak & Blue Point to see endemic plants & habitats (*4hrs*); high central ridge, taking in the walk to Diana's Peak (*4hrs*); & a geology & ecology tour (*4hrs*). All are accompanied by a knowledgeable guide. *£20pp 1–2 people, £15pp 3 or more; max 8*

**Stedson's Renault Scenic Tours** 24270; e stedson.francis@helanta.co.sh. Stedson Francis, who lives in Blue Hill & was a local councillor for 12yrs, offers a round-the-island trip taking in all the main sites & plenty of scenic grandeur. *3hrs; £50 up to 4 passengers*

**SUGGESTED ITINERARIES** Options for individual itineraries from Jamestown are many and varied, depending on your interests and the time available. These three suggestions take in some of the major sights, but all can be extended to incorporate some of St Helena's spectacular scenery. If you don't have your own vehicle, most taxi drivers (page 66) will be happy to follow your suggested route – or come up with their own.

**One hour** Drive up Ladder Hill Road, pausing at the top of Jacob's Ladder for a great view over James Bay. Continue to High Knoll Fort, for a sense of the island's military history and more superb views, this time right across the island. If you're not in a hurry, stop to look at the governor's residence, Plantation House, and perhaps see the giant tortoises.

**Two hours** Drive up Ladder Hill Road to Plantation House, the governor's residence and home to several giant tortoises. From here, a five-minute walk brings you to St Paul's Cathedral. Return via the Boer Cemetery (and the distillery if you've extra time), passing the Heart-shaped Waterfall on your left, and Briars Village in the valley below, before you descend down Side Path.

### Three hours
***Napoleonic sites*** From Jamestown, take Side Path to The Briars Pavilion, then on to Napoleon's tomb in Sane Valley, a 10–15-minute walk down a wooded path. From here, head out to Longwood House, where Napoleon spent the majority of his exile. Do check opening times of the Napoleonic sites in advance; at the time of going to press, these were being extended, but were still not confirmed. If you've extra time, consider continuing from Longwood House out to the Millennium Forest, or stopping at the distillery on your way back to Jamestown.

## HALF TREE HOLLOW

The rapidly growing settlement behind Ladder Hill would be almost a suburb of Jamestown but for one thing: it's a good 650ft (200m) above the town, and a very steep walk – either along the road or (steeper still) up Jacob's Ladder. Even the relatively short drive takes about ten minutes, since it follows Ladder Hill Road: a narrow, single-track road with several blind corners and only a few passing places.

The views from Half Tree Hollow to the sea are spectacular, taking in the sweeping panorama of James Bay. It's a great spot to chart the progress of the RMS *St Helena* and other boats as they approach or leave the island.

 **WHERE TO STAY AND EAT, AND NIGHTLIFE** *Map, pages 100–1*
Sadly the hospitable Harlyn's is no longer open for B&B (although owner Patsy Flagg still offers self-catering, as well as home hosting; page 81), but Half Tree Hollow has one excellent newcomer, and a good new restaurant too.

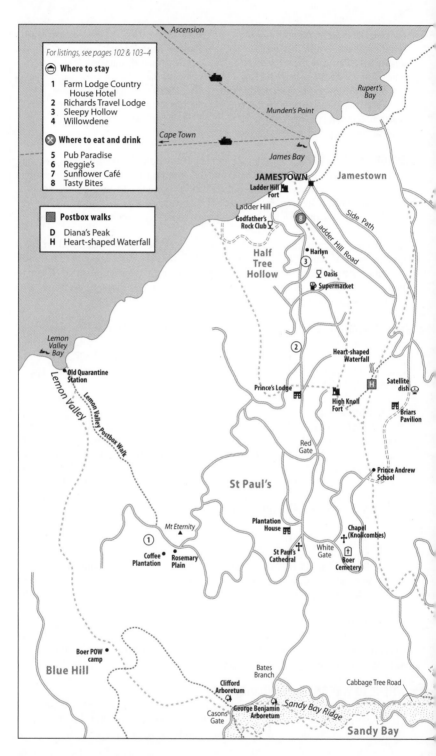

For listings, see pages 102 & 103–4

**Where to stay**

1 Farm Lodge Country
   House Hotel
2 Richards Travel Lodge
3 Sleepy Hollow
4 Willowdene

**Where to eat and drink**

5 Pub Paradise
6 Reggie's
7 Sunflower Café
8 Tasty Bites

**Postbox walks**

D Diana's Peak
H Heart-shaped Waterfall

Ascension

Rupert's
Bay

Munden's Point

Cape Town

James Bay

**JAMESTOWN**

Ladder Hill
Fort

Ladder Hill

Godfather's
Rock Club

Jamestown

Side Path

Half
Tree
Hollow

Harlyn

3

Oasis

Supermarket

Ladder Hill Road

Lemon
Valley
Bay

Old Quarantine
Station

Lemon Valley

Lemon Valley Postbox Walk

2

Heart-shaped
Waterfall

Satellite
dish

Prince's Lodge

High Knoll
Fort

Briars
Pavilion

Red
Gate

St Paul's

Prince Andrew
School

Mt Eternity

1

Coffee
Plantation

Rosemary
Plain

Plantation
House

Chapel
(Knollcombes)

St Paul's
Cathedral

White
Gate

Boer
Cemetery

Boer POW
camp

**Blue Hill**

Bates
Branch

Cabbage Tree Road

Clifford
Arboretum

Casons
Gate

George Benjamin
Arboretum

Sandy Bay Ridge

**Sandy Bay**

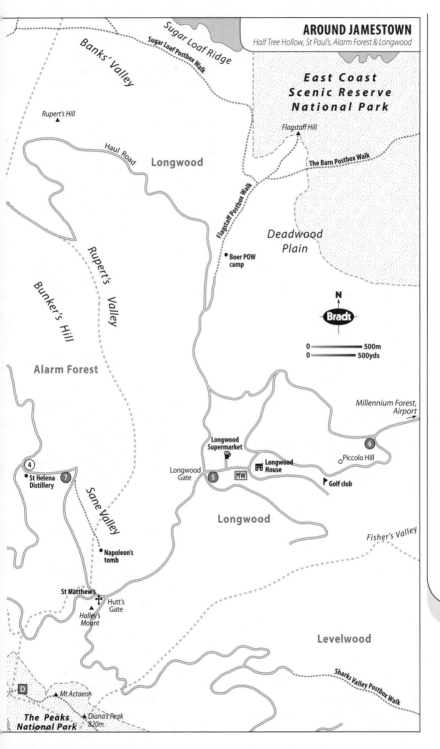

Sugar Loaf Ridge

Banks' Valley

Sugar Loaf Postbox Walk

East Coast
Scenic Reserve
National Park

Rupert's Hill ▲

Flagstaff Hill •

Haul Road

Longwood

The Barn Postbox Walk

Flagstaff Postbox Walk

Deadwood
Plain

Rupert's Valley

Bunker's Hill

• Boer POW
camp

N

**Bradt**

0 ══════ 500m
0 ══════ 500yds

Alarm Forest

Millennium Forest,
Airport →

Longwood
Supermarket

④

• St Helena
Distillery

⑦

Longwood
House

⑥

○ Piccolo Hill

Longwood
Gate

⑤

MW

▶ Golf club

Sane Valley

Longwood

Fisher's Valley

• Napoleon's
tomb

St Matthew's ✝
Hutt's
Gate

Halley's
Mount ▲

Levelwood

☒ D

▲ Mt Actaeon

Sharks Valley Postbox Walk

The Peaks
National Park

▲ Diana's Peak
820m

**Sleepy Hollow** (1 room) ☎23987; e jgaccomodations@gmail.com. Julie George's experience as a steward on the RMS *St Helena* has translated into a small, stylish B&B with clean, modern lines. Sliding doors lead from a sheltered private veranda, with table & chairs, & sea views, into a spacious bedroom. Neutral décor is offset by black-&-white photos & there's a large en-suite shower. B/fast, including homemade muffins, is taken in Julie's equally unfussy living room. Free Wi-Fi. Packed lunches & evening meals on request. **££**

**✗ Tasty Bites** ESH Business Park; ☎23116; ⏰ 09.00–15.00 & 18.00–21.00 Mon–Sat. Eat inside, or at picnic tables on the veranda with sunset views out to sea. A comprehensive menu of b/fasts, light lunches, steaks & other grills includes delicious fresh fish, & occasional specials such as fishcakes. You can come for coffee & cakes, too. If you're staying in Jamestown, & without transport, the owner will be happy to drive you without charge. Wi-Fi. Booking advised but not essential. **£–££££**

**♀Oasis Bar** Cow Path; ☎23607; ⏰ 17.00–01.00 daily. Traditional bar & disco with occasional fast food such as pizza & chips.

**♀Godfather's Rock Club** ☎23059; ⏰ Fri–Sun evenings. A popular local spot with planned activities that include euchre, country & western night, bingo, skittles & dances. You'll need to ask around for what's on offer.

**SHOPPING** Half Tree Hollow does relatively well for food shops, with a reasonable branch of Solomon's that's also open on a Sunday morning, a couple of smaller groceries selling the basics, and a fuel station. For most other things, though, and certainly anything out of the ordinary (with one notable exception), you'll have to head down to Jamestown.

**G-Unique Designs** Unit 8, ESH Business Park; ☎23935; www.g-unique.org. Beaded & silver jewellery is Giselle Richards's speciality – either to her design or your own. Prices are excellent, service good, & the turnaround very speedy.

**WHAT TO SEE AND DO** Half Tree Hollow is more of a staging post than of interest in its own right, but it is notable for being at the top of Jacob's Ladder (pages 94–5). Whether you climb the ladder, or approach along the road, you'll end up in the same spot: **Ladder Hill**. Either way, the climb is worth the exertion, affording a very good vantage point over Lower Jamestown and beautiful sea views. It's also a great place to look out for the red-billed tropicbird, especially in the late afternoon.

Ladder Hill Fort itself, once the island's main fort and with a commanding position above Jamestown, is rather disappointing. The former barracks and battery now serve largely as private houses or offices, and much of the site has been earmarked for tourist development.

A little further along the road, though, continuing straight ahead where the road goes sharply left to Half Tree Hollow, are two six-inch calibre guns. Requested by the garrison in 1902, when Boer prisoners of war were on the island, they didn't arrive until 2003, too late to be of any use in that context. Nevertheless they were installed up here, and have stood guard over James Bay ever since, gradually corroding until, in 2015, they were given a fresh lick of paint.

## ST PAUL'S, ALARM FOREST AND LONGWOOD

Easily accessible from Jamestown, and featuring the majority of places of tourist interest, the districts of St Paul's, Alarm Forest and Longwood offer much to interest and challenge the visitor. Top of the list for many visitors are the three key Napoleonic sites: Longwood House, The Briars Pavilion and Napoleon's tomb.

Outside of Jamestown and Half Tree Hollow, most of the island's tourist accommodation – which is still very limited – lies in this north-central part of the island, with easy access to several visitor attractions. However, unless you're happy to stay put, or to explore within a relatively small area with occasional use of the limited bus service, your own transport would be a big plus – not least as all guided tours start and end in Jamestown.

Aside from Jamestown, the districts of St Paul's and Alarm Forest offer the bulk of the **self-catering** accommodation on St Helena. Most are relatively simply bungalows, often with their own gardens and verandas, and some with superb views out to sea. As in Jamestown, many landlords will collect visitors on arrival in Jamestown, and return you to the port on departure, but do check this – and any arrangements once the airport is open – at the time of booking. For general details on self-catering accommodation, see page 68.

Closest in terms of self-catering options is **Briars Village**, about a mile from the town, up Side Path. It's a peaceful spot, well situated for The Briars Pavilion and offering an alternative route to the Heart-shaped Waterfall walk (pages 95–6), and thence perhaps to Jamestown. Houses in **St Paul's**, approached along Ladder Hill Road, are also relatively easy to access, and many have superb views out to sea. And if you're feeling really swanky, you can rent the Victorian-style Drake Cottage in the grounds of Prince's Lodge (page 104) – or indeed the lodge itself.

🏠 **Farm Lodge Country House Hotel**
(5 rooms) Rosemary Plain, St Paul's; ☏ 24040; e farm.lodge@helanta.co.sh. Built in the late 17th century as an East India Company planter's house, Farm Lodge was impressively restored in the 1990s by Stephen Biggs, a former purser on the RMS, who is originally from England, & his St Helenian partner, Maureen Jonas. It is set in a valley within 12 acres of lawns, tropical gardens & farmland: private & peaceful, with the feel of a small country house.

The lodge is about a 30min drive from Jamestown, some 1,500ft (460m) above sea level, so is relatively cool even in summer. Access is alongside Rosemary Plain picnic area. Guests are met at the wharf on arrival, & airport transfers will be arranged on request. Car hire, too, can be organised – & for most guests is essential.

The house is tastefully furnished throughout, with some well-chosen antiques including a chaise longue & wine cooler belonging to Napoleon, who is said to have been a visitor. There's plenty of space to relax inside & out (& plenty of books, too), or you can explore the gardens & surrounding area freely.

Pretty but uncluttered bedrooms – 3 twins & 2 dbls – are all en suite, & very comfortable. Two are on the ground floor, so potentially suitable for those with limited mobility. Note, though, that the number of guests is normally limited to 8.

Full English b/fast & mid-morning coffee are served, with packed lunches, or a light lunch, available on request, but central to any stay at Farm Lodge is their 5-course dinner (£££££). Elegantly served at a beautifully polished dining-room table, it's a convivial occasion, though the dinner-party atmosphere may not suit everyone. Stephen is an attentive host & Maureen an excellent cook, with much of the produce from the estate – eggs, honey, marmalade, figs, bananas, vegetables & coffee – & pork from the neighbouring farm. Note that dinner is primarily for hotel guests; those not staying here will need to book well in advance. Cash only, but bank transfers possible. ££££

🏠 **Richards Travel Lodge** (2 rooms)
St Paul's; ☏ 24620, 22666; e office@islandimages. co.sh; www.islandimages.co.sh. Derek & Linda Richards branched out in 2015 with a new B&B at their spacious, modern clifftop home. Both dbl rooms are en suite, 1 with a stupendous ocean view, the 2nd looking out to the back. Facilities inc flat-screen TV & DVD & internet access in each room, & a small kitchenette. As well as b/fast, there is the option of full board, with excellent traditional meals & BBQs featuring home-grown vegetables, either inside, or on the lawn looking out to sea. There's also the possibility of day trips with a gourmet picnic to somewhere scenic, such as South West

Point. Also have a simple self-catering bungalow with great views at New Ground. **£**

🏠 **Willowdene** (2 rooms) Gordon's Post, Alarm Forest; 📞 22619, 24307; e patmusk@outlook.com. A spacious & very comfortable family home within large, landscaped gardens, Willowdene is owned by the very hospitable Pat Musk. Bedrooms – an African-themed en-suite dbl & a sgl with basin & private bathroom – are downstairs, but guests have the run of much of the house. As well as the dining room & a lovely family lounge, there's an extensive veranda, with views to Flagstaff & the sea. The B&B is well placed for walks to St Paul's Cathedral, Sane Valley & Longwood, & there's a bus that stops at the end of the drive. **£**

✖ **Sunflower Café** Woodlea, Alarm Forest; 📞 24145; ⏰ 19.00 Mon–Fri, 12.30 & 19.00 Sat/ Sun. Millie Stopforth's plentiful home-cooked 2- or 3-course meals (£14/16) are legendary. Professionally served to individual tables in the comfort of her living room, they offer the added bonus of dining in a typical St Helenian home. If the option's there, don't miss her tuna curry pie, & the homemade ice cream is good, too. Outside, the covered veranda is a good spot for a pre-dinner drink, with magnificent views over James Bay. Reservations & menu choices must be made at least a day ahead. **£££**

✖ **Pub Paradise** Longwood Gate; 📞 24083; ⏰ 17.30–21.00 daily (or 01.00 if sufficient customers). Friendly & very low key, Pub Paradise serves burgers & pizzas all week, but you'll need to book ahead for a steak or curry. The cavernous bar area extends into a marquee-covered exterior, giving plenty of space for the crowds, especially on Sat night when there's a DJ or live music to 01.30. **£–£££**

✖ **Reggie's** ⏰ 11.00–18.30 Mon–Sat. Take-away burgers, etc, similar in style to its sibling in Jamestown. **£**

**OTHER PRACTICALITIES** There's a large grassy area opposite Longwood House, with plenty of picnic tables. If you've come without lunch, pop into **Longwood Supermarket** (⏰ 09.00–18.00 Mon–Sat, 09.00–13.00 Sun) on the other side of the green, where there's also a fuel station with the same opening hours.

**ST PAUL'S** Approached from Jamestown up Ladder Hill Road, and wrapped around two sides of Half Tree Hollow, St Paul's is significant in both residential and tourist terms. Key to the latter are High Knoll Fort, Plantation House and St Paul's Cathedral, while right on the edge of the district is the popular bay at Lemon Valley.

Attractions here are listed broadly as if following the road from Jamestown and Half Tree Hollow: south, and then west.

**Prince's Lodge** (📞 23939; ⏰ *by appointment only or through tourist office; £1/ US$2*) This rather lovely Georgian country house in St Paul's was formerly home to both the bishop of St Helena and the island governor. Restored by English historian and poet Robin Castell, it is home to his collection of St Helena prints, maps, engravings and aquarelles. Robin, who describes himself as a 'staunch monarchist, with a passionate desire for real freedom, intelligent self-expression, free enterprise and a lasting peace for all mankind', is based in South Africa, but visitors are welcome to view the collection, which is on permanent display in the ground-floor rooms of the house. Said to be the largest such collection in the world, it is by turns interesting, informative and intriguing.

For those who want to spend some serious time there, it's possible to rent the house, or the two-bedroom Drake Cottage in the grounds, on a self-catering basis. The well-maintained two-acre (0.8ha) grounds with views to the ocean are a further attraction.

**High Knoll Fort** (*National Trust;* 📞 22190; *guided trip £5pp*) Originally built in 1798, but significantly extended between 1857 and 1874, High Knoll Fort offers superb views right around the island, and on a clear day is worth visiting for that alone.

The fort was constructed as part of the island's defence network, but in 1811 it was brought into service as a makeshift prison for a group of mutineers, who had risen in protest against alcohol rations for the garrison. For their part in the mutiny, six of the rebels were hung at High Knoll.

In 1900, the fort again served as a prison, this time to secure Boer prisoners of war who were causing unrest in the less secure camps. Later it was used as a quarantine centre for animals that had arrived at the island.

Time has taken its toll on the structure of High Knoll, rendering it unsafe for several years, but in 2015 the National Trust was working to stabilise the walls and make it more accessible. As well as improving safety, there are plans for new signage, while at the same time protecting those endemic plants that shelter among the foliage. It is hoped that the fort will eventually become the occasional venue for concerts and other outdoor events.

Visitors may just turn up at the fort and wander round, but if you want to go inside, you can get the key from the National Trust in Jamestown (pages 98–9). Torches may be borrowed against a refundable deposit of £5.

**Francis Plain**  Named after Henry Francis, who owned the land in 1692, Francis Plain is one of the few absolutely flat areas in the centre of St Helena. Not surprisingly, then, it is the hub of the island's field sports: football, rugby and cricket. It is also the sight of the only secondary school, Prince Andrew's. Sadly the annual sports day, which used to take place here on New Year's Day, was abandoned in 1998, thus ending a 50-year-long tradition.

During Napoleon's captivity Francis Plain was used as one of the main military camping grounds. Later, from 1890, it was home to the Zulu chief, Dinizulu, and his family for the last two years of his exile.

**Plantation House** (⊕ *11.00 Tue, tours by arrangement only through tourist office; max 10; no children under 10; no photos inside house; paddock viewing area* ⊕ *08.30–18.30 daily; free*) The official residence of St Helena's governors for more than 200 years, Plantation House is a rather splendid Georgian structure which was built for that purpose between 1791 and 1792. The original was built in 1673, but it fell into disrepair and was replaced in 1722. The second house, initially the home of the plantation manager, in time became the governor's summer residence. But this house, too, was plagued with problems, and eventually the East India Company agreed to build a new governor's residence, which was completed in 1792 for the princely sum of £3,020. During his tenure, between 1816 and 1821, Napoleon's custodian Governor Hudson Lowe added a library and billiard room, with a nursery above them appropriately known as 'Chaos'.

Inside, the house is surprisingly light, with an air of tasteful elegance. In the entrance hall are photographs and paintings of the British royal family going back to Prince Albert, and rarely seen photographs of the Duke of Edinburgh sporting a beard. Of the 35 rooms, visitors see just three or four on the ground floor. Typically these included Hudson Lowe's comfortable library, restored in 2012 to reflect the original décor; the 'blue' lounge; and the particularly impressive dining room, one of the largest rooms in the house. Over the years, many distinguished visitors have been seated around the table, including the Duke of Wellington, Lord Curzon and one of Napoleon's companions in exile, the Comte de Montholon.

Roaming the large lawn, or paddock, in front of the house are five **giant tortoises**, which visitors may watch from a fenced-off viewing area without appointment. This is where you'll find Jonathan, the last surviving Aldabra tortoise, who – at the last estimate in 2015 – was said to be 186 years old. That said, no-one really knows his age, despite far-fetched claims that he was already here when Napoleon arrived. In reality, it's likely that he arrived around 1882, possibly brought from the Seychelles when he was fully grown. Whatever the date, age is beginning to take its toll, and today he is hand fed twice a week by the gardeners to ensure that he is properly nourished.

In recent years, a viewing corridor has been erected across the bottom of the paddock, so visitors may no longer approach the tortoises – though they may well approach you. If he comes close enough, you can tell Jonathan from the cararact on his right eye. His compatriots – Emma, David, Myrtle and Fredrika – are relative newcomers, having been brought to join him between 1969 and 1972.

If you follow the fence to the end, you can walk down into **Plantation Forest**, where paths lead through some groves of huge bamboos. In one of these are the Butchers' graves, two headstones marking the burial site of Francis and Margaret Butcher, who died in 1777. From here, there's a good view back towards Plantation House, framed in its natural setting.

## Boer War Prisoners' Cemetery

A turning off the main road leads down to this dignified cemetery. It's then a short walk, but on the way you'll pass the small Baptist cemetery at Knollcombes, where St Helena's second and last island-born governor, Hudson Ralph Janisch, is buried. The Boer War cemetery itself is a sobering sight, even from the road. Marching down the hill, the neatly organised rows of graves look like so many broad white steps cut into the slope. The names of those buried here are inscribed on two stone memorials at the foot of the site.

## St Paul's Cathedral

More of a country church than a cathedral in style, St Paul's was built in 1851, and in 1859 became the cathedral church of the Diocese of St Helena. While the walls are constructed of local stone, most of the rest of the building was assembled from prefabricated materials shipped from England.

The current building, however, belies a chequered past. A churchwarden was appointed in 1678, which dates the original church more or less concurrently with St James's. Decaying timbers meant that it soon had to be rebuilt, yet though this took over 30 years, the timbers rotted once more, and once more it was pulled down. In its place was erected an apparently impressive stone structure with a gallery and pews for the governor, his family and senior officials, but this building, too, came to grief – resulting in the structure that you see today. Take a look inside for the window behind the pulpit, which depicts St Peter with people working in the fields and St Paul with Governor Bain-Gray helping the survivors of the SS *Cairo*.

Although many of the gravestones are broken and on some, the writing is no longer legible, it's well worth a wander around the large graveyard. One stone, in particular, clearly commemorates two infant children of the Zulu chief, Denizulu, who spent seven years in exile on St Helena at the end of the 19th century.

## Ridges Roads circular walk

The quiet roads around St Paul's form a lovely circular walk with fantastic views over the centre of the island. Following the route clockwise, you'll pass the Boer Cemetery at Knollcombes then on to Stitches Ridge and Sandy Bay Ridge, before returning to St Paul's. Allow about an hour and a half, and be prepared for a couple of steep hills, at Cabbage Tree Road and Knollcombes.

## Rosemary Plain

Well situated for walkers or those visiting the coffee plantation, Rosemary Plain is just a stone's throw from Farm Lodge and is a lovely spot for a picnic. A short stroll up through pine woods brings you to the lichen-encrusted ridge of Mount Eternity, with views through the trees down to Sarah's Valley. The plain is also close to the start of Lemon Valley Postbox walk (below).

***Rosemary Gate Coffee Plantation*** (✆ *22015, 24371; ℯ bolton01@tiscali.co.uk, bolton@helanta.co.sh; ⊕ daily by appointment; free*) One of a small number of coffee plantations on St Helena, this private estate welcomes visitors; access is alongside the picnic area on Rosemary Plain. Having walked along the rows of coffee bushes, perhaps checking for fruit and flowers, owner Bill Bolton will take you through the processes of pulping, washing, drying, hulling and roasting. For a verdict on the final result, though, you'll have to make your way to the St Helena Coffee Shop in Jamestown.

## Lemon Valley
The valley was probably named for the abundance of lemons found here by early visitors to the island, though sadly no more. It has also served as a base for liberated slaves and a quarantine station, the ruins of which can still be seen behind the narrow stony beach.

Today, the sheltered bay with its calm, clear waters is justifiably popular with swimmers and snorkellers, and is a great place for rock pooling. Natural rock ledges provide at least some shade, and cover for a few basic barbecues, so it's a good spot for a picnic, too. It's all pretty rudimentary – but then that's part of the appeal. Toilets, though, are basic in the extreme.

Most people access the bay by sea – either by motorboat or by kayak (page 80). For a small boat (up to four passengers), you can expect to pay about £30 return, or £100 for something larger.

The alternative is to descend from near Rosemary Plain along the fairly strenuous **Lemon Valley Postbox walk** (*6/6; 2hrs 45mins; see page 75 for grading explanation*). The walk itself starts in Sarah's Valley, a pleasant meander downhill with beautiful views across the valley, before it becomes steeper, with loose rocks making it potentially hazardous. If you don't fancy the strenuous climb back up in the heat, you could arrange for a boat to pick you up later in the day.

## ALARM FOREST AND LONGWOOD
Unlike Half Tree Hollow and St Paul's, Alarm Forest and Longwood are usually approached from Jamestown along Side Path. The road climbs above Briars Village and heads towards Napoleon's tomb in Sane Valley (page 109), Hutt's Gate and St Matthew's Church, before continuing on to Longwood House, passing the distillery *en route*.

Alarm Forest takes its name from its strategic location high up on the cliffs. In times of impending danger, semaphore messages would be relayed from stations around the island to the (now bright pink) Alarm House, which would respond with two blasts on the cannon.

Longwood is in many ways very different – as Napoleon would have testified. Largely barren, and frequently shrouded in mist, it might appeal to today's visitor in search of wide open spaces, but to a Frenchman used to the cut and thrust of military or Parisian living, confinement to its harsh, rock-strewn landscape was sorely trying. He, at least, would have appreciated the airport on Prosperous Bay Plain.

In 2015, almost the entire coastal area of Longwood, from Flagstaff in the north right round to the area of Levelwood south of the airport, were united within the protection of the East Coast Scenic Reserve National Park, which in turn takes in several of the postbox walks.

**Napoleonic sites** Until now, access to the various Napoleonic sites has been strictly controlled and for pre-arranged groups only, albeit free of charge. In 2016, however, this is set to change. In future, opening hours will be increased, possibly to three or four hours a day, Monday to Friday, and there will be access for individuals as well as groups, but for the first time there will be an entrance fee. It is anticipated that there will be a one-off charge for all three sites, to include a guide, and a guidebook in English and French to all the Napoleonic sites on the island, but details have yet to be confirmed. In the meantime, the information given here was correct at the time of research in 2015.

**Longwood House** (\ *24409; tours 11.00 Mon–Fri, book through tourist office 1 day in advance; wheelchair access possible; no photographs inside house; free*) This is well known as the place where Napoleon Bonaparte (pages 12–17) spent the majority of his exile on St Helena. Perched on an exposed plateau, it can be a depressing place in poor weather, but a visit to Longwood House is a must.

Since 1858, the property – along with the site of Napoleon's tomb – has been owned by the French government, sold to them for the princely sum of £7,100 by agreement with Queen Victoria. Today it is maintained by the Honorary French Consul, Michel Martineau, and is presented much as it would have looked at the end of Napoleon's life, in 1821. On a sunny day, it is hard to picture the house as it would have been 200 years ago, its walls often dripping with damp, its floors rotten, and fires smoking in every grate.

Many of the pieces of furniture that can be seen at Longwood House date back to Napoleon's lifetime, but in 2015, 32 of the best pieces were shipped to Paris for restoration and to feature in an exhibition at Les Invalides during 2016. These include the billiard table that dominated the entrance, the dining-room table where Napoleon and his entourage endured short but formal dinners every night, and the deep copper bath where he spent an increasing amount of time, as well as the bed in which he died. All will be returned later that year.

Outside, the generals' apartment has been refurbished and will be open to the public at the end of 2015, as well as being available for private functions. The gardens, designed by Napoleon towards the end of his exile, provided him with an all-too-brief period of renewed activity before his health further declined. Today, their pleasantly informal planting warrants exploration, with mature trees providing an attractive frame for Flagstaff beyond. Nothing, however, is left of Longwood New House, constructed for Napoleon close by but never inhabited by him, and long ago demolished.

**The Briars Pavilion** (*tours 10.00 Mon–Fri; book through tourist office 1 day in advance; no wheelchair access; free*) Napoleon spent his happiest time on St Helena at this small pavilion, in the grounds of a house owned by the Balcombe family, with views across to James Bay. Their house is long gone, but the pavilion – gifted to the French government in 1959 – was being fully restored in 2015. Once complete, its décor – as at Longwood House – will reflect the house at the time of Napoleon's death. In addition, the attic area, which during Napoleon's two-month stay was used by Comte de Las Cases and his son, was being sensitively rebuilt from the original plans. The gardens, too, have been re-established, but what is left of the original furniture from the pavilion will be on display at Longwood rather than here.

An interesting experiment carried out at The Briars shortly after Napoleon died relates to an attempt by the governor to establish a silkworm farm here. A Chinese labourer who claimed to understand the breeding and care of silkworms was sent to China to procure some, but much to the disappointment of the governor, the project ended in failure.

**Sane Valley**  (⊕ *09.00–16.00 Mon–Fri; free*) It is said that Napoleon himself chose Sane Valley as his final resting place – though this was not quite how it turned out. Approached down a sometimes slippery track that was originally cut for the funeral cortege, the original (and now empty) tomb is quite well hidden, about 10–15 minutes' walk from the road. Today, a fence separates visitors from the tomb itself, somewhat accentuating its isolation in this lonely but serene spot.

At the time of Napoleon's interment the tomb was surrounded by willows, but these have now been replaced by Norfolk Island pines, backed by a profusion of well-tended but natural-looking shrubs. Still standing in its original spot, though, is the guard shack: even after Napoleon's death, the British kept a close watch over the former emperor. His memorial stone bears no inscription, for the simple 'Bonaparte' was rejected by Hudson Lowe, and the French were insulted by his counter-suggestion of 'Napoleon Bonaparte'. Napoleon's body, securely encased in four separate coffins, remained here for nearly 20 years until, in 1840, it was removed and taken back to France, where it resides with due decorum at Les Invalides in Paris.

## St Helena Distillery  (*Alarm Forest;* ✆ *24210;* e *tungiman@gmail.com;* ⊕ *09.00–17.00 Mon–Fri; free*) Widely billed as the 'world's most remote distillery' (and who would doubt it?), this is the brainchild of British owner Paul Hickling and his St Helenian wife, Sally. Having started life in Jamestown in 2006, it is now based at their home in Alarm Forest, where visitors are able to taste and buy their products.

The distillery can probably also lay claim to the world's most unusual spirit, Tungi (pronounced 'toonchi'). Made by hand from the widely available fruit of the prickly pear, which ripens between March and May, it's best drunk very cold, or with fruit juice or – as a Holdfast Tom cocktail – with tequila and apple juice. Drawing further inspiration from the distillery's local roots, Paul has also developed White Lion, a nice line in spiced rum that's good served with Sprite; Lemon Valley, a liqueur reminiscent of limoncello, using local lemons; and Midnight Mist, a coffee liqueur based on St Helenian coffee. Even the local juniper comes into its own for Jamestown gin, which connoisseurs say is delicious as a standalone drink. All are currently marketed in a distinctive stepped bottle, though stocks are running out fast.

More recently, Paul has also turned his attention to wine, based on grape juice imported from South Africa and, and sold as Mount Actaeon (red) and Diana's Peak (white).

As an adjunct to the distillery, the Hicklings are planning to open a café above, serving coffee, cakes and light bites, as well as sundowners – using their own products, of course. We understand that there's beer brewing, too.

## Deadwood Plain  Backed by the triangular peak of Flagstaff, the soft green hills, cropped grassy fields and grazing cattle around Deadwood Plain almost justify comparison with Devon. Once populous with gumwoods, the plain was over the years stripped of vegetation as a result of interference by man and wild goats. For once, though, desecration has had its upside, for this is now one of the best places to see the wirebird, St Helena's iconic plover favours dry grasslands and semi-desert areas, and is regularly seen here. Look out for a striking, long-legged plover moving hurriedly the grass, or join one of the National Trust's excellent wirebird tours (pages 98–9).

Between 1900 and 1902, Deadwood was also the site of the first **Boer prisoner-of-war camp**, with a second camp established in 1901 at Broad Bottom to ease the conflict between two groups of prisoners, the Freestaters and the Transvaalers. At its height, each camp held more than 3,000 men. It's interesting to note that prisoners from the Boer War were sent to places where the climate was similar to their homeland – with St Helena being on a list that also included Bermuda, Sri Lanka and the Northwest Frontier Province (now in Pakistan).

More recently, Deadwood has acquired a series of wind turbines which, together with a solar farm at Half Tree Hollow, are expected in time to contribute some 40% of the island's energy requirements.

**Piccolo Hill**  Built during the 1960s to house the staff of the Diplomatic Wireless Service, Piccolo Hill lies adjacent to St Helena Golf Course (page 76). With the aid of an aerial complex on Prosperous Bay Plain, the Diplomatic Wireless Service was able to monitor most west African radio communications, but has since been rendered obsolete. Today the small complex of buildings is home to government employees.

**Millennium Forest**  (*St Helena National Trust;* \ *22190;* e *sth.nattrust@helanta. sh; www.nationaltrust.org.sh;* ☺ *daily; free*) Founded in August 2000 to re-establish at least in part the island's once dense forest of gumwood trees (*Commidendrum robustum*), the Millennium Forest, set high above Prosperous Bay, was a significant marker for a new era. At the beginning of the millennium, every school child on St Helena, and many adults too, planted a tree on the barren 79-acre (32-hectare site) at Horse Point. Some 15 years later, and now in the care of the St Helena National Trust, the forest has been extended to 94 acres (38 hectares) with more than 10,000 trees: still no more than head height, but gradually spreading and thickening up to form an early tree canopy. For visitors, there's an information shelter at the entrance, and a children's nature trail.

Once this whole area was part of the Great Wood, itself part of a belt of gumwood forest that went all round the island. Then many years of felling for timber, fodder and fuel took their toll, and the forest all but disappeared. This, in turn, contributed to the loss of numerous species of plants, birds and insects from the area, and led to serious soil erosion. Along with the reforestation, it is anticipated that this area can once again support other species of plants, birds and insects. With this in mind, many of the island's other endemic plants – such as ebony and hairgrass – are being used to underplant the new gumwoods, and a dedicated area has been established to nurture and study individual specimens. To sponsor a tree costs just £10.

Hikers might like to combine a visit to the Millennium Forest with one of the postbox walks: Cox's Battery (which starts at the nearby meteorological station), or Prosperous Bay, which starts beyond the forest. For details, see pages 111–12.

**Prosperous Bay Plain**  Now the site of the new airport, Prosperous Bay Plain is a particularly desolate area, dotted with cacti and sisal plants but otherwise rough and cratered. The name is derived from a ship that landed at the bay, and is not a reference to the fertility of the area, despite the bright green vegetation that demarcates the centre of the valley. The plain is of interest for other reasons, too – not least, but rather gruesomely, that gypsum from here was probably used to make Napoleon Bonaparte's death mask.

In 1673, a group of English soldiers landed at Prosperous Bay with the aim of reclaiming the island from the Dutch. To help secure their approach, one of the men, Tom, climbed up the cliff and let down a rope to his companions. He, and the location, have since been dubbed 'Holdfast Tom'. The difficulties experienced by the English meant that they considered it unnecessary to fortify the beach, but years later small batteries were constructed and their ruins can still be seen.

Looking east across the plain, the shallow V-shape of Dry Gut would once have framed a view to the sea. Now the gut has been filled, a masterpiece of engineering that was needed to give sufficient length to the airport runway, looming over the valley like a huge dam wall. Yet despite the loss of view, the striped infill of crushed natural rock, hewn from the surrounding area, is in itself awe-inspiring.

**Postbox walks** The coastal area of Longwood features four of the postbox walks, plus the Sugar Loaf, which falls just outside. See page 75 for essential background information on these walks, including an explanation of the two-part grading system.

**Sugar Loaf** (*6/6 from Deadwood, 5/6 from Rupert's; both 3hrs 30mins*), At the most northerly tip of St Helena, the Sugar Loaf falls outside Longwood, but is included here as, like the walks to Flagstaff and The Barn, it is best accessed from Deadwood Plain.

The Sugar Loaf was once an important signalling station, whose ruins at the summit are still visible. The route from Deadwood Plain starts as if to Flagstaff, then turns off through dry coastland before climbing to the summit. From here, the path descends to Banks', where there is a well-preserved series of military batteries, and where it's possible to swim if the sea is calm. From there, continue to the end in Rupert's Bay.

**Flagstaff** (*2/2; 1hr 15mins*) With its classic triangular 'volcano' shape, Flagstaff, at 2,257ft (688m), is visible from many parts of St Helena, which explains why it was once the site of a signalling station. What the signallers didn't take into account was that the hill is frequently shrouded in mist, so the station was eventually abandoned, though it was briefly brought back into service during Napoleon's captivity.

One of the most straightforward of the postbox walks, Flagstaff takes you across Deadwood Plain (pages 109–10), up a steep woodland path and out on to a tiny promontory topped by Bermuda cedars. The views to Sugar Loaf and Turk's Cap are superb, and the drop off sheer. If time is short, and you have a suitable high-clearance vehicle, you can drive part of the way and walk just the last 15 minutes or so.

**The Barn** (*8/9; 4hrs 15mins*) The first piece of land that appears over the horizon when approaching St Helena from Ascension, The Barn is believed to consist of the oldest rocks on the island, some formed before the island emerged from the sea. It's a formidable sight, from land or sea, and one that Napoleon is said to have found deeply depressing. As an aside, it was also one of the last bastions of the island's wild goats, before they were finally eradicated.

The postbox walk to The Barn is considered one of the hardest, even for experienced walkers. As for the Flagstaff and Sugar Loaf walks, it starts on Deadwood Plain, but this hike takes you across unforgiving volcanic terrain, culminating at the Haystack, at the top of The Barn – where the views are stupendous. Keep an eye out for the weather; if the mist rolls in, it's easy to become disorientated, with consequent risk.

**Cox's Battery** (*3/2; 1hr 45mins*) This fairly straightforward walk shares its start near the Millennium Forest with that of the new mountain-bike trail. Initially

5

both run along the same track, past a pattern of smooth, richly coloured rocks and skirting the edge of the Millennium Forest, before diverging and descending into a valley. From here, walkers climb gently up onto the ridge, parallel with but below The Barn, to gain a bird's-eye view of Turk's Cap – far more fulfilling than the crumbling ruins of the battery. Do follow the directions in the postbox walks book carefully as it's easy to get misled by the mountain-bike signposting in the valley, but note that at point 5, you follow the slope on the *left* 'of this shallow valley', not the right.

**Prosperous Bay** *(7/8; 3hrs 30mins)* From its start beyond the Millennium Forest, the route follows a long valley past a series of waterfalls – though they're frequently dry – and down to the beach. You can paddle in the pools in the bay, but it's not normally deemed safe to swim from the pebble beach. Note that because the walk crosses the area now occupied by the airport, security clearance may be needed.

## THE PEAKS NATIONAL PARK

This 1,124 square-mile (2,911km²) area was extended in 2015 from the original Diana's Peak National Park to incorporate much of the central ridge, including both the George Benjamin and Clifford arboretums, and High Peak.

At its heart are the central three peaks: Cuckold's Point, Mount Actaeon and the highest point on the island, Diana's Peak, at 2,690ft (820m). Whereas the top of Diana's Peak is treeless, each of the others is marked by a lone Norfolk Island pine.

The national park, its higher terrain regularly swathed in mist, represents the last stronghold of many of the island's surviving endemic species, including the last remaining wild specimen of the St Helena olive, which was discovered on Mount Actaeon in August 1977. It also bears the scars of the flax industry, for following the industry's demise, New Zealand flax grew wild over this area for many years, in turn destroying many native plants. In recent years, much work has gone into controlling the flax in order to restore the habitat for native flora.

If you're planning to visit the Peaks, do wait for good weather and come prepared. When the mists roll in, visibility is limited to only a few yards/metres, which could prove dangerous for those unfamiliar with the terrain.

**DIANA'S PEAK POSTBOX WALK** *(5/5; 2hrs; see page 75 for general information)* Although the signboard at the start of the walk, on Cabbage Tree Road, indicates that there are three walks from this point, these are for practical and conservation reasons effectively now limited to one: the Snail Circuit.

It's a steep but not particularly difficult hike up through dense vegetation, along the trail of the endemic blushing snail (page 45), which is easily spotted on the cabbage trees – though it's often very, very small! There's no real likelihood of getting lost, but a knowledgeable guide is invaluable as along the way you'll pass several of the island's endemic plants, tree ferns, he, she and black cabbage, and many more, and you'd almost certainly miss out on countless invertebrates seen nowhere else in the world. As you near the top, where the mists of the cloudforest start to come down, the walk takes in St Helena's three highest peaks: Mount Actaeon, Diana's Peak itself, and Cuckold's Point – though the order of the two lower peaks has long been a subject of dispute. From the top of Diana's Peak there are breathtaking views of St Helena and far out to sea – potentially over more than 12,740 square miles (33,000km²) – as well as down onto a thicket of cabbage trees, dogwoods and whitewoods. The highest postbox in the South Atlantic is located up

In November 1676, the 20-year-old astronomer Edmund Halley, who we now know as the discoverer of Halley's Comet, came to St Helena to work. Thought to be the first scientist to have visited St Helena, he carried out some significant work mapping the stars of the southern hemisphere, despite the vagaries of the St Helenian weather. In November 1677, he made the first complete observation of a transit of Mercury across the sun. He returned to England the following year, but visited St Helena again in 1699 as commander of the expedition ship HMS *Paramour*, which was exploring the Atlantic seaboard. Halley later went on to become England's second astronomer royal.

More than 60 years later, another future astronomer royal, Dr Nevil Maskelyne, was sent to St Helena to observe the transit of Venus. Unfortunately, the observatory was set up on the high ridge behind Alarm House (page 107) where, shortly before the event was to occur on 6 June 1761, a passing cloud obscured the view. It is said, however, that several people witnessed the event down in James Valley.

Fascination with the stars continued unabated, and in 1823, the East India Company sent another British astronomer, Manuel Johnson, to St Helena. During his stay he was responsible for construction of an observatory at the top of Ladder Hill, and went on to become its superintendent. The culmination of his work on the island was a catalogue of the stars of the southern hemisphere, published in 1835.

here, too, along with the standard postbox stamp so you can authenticate reaching the highest point of St Helena.

Although there is in theory a circular route taking you back to the start, walkers are requested to return along the same path to avoid damaging the newly established and still-fragile tree-fern thicket.

**HALLEY'S MOUNT** A splendid view of the southeast of St Helena is to be had from Halley's Mount where, in 1677, Edmund Halley (see box, above) set up a small stone observatory to catalogue the southern stars and observe the transit of Mercury. Built on a northeastern spur of the central ridges, it was in an area that is frequently covered in clouds, but despite that Halley was able to carry out a good amount of work. Today, what is left of the observatory is being converted into an information shelter.

**GEORGE BENJAMIN ARBORETUM** In an area widely known as Cason's (and with an old sign proclaiming Hardings and Cason's National Forest), the George Benjamin Arboretum was opened in 1995. Named after the indefatigable island conservationist George Benjamin, who died in 2012, it is planted with several of St Helena's endemic plants. Sadly many of the labels have now disappeared, and the paths are rather overgrown, but the plants remain, including she and he cabbages, jellico, rosemary and small bellflower.

Better maintained is the **nature trail** through the arboretum, to the left of the planting area. Allow about half an hour for this pleasant walk, which takes you steeply up through pine and cypress woodland, the trees alive with fairy terns. At the top, picnic benches afford a view through the flax towards Sandy Bay. From here, take the left-hand path (the other is a dead end), and continue down towards the road, from where it will take about five minutes to return back to the start.

Parking is limited; try the field opposite the picnic benches, near Fairyland, just by the 'welcome to Blue Hill' signpost (known as Cason's Gate). From the picnic site there are great views towards Sandy Bay.

**CLIFFORD ARBORETUM** Despite its proximity to the George Benjamin Arboretum, this older sanctuary has a very different feel. Opened in 1977 to mark the Queen's Silver Jubilee, it is notable for its trees, including three species of pine, underplanted with a range of plants, some of them endemics. It's also the start of the **Mackintosh Trail**, a 3¾mile (6km) out-and-back walk that runs through the woods before descending steeply into pastureland in the valley below. As an alternative, it's possible to form a loop with the **Spring Gut Trail**, which stays within the forested area.

**HIGH PEAK POSTBOX WALK** (*3/2; 30mins; see page 75 for explanation of gradings*) Continuing southwest along the ridge you'll come to High Peak (not to be confused with the very different High Hill, further west). The short but steep climb to the rocky summit is rewarded with some excellent views when the weather is clear. A longer, round-trip walk (*3/3; 1hr 15mins*) also takes in the lush vegetation below the cliff face. There's limited parking by the picnic area at the bottom.

## LEVELWOOD, SANDY BAY AND BLUE HILL

These three sparsely populated districts make up the whole of the southern part of the island, extending from Lemon Valley in the northwest right round to Gill Point in the east, below the airport. That much of this area has recently been incorporated into two new national parks – the southern part of the East Coast Scenic Reserve National Park and Sandy Bay – simply serves to underline the importance of the landscape and the terrain, both scenically and in terms of habitat.

Visitor attractions focus on the extraordinary landscape, as well as Sandy Bay itself, and 12 of the 21 postbox walks.

**PRACTICALITIES** Staying in these remote districts is not particularly realistic at the moment. True, there's a simple campsite at Thompson's Wood, and another at Horse Pasture, but they're geared to the locals, who have a tradition of camping at Easter and Christmas; neither is set up for tourists. One project that would have changed the whole dynamic was an upmarket eco-lodge hotel and golf complex which was on the table for many years, but has now been shelved.

**Bars** For now, just a trio of bars vie for custom at weekends, and a few isolated shops serve their local communities.

☿ **Colin's Bar** Sandy Bay; ☏ 23722; ⊕ 13.00– late Sat. The only place on the island to serve draught beer, & Guinness, Colin's has a DJ or live music on Sat nights, & sometimes a DIY BBQ. Parking is very limited.
☿ **Moonshines** Blue Hill; ☏ 24571; ⊕ 18.00– late Fri–Sat, 15.00–late Sun. A good spot for a drink with a view from their veranda.
☿ **Silver Hill Bar** Silver Hill, Levelwood; ☏ 24663; ⊕ 11.00–late Fri/Sat. Alongside Silver Hill shop, the bar has a disco at weekends, with a noisy line in country & western.

**LEVELWOOD** Whoever named the district of Levelwood had surely taken leave of his senses. Far from being level, the roads rise up in front of you, only to fall sharply away. Forests of eucalyptus give way to great clumps of aloes and they in turn to slopes clothed in uniform green flax – or simply to naked rock. From a vehicle, it's not difficult to appreciate the scenery, which features some superb hiking.

Much of the coastal fringes of this peaceful district have been incorporated into the newly gazetted East Coast Scenic Reserve National Park, and are best explored on foot. But the valleys and hills outside the park are worth investigation too, with a further two postbox walks, and the **Bellstone**. This hefty rock of trachyandesite lies in woodland, shady and cool, with a bench and even a tap for fresh water. The Bellstone also marks the start of the walk to Great Stone Top (below).

**Postbox walks** For general details, including explanation of grading, see page 75.

**Shark's Valley** (*6/8; 3hrs 30mins*) The walk from Silver Hill down this scenic valley is enhanced by a permanently flowing stream, but rampant wild mango can be a pain. Having crossed the stream in a few places, it finishes on the coast beneath Great Stone Top, where a small pool is a good place to cool off before the return walk.

**Great Stone Top** (*5/5; 2hrs 30mins*) Starting in the woods by the Bellstone, this varied, uplifting walk passes around Boxwood Hill and Little Stone Top, before climbing up the rocky slopes of Great Stone Top itself, topping out at 1,621ft (494m). The views over Shark's Valley and down to George and Shore islands are superb, though do be aware of a very steep drop at the top.

**SANDY BAY** Even on the island, the approach road to Sandy Bay is spoken of with respect: a steep, narrow, winding slip of a road which is one of the most testing on St Helena. But make your way slowly down, past the flax, the buddleia, the coffee plantation, the tiny Baptist church, and the thorn trees laden with shimmering morning glory, and you'll understand why it's worth the effort. In practical terms, there are three small shops, helpfully with different opening hours, but – aside from Colin's Bar – there is nowhere for a drink or meal.

**SHAPE** (*St Helena's Active Participation in Enterprise; Sandy Bay;* ✆*24690;* e *shape@ helanta.co.sh;* ⏰ *09.00–15.00 Mon–Fri*) St Helena's first social enterprise, SHAPE works with disabled and vulnerable people of working age to help them lead independent and fulfilling lives. As well as learning basic skills such as maths and English, many of the clients work on a range of crafts, from baskets and tortoises carefully woven out of aloe to handmade paper from flax and unwanted cotton fabric. Others are involved in tasks such as making compost, spinning and carding wool, recycling paper and producing candles, soaps and handwash.

Visitors are welcome, not just to the shop, which sells SHAPE produce, but also to the centre, where you can meet the people who work here. There's a café planned, with information posters about the district, including its geology, settlement and Jenkins' cottage – once home to Captain Robert Jenkins who was brought in to sort out the embezzlement scandal involving Governor John Goodwin and his aide, Duke Crispe.

The centre is on the left of the road leading down to Sandy Bay. You can find some of their products in the Art & Crafts Centre, next to the tourist office in Jamestown.

**Sandy Bay** Sandy Bay – the bay itself, rather than the district – occupies a spectacular southern location, its beach dominated by the barren rock formations that culminate in Lot and Lot's Wife. The surrounding landscape varies from lush greenery to barren rock, sometimes changing abruptly, sometimes in subtle gradations.

To envisage this 'sandy bay' could be slightly misleading. It is indeed a bay, neatly enfolded within steep volcanic cliffs; and there is indeed sand – but that's where the picture goes awry. As on the island of Lanzarote, the sand at Sandy Bay is black – and to detract further from the image, it's not a safe place to swim. (Jellyfish don't help, either.) Despite that, it's an interesting area to explore. The remains of fortifications and the lines of rusting cannons lining the beach hint at the vulnerability of the island at this point. The battery is still standing but much of the wall which once connected the fortifications at Sandy Bay has eroded due to weather, time, and poor construction. There's also the remains of an old lime kiln, built so that limestone discovered here in the early 18th century could be fired and converted to lime to mix with mortar. It was a great find at the time, making it possible to repair fortifications and buildings that had started to crumble because the mortar used in them was of such poor quality.

Do note, if you're planning to come down here, that if turtles are found to be nesting on the beach – usually in the first half of the year – the beach itself is put off-limits, but visitors can still take a look at the fortifications, and walk in and around the area.

**Postbox walks** See page 75 for general information on these walks, and an explanation of the grading.

*Lot's Wife's Ponds* (6/8; 2hrs 30mins) The end of the track leading down to Sandy Bay is the starting point for this, justifiably the most popular of the postbox walks. The narrow path winds up and over a multi-coloured ridge: millions of years of geology right at your feet. The views are spectacular. And while the walking's challenging, there's a reassuring rope at one of the trickier points, and another beyond the postbox to help you climb down the low cliff to those ponds. Sheltered from the waves by natural rock, they're large, deep and crystal clear. Don't forget your swimming things.

*Powell's Valley* (9/9; 2hrs 30mins) There are those on the island who consider this walk to be positively dangerous, but others relish the challenge of the steep slopes with their loose rocks. Either way, it's graded the highest of all the postbox walks, so be warned. It finishes by the sea, where if you're happy to climb down to the beach, you may be able to swim in a small pool.

*Sandy Bay Barn* (5/6; 2hrs 15mins) With views that are said to be as impressive as those from The Barn, this also has its challenges, especially at the end where there's an alternative route for those with no head for heights. Note that near the beginning of the walk, the route crosses private property, so prior permission is required for access.

**BLUE HILL** More than any other area of St Helena, the heart of Blue Hill comes close to the pastoral idyll. At the western end of the central ridge, a couple of narrow roads twist and turn through rolling hills. Head broadly west and you'll pass the little church of St Helena of the Cross and the Donkey Home. North will bring you to Broad Bottom, which between 1900 and 1902 played host to some 3,000 Boer prisoners of war. And right across the land, enticing postbox walks afford dramatic views down to the sea.

**St Helena Donkey Home** (*Blue Hill;* ⧵ 24552) Donkeys have long played an essential role in the life of the island. They have carried people, food, and provisions for both locals and visiting ships. The flax industry was carried and powered by them. Now, as a result, there are a large number of neglected donkeys. The St Helena Donkey Home was set up to provide a haven for the full care and protection of these donkeys. Volunteers are welcome, and there are donkey walks every Saturday morning at 10.00. You can also adopt a donkey for £20 a year.

**Postbox walks** For general information and an explanation of the grading system, see page 75.

**High Hill** (*3/4; 1hr 15min*) For the most part cool and shady, with a welcoming breeze at the top, this is a particularly good choice on a hot day. It's an attractive walk through pine forests, somewhat redolent of the Mediterranean, culminating in a steep climb to the summit. Here, the rocks fall away in all directions to reveal on one side a deep green valley, on the other, South West Point. But do take care; although wooden steps help along the hardest sections, pine needles can make the path slippery and the drop in places is precipitous.

There's a small parking area at the beginning of the walk, just beyond the Blue Hill Store, which could be handy for drinks and snacks.

**Lot** (*7/9; 3hrs*) The large outcrop of phonolite rock that is Lot is quite a hike down from Sandy Bay Ridge – and even more challenging on the way back.

**Blue Point** (*3/3; 1hr 20mins*) One of the newer walks, this follows the edge of the wonderfully named Gates of Chaos. Characterised by eroded volcanic terrain (and strong winds!), it opens out to give views over Sandy Bay and Speery Island.

**Peak Dale** (*3/2; 1hr 45mins*) From the signpost to Fairyland, near the boundary with Blue Hill, the walk runs through areas of flax, pasture and woodland that characterise the hillside below the Sandy Bay Ridge, with views down to Sandy Bay itself. Several potential add-ons make a longer walk possible.

**Manati Bay** (*8/7; 3hrs*) Starting close to the beginning of the South West Point walk, this is an entirely different option – described by at least one islander as 'extreme'. The scenery is impressive but the path is steep and potentially slippery. It's sometimes possible to swim in one of the small ponds beyond the postbox.

**South West Point** (*4/3; 2hrs 30mins*) It's hard to resist the allure of this lovely long walk to the westernmost point of the island, with dramatic views down to Speery Island. There's plenty to appeal to the naturalist, too, with patches of wild bilberry and the blue-flowered gobblegheer on the approach track and the likelihood of seeing the wirebird as the path opens out onto undulating pastureland.

**Thompson's Valley** (*8/7; 3hrs 15mins*) Like Manati Bay, Thompson's Valley is another challenging hike, this one starting in woodland then descending a rocky valley to the sea. At the bottom, you'll be rewarded with a range of military fortifications, and it's possible to swim in calm weather.

5

# SOUTH ATLANTIC SPECIALISTS

Island Holidays has been operating to South Atlantic islands for nearly 30 years (as at 2015)

For expert advice on your holidays to

**ASCENSION ISLAND**

**ST HELENA**

**TRISTAN DA CUNHA**

**FALKLAND ISLANDS**

contact Libby Weir-Breen  E:  libby@islandholidays.co.uk

Tel. 01764 670107 or text on 07808 010939

Island Holidays, PO Box 26317, Comrie, PH6 2YL, Scotland, UK

# Part Two

## ASCENSION ISLAND

## ASCENSION AT A GLANCE

**Location** South Atlantic Ocean, 703 miles (1,131km) northwest of St Helena; about halfway between Brazil and Angola
**Size** 34 square miles (88km²)
**Highest point** 2,817ft (859m)
**Status** British Overseas Territory, with St Helena and Tristan da Cunha
**Capital** Georgetown
**Currency** St Helena pound or pound sterling, US dollar also in use
**Population** 831 (2014), but no permanent residents
**Language** English
**Religion** Predominantly Christian
**Time** GMT
**Electricity** 240V, 50Hz; standard UK electrical socket
**International dialling code** +247
**Emergency telephone** 999
**Flag** Blue with flag of UK in upper left quadrant and Ascension shield centred on outer half of flag. The shield features Green Mountain with three wideawake birds (sooty terns), flanked by a pair of green turtles and topped by a three-masted sailing ship.
**Public holidays** 1 January, Good Friday, Easter Monday, 40th day after Easter, Whit Monday (day after Whitsuntide), 2nd Saturday in June, last Monday in August, 25–26 December
**Website** www.ascension-island.gov.ac

# 6

# Background Information

Ascension Island does not fit into any normal geopolitical pattern. It is essentially a multi-national communications and military hub, but from a political point of view it forms part of the British Overseas Territory of St Helena, Ascension and Tristan da Cunha.

For many years Ascension Island was inaccessible to tourists because of the military installations that have their home here. On the one hand, the United States Air Force (USAF) leases the Wideawake Airfield from the British government, operating it as the southernmost tracking station of the US Government Eastern Test Range. On the other, the British Ministry of Defence (MOD) maintains a base here as an air link between the United Kingdom and the Falkland Islands – a strategy that was to prove definitive during the 1982 Falklands conflict.

For most of its history, Ascension has been run as a 'working island'; despite being an invaluable source of employment for St Helenians, nobody actually 'lived' here. During the 1990s, it looked as though this was going to change, but an abrupt about-turn in 2005 returned the island to the status quo. Today, despite considerable political toing and froing, there is still no permanent population, and still no private property – and a change of policy seems unlikely.

## GEOGRAPHY

Just south of the Equator, at ✪ 07°55.998'S, 14°22.002'W, Ascension is a rocky peak of purely volcanic origin, its base just west of the Mid-Atlantic Ridge. The nearest land is St Helena, some 703 miles (1,131km) to the southeast, but to reach the nearest mainland, the coast of Brazil, you'd have to travel west for around 1,367 miles (2,200km).

At just 34 square miles (88km²), the island is smaller than St Helena: a mere eight miles (13.5km) long and five miles (8km) wide. Barren volcanic rock characterises much of the terrain, punctuated on the west by sweeping bays, some blessed with golden sandy beaches, others with a jumble of rocks. Its highest point, Green Mountain, at 2,817ft (859m), while once also barren, is today covered with lush, dense vegetation that increasingly spreads down through the island during the rainy season.

**GEOLOGY** Ascension is the tip of a shield volcano that rises a staggering 1.8 miles (3.2km) from the seabed. Geologically it is very young (the oldest exposed rocks date back only about a million years) and the last major volcanic eruption took place only within the last several thousand years. Indeed, with 44 dormant craters, the possibility of volcanic activity can never be completely ruled out.

Much of the ground remains covered by basalt lava flows and cinder cones, giving the impression of a moonscape. Beneath the surface, numerous caverns, lava tubes and fumaroles are further testament to the violent activity that created the island, with some sea caves – as at Hannay's Beach – manifesting themselves in blow holes.

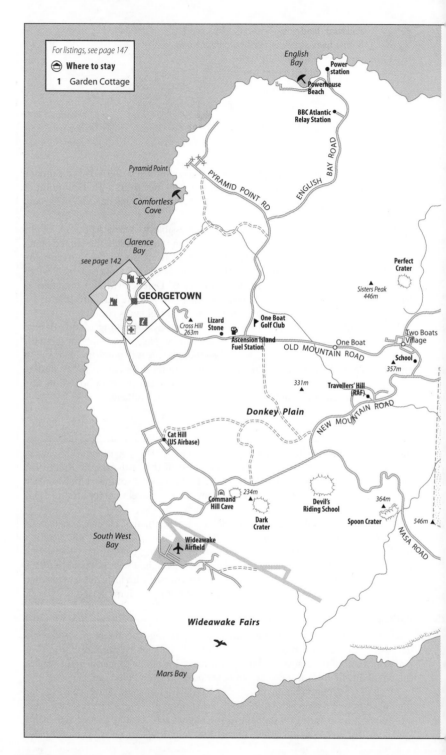

For listings, see page 147

**Where to stay**

**1** Garden Cottage

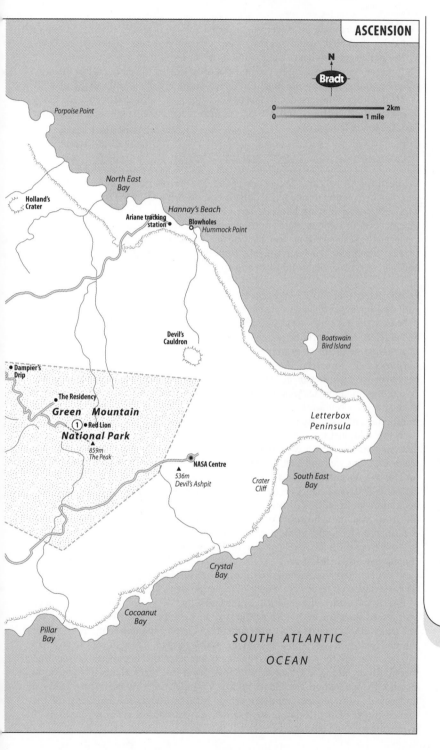

N

**Bradt**

0 ————————————————— 2km
0 ————————————————— 1 mile

Porpoise Point

North East
Bay

Holland's
Crater

Ariane tracking
station

Hannay's Beach

Blowholes
Hummock Point

Devil's
Cauldron

Boatswain
Bird Island

Dampier's
Drip

The Residency

Green Mountain

(1) Red Lion

National Park

▲
859m
The Peak

Letterbox
Peninsula

▲ NASA Centre
536m
Devil's Ashpit

Crater
Cliff

South East
Bay

Crystal
Bay

Cocoanut
Bay

Pillar
Bay

*SOUTH ATLANTIC*

*OCEAN*

6

**CLIMATE** The climate on Ascension may be sub-tropical, but it is much cooler and drier than that would suggest, with temperatures kept relatively moderate by the persistent southeast trade winds. At sea level, they average around 79°F (26°C) year-round, peaking in the mid 80s (30s) during the early part of the year, when humidity can be quite high. On Green Mountain, it's usually about 10–15°F (4–7°C) cooler. Showers occur throughout the year, with a tendency to being heavier around February and March, but Green Mountain is considerably wetter than the lower-lying areas.

## NATURAL HISTORY AND CONSERVATION

Before the 19th century, Ascension Island had no mammals and few plants. It was, however, home to one of the largest seabird colonies in the tropical Atlantic, with millions of nesting boobies, terns and frigatebirds. Change came with the introduction of various plants and animals, including feral cats, which wrought havoc on the seabird population. Despite this, the island still has a range of endemic species: seven vascular (leafy) plants, some 15 bryophyte species, such as mosses and liverworts, one seabird, 11 fish and an estimated 28 invertebrates.

**FLORA** Ascension has 25 indigenous plants, of which seven are endemic, and countless introduced plants – especially on Green Mountain (page 147).

Most of the endemics are also confined to Green Mountain, and all are considered endangered. Most prolific is the **Ascension Island spleenwort** (*Asplenium ascensionis*), with many examples here. Near the summit, a large fern, *Ptisana purpurascens* (formerly *Marattia purpurascens*), takes two forms. In densely shaded areas it grows beneath larger vegetation, whereas in areas of cloudforest it is found as an epiphyte. *Stenogrammitis ascensionense*, too, has taken advantage of the recent cloudforest cover on the mountain, extending its range from the traditional damp, exposed sites to new growth in the trees.

In the wild, just two small populations remain of the bracken-like fern, *Pteris adscensionis*: on Green Mountain and in Cricket Valley. Fortunately, cultivated plants are doing well and have recently been reintroduced to the wild. It's good news, too, for the **Ascension Island parsley fern** (*Anogramma ascensionis*). Considered extinct in 2003, this pretty green fern was rediscovered six years later and has since been successfully cultivated and re-introduced. With a preference for exposed sites on Green Mountain, however, one of the endemic grasses, *Sporobolus caespitosus*, is easily dislodged, so is at the mercy of grazing sheep.

Away from the hills, small colonies of the low-growing **Ascension Island spurge** (*Euphorbia origanoides*) may be found in remote locations, from Letterbox to Comfortless Flats. Its greenish-red flowers are similar to the English spurge, and – when snapped – its prostrate vermilion stems ooze a thick, poisonous milky sap.

Endemics aside, the majority of plants on Ascension today have been introduced since the early 19th century; some because of their visual attractions, but many others as part of an experiment on Green Mountain conducted by Sir Joseph Hooker, in part with a view to increasing rainfall. A few, however, have had catastrophic environmental consequences, not least the impenetrable Mexican thornbush or mesquite (*Prosopis juliflora*). From just three plants introduced to stabilise the land when Two Boats Village was built in the 1960s, it spread almost unchecked, with serious implications for turtle-nesting sites and some of the island's fragile plants. Today, in such sensitive areas, control measures are in place to prevent ongoing damage.

# BIRDS

**Seabirds** When Ascension was first inhabited in 1815, it was thought to host millions of individual seabirds, but then came the introduction of domestic cats. Brought to the island in 1815 to get rid of the black rats that had survived shipwrecks, the cats instead developed a preference for birds. As the cats thrived, they became wild and multiplied rapidly, with devastating consequences for the bird populations on Ascension. The drastic decline in seabirds was not helped by the arrival of men, who harvested birds and their eggs and mined their guano. Indeed, remnants of the guano-mining venture established by an English company in the 1920s still exist. Goats and rats contributed further to the birds' woes.

As feral cats continued to haunt Ascension, almost the only place to find full-time ground-nesting birds on Ascension Island for close on 200 years was the tiny Boatswain Bird Island off the east coast. Until, that is, the introduction in 2001 of the **Ascension Seabird Restoration Project**. Implemented by the Ascension Island government, and overseen by the Royal Society for the Protection of Birds (RSPB) with £500,000 funding from the British government, it succeeded in a total eradication of feral cats from the island. Since 2004, although domestic cats have been allowed to remain under strict control, no feral cats have been recorded on the island.

The impact on seabirds was immediate. Seabird recolonisation of the main island was first recorded in May 2002, and numbers have since increased steadily. By 2011, five of Ascension's 11 seabird species had returned to nest on the main Ascension Island. Most were occupying sites immediately adjacent to existing offshore colonies, although the masked boobies were more widely dispersed.

Meanwhile, seabirds suffer threats from another quarter: fishing. Frigatebirds and boobies are known to scavenge bait from behind local sportfishing boats, and occasionally get caught on the hooks, though most are successfully released. When the scale of fishing is magnified, as in the long-line operations carried out in Ascension waters by Asian vessels since 1988, many seabirds have become ensnared and have subsequently drowned. Overfishing of the yellowfin tuna, too, may have indirect effects on seabird populations, since the birds feed on shoals of small fish that the tuna herd to the surface for their own consumption. Thus any reduction in the tuna population could result in a reduction in food for the seabirds. In order to address this, in 2013 the Ascension government suspended the sale of commercial fishing licences while they reviewed the options for sustainable marine management.

Today, of the 11 seabird species that breed on Ascension Island, just one is endemic: the **Ascension frigatebird** (*Fregata aquila; wingspan 6ft 6in/200cm*). Until recently, Boatswain Bird Island supported the entire population of this, the smallest frigatebird in the world. Following the successful eradication of feral cats from the main island, however, at least 12 frigatebird pairs – of a total of around 6,000 – nested on Letterbox Peninsula in 2013, rising to 44 in 2014–15.

With a hooked beak and forked tail, these are distinctive birds, but never more so than during courtship rituals, when the male inflates the prominent scarlet pouch at his throat. Frigatebirds lay just one egg at a time, usually in alternate years. They feed on the wing, and while they do take fish from the surface, they are also piratical by nature, stealing food from boobies in particular, and helping themselves to both baby turtles and sooty tern chicks. It's not surprising, then, that they are frequently seen scanning the ground above Long Beach, where the turtles nest, and the Wideawake Fairs, home to a huge sooty tern colony.

Most of the other seabird species are also found on St Helena, so are described in more detail in *Chapter 3*. Among them are two species of booby. Most visible is

6

the attractive **masked booby** (*Sula dactylatra*; page 44), also known as the white booby, which nests on Letterbox Peninsula and Boatswain Bird Island. Found in far fewer numbers is the **brown booby** (*Sula leucogaster*; page 44), often seen off Long Beach, but altogether less common is the similar-sized **red-footed booby** (*Sula sula; wingspan 3ft 3in/1m*), which is not found on St Helena, but can be seen in two morphs, or colorations, on Ascension: brown, and the very rare white.

Surely the most elegant of seabirds, the terns are represented on Ascension by four species. Large numbers of the **sooty tern** or 'wideawake' (*Onychoprion fuscata*; page 44) settle on the Wideawake Fairs, on the southwest coast, to hatch their eggs. The colony, currently about 200,000 pairs, was seriously affected by feral cats during the breeding season, but that threat, at least, is no longer. A few **white terns** (*Gygis alba*; page 43), also locally referred to as fairy terns, can be found nesting on the cliffs and in eucalyptus trees on Green Mountain.

In the same family are two noddy terns. The **black noddy** (*Anous minutus*; page 44), which nests in good numbers on coastal cliffs, including at Pillar Bay, and the less populous **brown noddy** (*Anous stolidus*; page 44), which can sometimes be observed nesting alongside the sooty terns at the Wideawake Fairs.

Another pairing comes with the tropicbirds or boatswains: the **red-billed tropicbird** (*Phaethon aethereus*; page 44), which is also found on St Helena, and the slightly smaller and more populous **yellow-billed tropicbird** (*Phaethon lepturus; 31in/80cm*), which is not. Both are hole nesters, and both sport magnificent tail feathers that are over half the length of their body. Look out for them around Boatswain Bird Island and Pillar Bay.

Completing the seabird picture is the **Madeiran storm petrel** (*Oceanodroma castro*; page 44), which numbers around 3,000 breeding birds, probably all on Boatswain Bird Island.

**Landbirds** Before the 19th century, the only known landbirds on Ascension were the small night heron and the Ascension flightless rail. Both are now extinct. The only evidence of the presence of the tiny flightless Ascension Island rail (*Atlantisia elpenor*), which was closely related to the Inaccessible flightless rail, is from a traveller's description of 1656, and skeletons found within the last century.

Today, only four non-seabirds exist, all of them introduced. The **common waxbill** (*Estrilda astrild*; page 42), and the **common mynah** (*Acridotheres tristis*; page 43), are often seen in Georgetown as well as in less urban surroundings. You'll also find the **yellow canary** (*Serinus flaviventris*; page 42), introduced in the 1860s and the raucous **red-necked francolin** (*Francolinus afer; 14in/35cm*). The **cattle egret** (*Bubulcus ibis; 20in/50cm*) does not breed on the island. but is frequently spotted, along with a number of other passing vagrants.

**LAND ANIMALS** Also making their home on the island are rabbits, of which there are plenty, feral sheep (once part of the farm on Green Mountain), feral donkeys, land crabs, at least two species of lizard and black ship rats (*Rattus rattus*). Then there are the invertebrates, of which an estimated 28 species are endemic, including four spiders.

Arguably of greatest curiosity are the **land crabs** (*Johngarthia lagostoma*). Probably the earliest colonisers of Ascension, they were first recorded here in the 16th century. With their wide, unblinking eyes and slightly officious way of scurrying across the ground and through vegetation, they are curiously engaging to watch. Although they're relatively easy to spot, especially on Green Mountain, little is known about these crabs, but they inhabit high places, coming down to the sea only to breed. Then, when the time is right, sometime around February to May, they creep out of their hiding places in rocky crevices or holes in the sand, and cautiously make their way down to the water's edge. Here, they release their egg pouches, bulging with tiny eggs that appear black due to eye spots of the larvae, into the sea, where the developing larvae will drift for two weeks. If currents are favourable, they will then return to land as megalops – an intermediary between the larva and the true crab. After spawning, the adult crabs begin their journey back into the island's mountainous interior.

**MARINE LIFE** Frequently seen around Ascension are bottlenose and pan-tropical spotted dolphins (page 45), with humpback whales (page 46) putting in an occasional appearance around September and October each year. But in marine terms, the island is best known for the **green sea turtle** (see box, below). As long as anyone can remember, Ascension's beaches have served as the second-largest breeding ground in the Atlantic of these turtles. Every year, the animals migrate to the island from their feeding grounds, some 1,367 miles (2,200km) to the west along the South American coast. Many of the females come ashore to lay their eggs on Long Beach in Georgetown, where there are regular turtle tours in season (pages 139–40). Out at sea, you may also see juvenile **hawksbill turtles** (*Eretmochelys imbricata*; page 46).

**Fish** Barracuda, sailfish, wahoo, bonita, tuna and marlin: all are regularly seen in Ascension waters, but there are 11 species of **endemic fish** here, too, along with 16 others that exist only around Ascension and St Helena. Among the Ascension specials are the brightly striped Ascension wrasse (*Thalassoma ascensionis*), the Ascension goby (*Priolepis ascensionis*), the mottled blenny (*Scartella nuchifilis*), the resplendent or splendid angelfish (*Centropyge resplendens*), and sea bream or 'old wife' (*Diplodus ascensionis*).

## GREEN SEA TURTLE

The green sea turtle (*Chelonia mydas*) is named after the greenish colour of its fat. Those that nest on the beaches of Ascension, between 2,000 and 5,000 a year, spend most of their lives in the sea off the coast of Brazil, returning hundreds of miles to their place of birth to lay their eggs.

Turtles are cold-blooded animals, requiring warm water to survive. The sex of the hatchlings is determined by the temperature of the sand – at around 82°F (28°C) a balance between males and females is to be expected; cooler than that and males will dominate; hotter and there will be a predominance of females.

In the wild, the green sea turtle nests every three or four years, when she lays between 600 and 900 eggs per season in six clutches: one every fortnight or so. In their first year, the hatchlings grow up to 6lb (2.7kg), and by the time they are three or four they can weigh up to 52lb (24kg). Fewer than one in 1,000 hatchlings can expect to survive to adulthood.

Turtles do not nest until they are at least 25 years old, when they lay their eggs deep in the sand. The eggs take around 60 days to hatch, at which time the hatchlings make their way after dark towards the sea, attracted by the play of moonlight on the waves, and set off for distant climes. Any foolish enough to attempt the short journey by day are likely to be taken by frigatebirds and predatory fish.

6

Added to the haul of endemics are two species of inland saltwater shrimp: *Typhlatya rogersi* and the larger, but less common *Procaris ascensionis*, both found in rock pools near Shelley Beach.

**CONSERVATION** Conservation issues on Ascension are monitored by the **Ascension Conservation Centre** (page 131), a government-linked body that has a practical and educational remit, and the voluntary **Ascension Heritage Society** (page 131).

In 2005, Green Mountain (pages 146–9) was designated a national park in recognition of its unique environment. Since then, many of the historical paths and tunnels, and associated buildings and structures, have been cleared of encroaching vegetation and rendered safe, with signage installed to make the park more accessible for visitors.

Further environmental protection came in 2014, when several additional protected areas were introduced: Boatswain Bird Island Sanctuary, Turtle Ponds Area of Historical Interest, and a series of six nature reserves: Long Beach, South West Bay, North East Bay, Letterbox Peninsula, Mars Bay and the Waterside Fairs.

The success of the Seabird Restoration Project has inadvertently created a new threat: rats. No longer predated by feral cats, the rat population is growing, with potential consequences for seabird eggs, small crabs and turtle hatchlings. While eradication is an unlikely scenario, so far the turtles and seabirds at least have been protected by the laying of poison, and the situation is being monitored.

Out at sea, there is considerable pressure from the RSPB and other environmental bodies to introduce a marine protected area within 200 nautical miles of Ascension. It's a controversial topic, not least because policing waters of that magnitude is too large a task for the island's limited resources. One alternative under consideration is to open a small-scale sustainable fishery with just a few licences, which would pay for overseeing that area, but as yet no decisions have been taken.

# HISTORY

**DISCOVERY AND A QUIET START** Ascension was discovered in 1501 by the Portuguese seafarer João da Nova, who named it Conception. Then, two years later, on Ascension Day 1503, it was effectively rediscovered by Alphonse d'Albuquerque, who named it to mark the date of his arrival.

Although the island was dry and barren, it did have its uses for passing ships. During the 17th century, captains started to call at the island to stock up with turtle meat and eggs to supplement their crew's diet. In return they would leave behind goats for later ships, a practice that continued into the 19th century. They'd leave letters, too, to be delivered by vessels heading in the opposite direction. While most ships stopped simply to take on supplies, there were also occasions where a wrongdoer would be marooned on the island as punishment.

**FIRST SETTLERS AND THE MILITARY** It was not until Napoleon was exiled to St Helena in 1815 that the first permanent inhabitants arrived on Ascension. To help deter any attempt at rescue, a small British naval garrison was stationed on the island. Back then, the island itself was dubbed by its occupiers as a 'stone sloop of war' of the smaller class, and was known as HMS *Ascension*. Their first settlement, on the northwest coast of the island, was called simply Garrison, but it went on to become what is today the island's capital, Georgetown.

By the time of Napoleon's death in 1821, Ascension had become a supply station and sanatorium for ships involved in the suppression of the slave trade around the west African coast. Two years later, it passed to the Royal Marines and remained a base for British naval operations until 1922, when it was made a dependency of St Helena.

**TELECOMMUNICATIONS AND STRATEGIC DEFENCE** In 1863, the Union Steamship Company began calling at Ascension to deliver and collect mail, but it was the laying of the first telegraph cable in 1899 that established the island as an important telecommunications station. Indeed, from 1922 until 1964 it was 'governed' by the Eastern Telegraph Company (which became Cable and Wireless in 1934), whose senior manager handled the day-to-day affairs of the island. It wasn't until 1964 that these executive duties were taken over by an administrator from the British government.

In the meantime, in 1942, the United States government, by arrangement with the British government, built Wideawake Airfield, which proved to be a considerable strategic asset during the second part of World War II. Between 1943 and 1945, more than 25,000 American planes made a stopover in Ascension on their way to north Africa, the Middle East and Europe, transporting troops and moving planes to serve in the war. The US wartime base, holding as many as 4,000 servicemen at one time, was centred on Command Hill overlooking the airfield.

After the war, in 1947, American troops left the island and the airstrip fell into disuse, but not for long. Just nine years later, an agreement was signed between Great Britain and the United States permitting the use of Ascension as a long-range testing ground for military missiles. In 1957, a US Air Force presence was re-established and the airstrip facilities were enlarged. The site is now a tracking station for intercontinental ballistic and space missiles. A NASA tracking station built in 1967, however, has since been shut down, although there is talk of NASA establishing further operations here.

In 1964, Ascension was used as a base for Operation Red Dragon (Dragon Rouge), when Belgian paratroopers were sent into the Congo to rescue hostages held by communist rebels. Then in 1982, Wideawake Airfield proved its value once again, this time during the Falklands conflict, when Ascension served as a staging post for RAF flights between Great Britain and the Falkland Islands. Shortly afterwards, in 1985, these flights became a regular fixture, used not just by the military but also by St Helenians to get to and from jobs on the Falkland Islands, and by a limited number of tourists and other passengers bound for St Helena.

## GOVERNMENT AND ADMINISTRATION

Ever since it was first settled in 1815, Ascension has been run as a company island. It was a status that suited everyone well enough for decades, but during the 1990s, the UK government decided to move towards a public-finance model. Taxation was introduced and representation followed, with the first Island Council elected in 2002. With democracy came promises from the British government that the right of abode and the right to own property would be enshrined in new legislation. Long-term residents spent money on their houses and invested in local businesses. Ascension set out towards constitutional democracy and began to plan for tourist development.

Then, in 2005, following a visit by Foreign Office and MOD officials to the island, the British Foreign Office announced that it no longer considered it 'appropriate' to grant right of abode or property ownership. It is not clear what caused this about-turn, and many long-term residents were deeply unhappy about it, but it seems very unlikely that the decision will be reversed.

**ADMINISTRATION** The day-to-day running of the island is the responsibility of the resident island administrator, who is advised by the Island Council and responsible to the territory's governor on St Helena.

The provision of public services on Ascension has since 2000 been the responsibility of the Ascension Island government, with the first Island Council elected on 1 November 2002. The council is made up of seven elected councillors, who are the only ones to have a vote, plus two ex-officio members, and the administrator in the chair.

**LAW** The island's legal system is based on English law with a mixture of Ascension and St Helena ordinances, adapted to conform to local circumstances. Most cases are heard by a magistrate, but appeals and more serious cases are referred to the chief justice, who is based on St Helena. Although there is a small jail cell at the police station, prison sentences meted out are served on St Helena.

The police station is staffed by a detachment from the St Helena police force. In addition to standard duties, they act as prison warders and are responsible for immigration.

## ECONOMY

Given that the right to stay on Ascension is granted only to those with a job, there is no unemployment here, and no real poverty.

Unlike St Helena, Ascension receives no financial assistance from the UK. The government derives its income from income tax, customs duties and business levies on the telecommunications based on the island, such as Sure (formally Cable and Wireless), Babcock (the BBC), and the Composite Signals Organisation (CSO). All property, except the church, is owned by the state.

**Tourism** is limited by the availability of flights, with advance purchase of tickets currently limited to just ten civilians per journey. That said, there is some income from military families taking a holiday here, particularly those based on the Falklands, as well as from passengers on the RMS *St Helena*, and from the occasional cruise ship. There is just one hotel group on the island.

## PEOPLE

Ascension has no indigenous population; even those who consider themselves to be Ascension Islanders have no legal status as such. The population of 800 or so is largely a mixture of British and American citizens, including many St Helenians, most of whom work for the military, the telecommunications companies, and the British government.

Regardless of nationality, only those who are employed on the island may live here, together with their partners and dependent children. There is no right to permanent residence, and – aside from the Church – no question of owning property. Despite a near-reversal of policy in the 1990s, everyone must leave on retirement, or on reaching the age of 18 unless they have secured employment. All the same, there are many people who have raised families on Ascension and consider it home, and some consider it a draconian arrangement.

Most of the island's inhabitants live within four settlements: the administrative capital of Georgetown, Two Boats Village, Traveller's Hill (where the RAF contractors live), and the US base at Cat Hill. The Residency on Green Mountain is home to the island's administrator.

# EDUCATION

Two Boats School, whose curriculum largely follows that of the UK, caters for all children between the ages of three and 16, after which there's a youth training programme. Those seeking further education must do so overseas. Of the 100 or so pupils, most are St Helenian children whose parents are employed on the island.

## TRAVELLING POSITIVELY

Visitors to Ascension with time on their hands may wish to get involved with some form of voluntary work, while others may like to remain in contact or to make a financial contribution to a particular cause. The following two organisations would welcome involvement on both fronts – though if you'd like to volunteer with the conservation centre, do make arrangements in advance of your visit.

**Ascension Heritage Society** http://heritage. org.ac. Founded in 1966, this friendly voluntary body is based at the museum, & takes full credit for its recent restoration. They are also responsible for the island's archives, & work with the Conservation Department to maintain access to the letterbox walks. Though it's best to phone first, volunteers can just turn up to help – & financial contributions are a bonus.

**Ascension Island Government Conservation Centre** ✎6359; e conservationenquiries@ ascension.gov.ac; www.ascension-island.gov.ac/conservation. By prior arrangement, volunteers are welcome to help out for a day or more with activities such as plant restoration, & monitoring seabirds & turtles. Their website boasts a wealth of accessible information.

**ST HELENA ONLINE**

For additional online content, articles, photos and more on St Helena, Ascension and Tristan da Cunha, why not visit www.bradtguides.com/sthelena.

# 7

# Visiting Ascension

First impressions of Ascension are not great. The largely barren, volcanic landscape has its own allure, but it's blighted by the paraphernalia of the modern telecommunications industry, and a slight air of impermanence. It doesn't take long, though, before the island's natural beauty kicks in: the quiet little town of Georgetown; Atlantic rollers crashing onto long, sandy beaches; nesting turtles that lay their eggs by starlight; seabirds in their thousands; and the densely vegetated slopes of a mountain that represent an extraordinary triumph of human intervention over the natural world.

Ascension Island may be a 'working island' but it is very much open to visitors. Some are *en route* to St Helena, others to or from the Falkland Islands; either way, it makes a very good stopover for a few days, or a holiday in its own right. While the tourist infrastructure is fairly modest, the few places to stay are comfortable, the island uncrowded, and there's no shortage of activities and places to explore. You will, though, need to be reasonably self-sufficient. With so few visitors, guided trips in particular can rarely be organised on the spur of the moment, so a little advance planning is well worth the effort.

## WHEN TO GO AND HIGHLIGHTS

There's no one 'good time' to visit Ascension. The climate (page 124) is relatively moderate all year, so more important is what you want to do, since that is far more likely to impact on your timing.

### HIGHLIGHTS
**Wildlife** Key to many a visit is Ascension's **birdlife** (pages 125–6), and specifically the seabird colonies of the Wideawake Fairs and Boatswain Bird Island (page 151). Up there with the best sights, too, is the endemic **Ascension frigatebird**. More seasonal, but equally unmissable, are the nesting **green sea turtles** (pages 139–40), which are usually here between January and June. To watch one of these lumbering females laying her eggs in the sand is one of the world's great wildlife experiences. The early part of the year gives the best chance of seeing **land crabs** when they are spawning, usually around February and March (page 139).

**Walking** With miles of designated paths, Ascension offers much to the walker. Terrain is varied, from clambers across volcanic rocks to hikes through dense vegetation on Green Mountain, and coastal walks with magnificent sea views. See also page 139.

**Watersports** As on St Helena, the seas around Ascension offer clear, unpolluted waters with some excellent diving and fishing opportunities year-round – provided you arrange things in advance. That said, between June and November gives the greatest chance of calm seas. See also pages 140–1.

**PUBLIC HOLIDAYS AND FESTIVALS** Ascension's public holidays are broadly as on St Helena (page 52), with the exception of St Helena Day. In its place is the annual Ascension Day, celebrated 40 days after Easter Sunday, so usually also in May. On public holidays, as for other events, the strong St Helenian population sets the tone with parades and all sorts of fanfare.

The considerable US presence on the island means that both American Independence Day, on 4 July, and Thanksgiving, on the fourth Thursday in November, are widely celebrated too, though neither is a public holiday.

## November
**Dew Pond Run** The seven-mile Dew Pond Run starts at sea level by the Turtle Ponds in Georgetown and ends at 2,817ft (859m), at the top of Green Mountain, so it's not for the faint-hearted.

## December
**Boxing Day Raft Race** Held at English Bay every year on 26 December.

## TOUR OPERATORS

The only dedicated overseas **tour operator** is Island Holidays (page 53), although one or two others that offer St Helena can also organise tailor-made trips to Ascension on request. For tourist information, see page 141.

## RED TAPE

Prior to making any travel arrangements, visitors wishing to stay on Ascension Island should apply for an **entry permit** to the administrator (e *aig.admin@ ascension.gov.ac; www.ascension-island.gov.ac; £20pp, under 12s £5*). The application form can be downloaded online, then submitted via email or through your tour operator. Accommodation must be pre-booked. On arrival, you will need to have a passport with at least six months' validity, comprehensive travel and medical insurance (see below), proof of onward travel, and sufficient funds to cover your stay on the island. Passengers on visiting cruise ships are required to pay a **landing fee** of £10 (under 12s free).

**Consular activities** are handled by the police (℡ *6412*), but there is no facility for issuing replacement UK passports or entry visas. See also page 54.

**TRAVEL INSURANCE** All travellers must have a valid medical insurance policy for at least £1 million, to include cover for medical evacuation.

**CUSTOMS** See page 54 for products that may be brought in duty free by visitors.

## GETTING THERE AND AWAY
### BY AIR
**From the UK** Ascension Island's airport is actually a US military base. The RAF, however, flies civilians to and from RAF Brize Norton, currently using an adapted Airbus A330, known as a Voyager. Usually only ten seats per flight are allocated to civilians, so advance bookings are essential. Even with a confirmed booking it is possible – albeit very unusual – for civilians to be offloaded in the event of military need. Conversely, tickets are sometimes available at very short notice if there are still free seats just a few

7

days before the flight. The plane, known as the South Atlantic Airbridge, makes a short stopover on Ascension, then continues to the Falkland Islands.

Tickets are available direct from the government-run **Ascension Island Travel Agency (AITA)** (✆ 6500; e *flight.bookings@ascension.gov.ac; www.ascension-flights. com*), or through a tour operator (pages 54 and 133). It is a condition of booking that you already have an entry permit (page 133) and comprehensive travel and medical insurance. Fares are £510 one way, or £969 return.

**Schedule** There are two flights a week in each direction: leaving Brize Norton on Wednesday and Sunday, and returning from Ascension on Tuesday and Friday. Flights in both directions depart at 23.00, arriving the following morning at around 08.00. That said, flight times are subject to change, so all UK departures should be checked both 24 hours and 12 hours in advance.

**Baggage allowance** Civilian passengers may check in baggage up to 27kg, plus one piece of hand baggage up to 8.8lb (4kg), with maximum dimensions of 18 x 12 x 9in (45 x 30 x 22.5cm). This must include all carry-on luggage, including laptop computers, handbags, etc.

**Getting to Brize Norton** Brize Norton is a military airport about 18 miles (29km) west of Oxford, or 60 miles (97km) from London's Heathrow Airport. The nearest railway stations are Oxford and Swindon (also 18 miles/29km), from where registered taxis can take passengers to/from the airport. If you are being dropped off, note that your driver will need to present two forms of identification, including a passport or photo driving licence.

Airport facilities are practical if not fancy. There's a branch of Spar that incorporates a coffee shop and snack bar, as well as internet access and free Wi-Fi, free secondhand books, televisions and gaming machines – including an Xbox game zone.

**From St Helena** Atlantic Star Airlines (*www.atlanticstarairlines.com*), who have announced operation of fortnightly flights between London and St Helena, is also planning to operate between St Helena and Ascension, although no details have yet been released.

**Ascension Airport** The airport at Wideawake Airfield goes under several names, including Ascension Island Base or simply the Airhead. Little more than a holding bay for passengers off the RAF flights, the small terminal is staffed in friendly fashion by British service personnel.

A minibus from the Obsidian Group (which operates all visitor accommodation on the island) meets incoming guests off the flights for the ten-minute drive to Georgetown, and transfers them back at the end of their stay.

## BY SEA
**RMS *St Helena*** The RMS *St Helena* (pages 55–7) service that shuttles between Ascension Island, St Helena and Cape Town is scheduled to cease in summer 2016. Until then, it remains a vital bridge between the three ports, bringing supplies from Cape Town to the islands, and transporting St Helenians who work on Ascension to and from St Helena when they're on leave.

The ship calls at Ascension twice a month, arriving at around midday, and departing that evening at about 19.00, though precise timings vary. The Obsidian Hotel will keep guests informed of the latest information, which can also be

**RADIO CONTACT** Call VHF Channel 08 (during office hours) for advice on anchoring and formalities, or VHF Channel 16 after 16.00 and at the weekend.

**ANCHORAGE** Visiting yachts should anchor north of the Pierhead, in front of the local boat moorings (✪ 07 55.200'S, 14 24.700'W), without obstructing ships arriving, departing or unloading cargo. Yachts should use their own anchor, and not pick up one of the vacant mooring buoys.

**FORMALITIES** Advance notice of arrival is not essential but it is encouraged. At the earliest opportunity within working hours (⊕ *08.00–12.30, 13.30–15.30*), the captain must register with the assistant harbourmaster at the Pierhead and pay light dues of £15, then should complete immigration formalities at the police station. Each person must have an entry permit, costing £20 and payable to the police, who will also require evidence of medical insurance. Once registration is complete, crew members may go ashore between 07.00 and 23.00, but may not stay on land unless they have booked accommodation on the island.

**DISEMBARKATION** Landing is at the Pierhead steps only.

**HARBOUR FACILITIES** Fresh drinking water is available at £1 for 45 litres from a coin-operated meter at the fishermen's bench near the landing steps, and there are good showers and toilets at Georgetown swimming pool. Waste, with the exception of gas cylinders, may be dumped in the skip at the bottom of the pier.

**OTHER PRACTICALITIES** No form of cooking gas is sold on Ascension, and availability of parts is very limited. Should any repairs be needed, contact the Ascension Island Works and Services Agency (✆ *6346*) for advice.

obtained at the port office. Baggage for departing passengers usually needs to be checked in at the port office early that morning. With fewer tourists on board, this leg of the ship's journey has a rather different feel from the Cape Town stretch, more of a practical trip than one with a holiday atmosphere. That said, the crew work exceptionally hard to make everyone feel welcome and it's still a great experience.

**Cruise ships** Ascension sees a handful of cruise ships each year, though with anchorage in the bay and a sometimes tricky landing, all too often passengers are not able to go ashore. When this happens, and weather permitting, the ship may circumnavigate the island with staff from the conservation and tourist offices on board to point out key features and places of interest. Souvenirs and stamps are also sold.

**Arrival and departure** All ships anchor in Clarence Bay, in front of Georgetown, with passengers transferred to and from the Pierhead in small boats. Only those who are steady on their feet should consider going ashore as even the slightest swell can make the transfer tricky. Sensible shoes are essential.

Visiting Ascension    GETTING THERE AND AWAY

7

## HEALTH AND SAFETY

Ascension has a small hospital (✆ *6000, 6252*) staffed by two doctors – a surgeon and an anaesthetist – and there's a separate modern dentist practice (✆ *6348, 6355*) in Georgetown. Medical care is not free to visitors, who should ensure that they have an adequate supply of prescription drugs. In case of serious illness, patients would be evacuated by air to the UK. The emergency telephone number is ✆ 999.

Water on the island comes from a desalination plant and is deemed safe to drink, though it has rather a chemical taste. For other health matters, see pages 59–61.

## WHAT TO TAKE

Suncream, insect repellent, a hat and a waterproof jacket should be top of your packing list. If you plan to hike, bring strong shoes and perhaps a walking pole. Masks, snorkels and fins may be available locally but sizes are erratic, so bring your own if you can. For divers, it's worth packing a wetsuit and dive computer, even if you plan to hire the rest of the kit. See also pages 62–3.

## OPENING HOURS

Aside from standard office hours (⊕ *08.30–16.00 Mon–Fri*), opening hours for shops, tourist attractions and other facilities are often extremely limited. Many places close at lunchtime, and shops may be open only one or two days a week. Even the tourist office is open only for a couple of hours in the mornings.

## MONEY AND BANKING

The official **currency** is the St Helena pound, which has parity with the British pound, although sterling is widely acceptable, and US dollars are the norm at the American air-base. Falkland Islands currency cannot normally be used.

**Credit and debit cards** are not widely accepted, except by the Obsidian Hotel group, and at the RAF NAAFI shop (page 149), where you can get cash against your card. With suitable photographic ID and a signature, you can also obtain cash against Visa and MasterCards at the tiny Bank of St Helena in Georgetown (*Ascension Island Govt Bldg*; ✆ *6123; www.sainthelenabank.com;* ⊕ *08.30–15.00 Mon, Wed & Fri, 09.30–15.00 Tue, 08.30–noon Thu, 09.00–noon Sat*), or at the airport (⊕ *09.00–14.30 Thu/Fri*). Travellers' cheques cannot be exchanged at the bank, and there are no ATMs.

The bank will also exchange notes in South African rand, US dollars and euros. It is advisable to change back any surplus local currency before leaving as it can be difficult to exchange outside St Helena and Ascension.

## MEDIA AND COMMUNICATIONS

**TELEVISION** Digital television came to Ascension in 2015, bringing with it six digital channels, including BBC 1, BBC2, ITV1 and Sky News.

**NEWSPAPERS** The weekly *Islander*, more of a parochial newsletter than a newspaper, is available both as a printed A4 edition (60p) and online (*www.the-islander.org.ac*). As well as news, interviews and job advertisements, it includes the week's TV guide.

Ascension has long been an important centre of communications. It was once a main relay point of the co-axial submarine cable system laid between the United Kingdom, Portugal and South Africa, with links to South America and west Africa. While this is no longer operational, it is still the base of the Sure (formerly Cable and Wireless) international satellite telecommunications service which operates the internal telephone service, and mans the Ariane Earth Station.

The BBC has had a presence here since the mid 1960s, as has the Composite Signals Organisation (CSO). Initially, the BBC established the Atlantic Relay Station to improve coverage of its short-wave broadcasts to Africa and South America. Three decades later, Merlin Communications International was appointed to operate its Ascension facilities, including the island's power and freshwater plants, and the work is now undertaken by Babcock International.

**TELEPHONE** Public phone boxes take phonecards that can be bought at both the Obsidian Hotel and Solomon's, though the Obsidian's room rates for overseas calls are slightly cheaper. Local calls cost 4p a minute; calls to St Helena 43p/minute, and £1.18/minute to the UK. You cannot make reverse-charge (collect) calls from public phones.

**INTERNET** Internet access on Ascension is slow, sporadic and very expensive. A few public spots, such as the Obsidian Hotel and Two Boats Club, offer Wi-Fi, but be prepared for a lengthy wait.

**POST** The post office (✆ 6260, 6583; e postoffice@atlantis.co.uk; ⏰ 08.30–12.30 & 13.30–15.00 Mon–Fri; airmail closing times 10.00 Tue & Fri) is in Georgetown, a small building where they also sell first-day covers of prized Ascension Island stamps (see box, page 138).

Airmail is received and dispatched twice a week via the RAF aircraft that flies between the UK and the Falkland Islands. Surface mail and parcels arrive every month from the UK on the Ministry of Defence chartered shipping service, also *en route* to the Falklands. Surface mail to and from Cape Town and St Helena, and surface mail to the UK, currently travels on the RMS *St Helena*, though when the ship is decommissioned in 2016, that service is in jeopardy.

There is no personal postal service within Ascension Island and just a single postcode: ASCN 1ZZ. Mail for staff of the various organisations is collected from individual boxes at the Ascension Government Building in Georgetown.

The cost of stamps is surprisingly reasonable: 50p for a postcard anywhere in the world, or from 55p for a letter.

## GETTING AROUND

There are no taxis on Ascension, and no public transport system apart from a bus that shuttles between the island's four clubs on Friday and Saturday nights (£1–2 one way) You can walk around Georgetown easily, but to explore much further afield you'll either need to hire a car, or to take a guided tour.

**CAR HIRE** Cars can be hired through the Obsidian Group in Georgetown (page 142), or Ascension Island Fuel Station (✆ 6241; e asc.fuelstation@atlantis.co.ac; ⏰ 08.00–noon Mon, Wed & Fri, 14.30–18.30 Tue & Thu, 08.00–14.00 Sat), about

The first supply of stamps was sent to the island in March 1867 by the UK Postmaster General. Then in 1922, in celebration of Ascension becoming a dependency of St Helena, sets of St Helena stamps overprinted with Ascension were produced, triggering the start of a worldwide interest in Ascension philately. The island's post office was inundated with requests for these first stamps, and demand increased when the first sets of Ascension definitive stamps rolled off the press in August 1924. In those days the post office was normally staffed by one or two wives of the workers of the Eastern Telegraph Company, so fulfilling the orders must have been quite a task.

Five sets of stamps are issued each year, with special and commemorative issues added if the occasion warrants it. A 'definitive' set is released every five years, and remains on sale until it is replaced, whereas the special and commemorative issues are withdrawn from sale 15 months after their release date. Stamps from St Helena in mint condition can also be purchased in Ascension, but first-day covers are fully serviced (ie: with stamp and postmarked).

half way to Two Boats Village. This is also the only fuel station, so always make sure you have enough fuel before you attempt to drive off the beaten track. At the time of research, in 2015, fuel prices were slightly lower than those in the UK: 98p a litre for petrol, or £1.22 for diesel. Cars are normally about half full of fuel when hired, and should be returned with a similar amount.

Vehicles are limited so it's important to reserve one well in advance of your trip. Expect to pay from £15 a day for an old, petrol-engine Ford Fiesta from either outlet, or £25–27 for a more up-to-date diesel from the Obsidian, all with fully comprehensive insurance (petrol is being phased out on Ascension, which explains the discrepancy). The Obsidian also has 4x4 vehicles at £25–35 a day. You'll need a full national driving licence, and the minimum age to hire a car is normally 25; for drivers aged 21–25 a 25% surcharge will apply.

**DRIVING** There may be no traffic lights, roundabouts or traffic jams, but driving on Ascension poses its own unique challenges. Sheep and donkeys have an annoying tendency to wander across the road without warning, especially at dusk or when the roads are wet. Wet roads can become very slippery. And many of the roads are narrow, winding and steep, especially on Green Mountain. Aside from exercising extreme caution on such throughways, note that vehicles going down must always give way to those going up.

The maximum speed limit is 40mph, reduced to 20mph in Georgetown and Two Boats Village, and 30mph on some approach roads. As on St Helena, driving is on the left, and it is tradition to give a friendly wave to cars travelling in the opposite direction.

**MAPS** The only commercially available map of Ascension is a small-scale inset on the Gizi map (page 67). One or two local outlets, including the tourist office, sell copies of the old 1:25,000 Ordnance Survey map which, although out of date, is generally more helpful. That said, there are so few surfaced roads that even a simple map should suffice for most ordinary journeys.

**GUIDED TOURS** Guided trips can be booked through the tourist office (✆ 6359; e tourism@ascension.gov.ac) or the Ascension Island Conservation Centre (e *conservationenquiries@ascension.gov.ac*) in the same office, but with the exception of the turtle tours, almost all must be organised in advance. Rarely can you just turn up and expect to arrange something on the spot.

Most popular is their **island tour** (*2½–3hrs, £80 for up to 6 people*), a scenic drive that is best started at around 08.30 before it gets too hot. Typically this takes in Georgetown, Long Beach, Green Mountain, Two Boats Village and Sisters Peak lava flow, but the itinerary is flexible. Other options include **turtle tours** (*Jan–Jun, £5pp; below*), **guided walks** on Green Mountain, and guided trips to the sooty tern colony on the **Wideawake Fairs** (page 151). For birders, a boat trip around **Boatswain Bird Island** (page 151) can sometimes be arranged, too, but at £300–400 for up to eight people, it doesn't come cheap. Those with an interest in **endemic plants** can ask for a tour of the Conservation Department's plant centre on Green Mountain.

Other guided walks (*£60; max 6 people*) can also be organised, taking around two hours, or you can arrange for a guide to escort you on one of the letterbox walks.

Another real draw, on a couple of nights in February, March and April, is to take a **land-crab spawning tour** (*£5pp*), but timing is linked with the phases of the moon, so this is one excursion that cannot be guaranteed. At the peak, in excess of 1,000 crabs can be observed releasing their eggs into the surf at any one time.

## ACTIVITIES

**WALKING/HIKING** Ascension is a great place for hiking, with a varied range of walks that take in volcanic landscapes, lush green cloudforest and challenging coastal paths.

There are numerous walks around the island, including a series of **letterbox walks**, similar in concept to the postbox walks on St Helena. While the walks are generally better waymarked than those on St Helena, don't depend on it; it only takes a sign to be obscured by vegetation and you could easily find yourself taking a wrong turning. Better by far is to get hold of a copy of the detailed *Ascension Island Walks* by Neil MacFall (page 194), which is an essential companion – not least for safety reasons. It's available from the tourist office, the museum and the Obsidian Hotel.

The idea of letterboxes derives from a 17th-century practice, when outward-bound ships would leave messages on the island for the next ship to take home. In 1913, the first letterbox, a green tin box, was placed at Letterbox, a peninsula at the easternmost point of the island. Notes were left by visitors at this spot and the next person to come along would take the letter to the post office. The modern set of boxes was set up in 1979, and each now contains a visitors' book and a handstamp, so that you can authenticate your achievement.

**BIRDWATCHING** There are literally thousands of seabirds nesting on Boatswain Bird Island (page 151), which are best seen from a boat, though you'll need to organise this well in advance. At much closer range are the sooty terns on the Wideawake Fairs (page 151), a relatively easy walk and a spectacle that is not to be missed. On foot, you can also see nesting masked boobies and views of Boatswain Bird Island from the mainland Letterbox Peninsula, although this is only recommended for serious hikers. And don't despair if you don't have transport. Just look skyward from Long Beach in Georgetown when the turtles are nesting and you'll almost certainly see the endemic Ascension Island frigatebird, keeping an eye out for his next meal.

**TURTLE WATCHING** During the nesting season, around January to June, green sea turtles (see box, page 127) can be observed after dark on Long Beach in

Georgetown, laying their eggs in the sand and then returning to the ocean. The turtles and their nest sites are fully protected and it is an offence to disturb them in any way. In particular, do not use a conventional torch or camera flashlight, as these will frighten the females and cause them to leave the beach without laying. It is far better, and far more interesting, to join one of the turtle tours operated by knowledgeable guides at the Conservation Centre (*approx 2hrs; 21.00 Mon & Thu; £5/2.50 adult/child*). Then if you return to the beach just after sunrise, you're likely to have time to watch the last of the turtles returning to the sea, a humbling sight and one that offers plenty of photographic opportunities.

## LAND-BASED SPORTS

**Golf** One Boat Golf Club (☎ 4451), about halfway between Georgetown and Two Boats Village, is a unique 18-hole course where the 'greens' – made of crushed compacted lava smoothed flat with diesel oil – are called 'browns' and the fairways are lined with large boulders of volcanic rock. The 19th hole, though, is the same the world over!

Most weekends see golf competitions held, and visitors are usually most welcome to take part for a small fee.

**Racket sports** Aside from the sports facilities at the two air bases, there is a badminton court near the Pierhead at Georgetown, and tennis courts in both Georgetown and Two Boats Village.

## ON THE WATER

**Swimming** Although the island is fringed with sandy **beaches**, there are just two where it is deemed safe to swim in calm weather: English Bay and Comfortless Cove. Strong underwater currents make swimming elsewhere on the coast potentially dangerous at any time.

Ascension Island has four **swimming pools** that are all open to the public. The first two, a saltwater pool in Georgetown (page 145) and a freshwater pool in Two Boats Village (page 146), are open most of the week. The other two, respectively at RAF Traveller's Hill and the US base at Cat Hill (page 149), are open only when a lifeguard is present.

**Diving and snorkelling** Ascension boasts clear, warm, unpolluted waters averaging 79–84°F (26–29°C) all year, which is great for diving and snorkelling. That said, sea conditions can change rapidly, particularly from November to May, when large swells can make diving impossible.

The fish life may not be quite as varied here as on St Helena, but it's certainly big on quantity. Take a look into the waters of any bay and you can't miss the hundreds of black triggerfish (*Melichthys niger*), or durgon, milling around in the shallows. Smartly striped sergeant-major fish vie for attention with squirrelfish, wrasse and resplendent angelfish, while rocky crevices hide moray eels and spiny lobster, and the occasional exquisite fireworm adds a touch of the exotic.

**Dive and snorkel sites** Without a boat, the best spots for snorkelling, as for swimming, are English Bay and Comfortless Cove (page 150). Most of the dive sites are a little way from land, but rarely more than a half-hour ride. If your focus is on the underwater world, get hold of a copy of Paul Colley's informative *Diving and Snorkelling Ascension Island* (page 194), which clearly sets out details of 21 sites, including seven wrecks. It's available at both the tourist office and the Obsidian Hotel.

**Practicalities** There are no rescue facilities on Ascension Island, and no decompression chamber, making it particularly important to adhere to conservative dive profiles and safety stops.

**Dive operators** Ascension Island has its own BSAC-affiliated dive club, Atlantis Divers (e *atlantisdivers@hotmail.com*), but this is open only to members with their own kit. For visitors, there are a few specialist dive operators, including:

**Seven South** ⬩6836; e cazandchris.yon@ gmail.com. PADI & BSAC-affiliated diver Caroline Yon operates the diving aspect of watersports specialists Seven South. As well as guided shore & boat dives for qualified divers, she offers courses from Discover Scuba to Divemaster. Dive kit can be hired, though fins & wetsuits are limited, so if you have your own, bring them with you. *Shore dive £15pp; boat dive £25/40pp 1/2 dives. Kit hire £15/day.*

**Fishing** Fishing goes on all around the island, both inshore ('rock fishing') and further out. Inshore, the most common catches are grouper, silver fish, soldier fish and moray eel, although sometimes a fisherman gets lucky and lands a yellowfin tuna. Offshore, sportfishermen are setting their sights on the big pelagics: tuna, sailfish and marlin. There are various size limits imposed on a catch, and it is prohibited to fish for spiny lobster when the females are in berry (have eggs).

One of the safest spots to fish is off the Pierhead in Georgetown, but fishing off the rocks carries the danger of being swept away. It's possible to hire a skippered boat with fishing gear, but don't expect this to happen instantly; most fishermen have jobs that preclude them going out during a working day. Ask at the Obsidian Hotel or tourist office, and expect to pay around £100–150 for a couple of hours.

The introduction of fishing licences was anticipated during 2015, with the aim of monitoring rather than restricting fishing activities. For the latest information, ask at the tourist office (below).

### Fishing operators

**Seven South** ⬩6522; e colinchester@ me.com; www.ascensionislandfishingcharters. co.uk. Fishing professional Colin Chester has a fleet of 6 boats, & specialises not just in sportfishing but also in freediving & spearfishing, as well as inshore trips – including to Boatswain Bird Island. Advance reservations are essential – & sometimes need to be made months ahead. *Fishing from £300/½ day inshore; max 5 passengers, but 3.*

## GEORGETOWN

Set against the backdrop of Cross Hill, the capital of Ascension is little more than a small village with three places to stay, a few shops and some bungalows. The town, originally just known as Garrison, was established in 1815 when a military presence was installed on the island during Napoleon's exile. It wasn't until 1829 that it was officially named Georgetown.

**TOURIST INFORMATION AND TOUR OPERATORS** The **Tourism Department** (*Georgetown;* ⬩ *6244;* e *tourism@ascension.gov.ac; www.ascension-island.gov.ac;* ⊕ *10.00–noon Mon–Sat*) is based in the Conservation Centre office, which it shares with the Conservation Department. In addition to organising tours, most of which need to be pre-booked (pages 138–9), they have a good range of books and souvenirs, particularly on natural history.

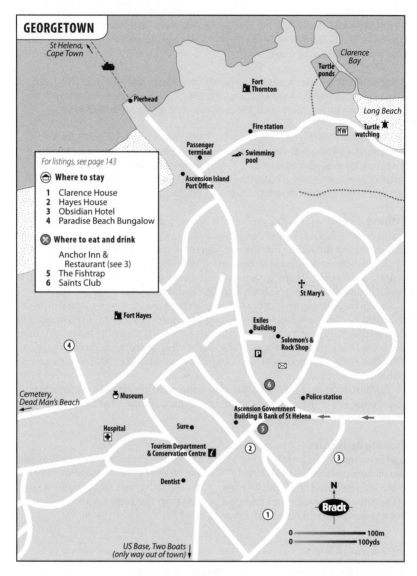

## GEORGETOWN

St Helena,
Cape Town

Clarence
Bay

Turtle
ponds

Pierhead

Fort
Thornton

Long Beach

Fire station

MW

Turtle
watching

Passenger
terminal

Swimming
pool

Ascension Island
Port Office

For listings, see page 143

**Where to stay**

1 Clarence House
2 Hayes House
3 Obsidian Hotel
4 Paradise Beach Bungalow

**Where to eat and drink**

Anchor Inn &
Restaurant (see 3)
5 The Fishtrap
6 Saints Club

St Mary's

Fort Hayes

Exiles
Building

Solomon's &
Rock Shop

4

P

6

Cemetery,
Dead Man's Beach

Museum

Police station

Ascension Government
Building & Bank of St Helena

5

Hospital

Sure

2

Tourism Department
& Conservation Centre

3

Dentist

N

Bradt

1

0                    100m
0                    100yds

US Base, Two Boats
(only way out of town)

Flights and passage on the ship can be organised through the **Ascension Island Travel Office** close to the Pierhead (\ 6244, 6500; ⊕ 08.00–12.30 & 13.30–16.30 Mon–Fri, or 16.00 Fri, & when RMS St Helena is in harbour). This is also where the harbourmaster is based, and is the place to come if you've any queries about your journey on the RMS.

### WHERE TO STAY  Map, above

Almost all visitor accommodation is in Georgetown; the only other option is a self-catering house on Green Mountain (page 147). All are administered by the **Obsidian Group** (\ 6246; e accommodation@atlantis.co.ac; www.obsidian.co.ac). Rates are significantly lower than on St Helena, from around £40 a night for a double at Clarence House, to upwards of £70 at the Obsidian, with breakfast.

**Obsidian Hotel** (17 rooms) The island's main hotel is in the heart of Georgetown, close to all amenities including Long Beach. Each of its comfortable rooms (4 sgls, 5 dbls, 8 suites) is en suite, with high ceilings & a simple balcony or patio, some with views to Cross Hill, others to the sea. They may not be stylish, but they're large, comfortable & well furnished, with AC, TV, phone, fridge, tea-making facility & a hairdryer as standard. The restaurant (see below) is good & the bar friendly. There's Wi-Fi in the main building & on the hotel's patio (£5/hr; £10/day; £50/wk). **£**

**Hayes House** (13 rooms). Simpler & far less spacious than the main Obsidian Hotel, but still comfortable, Hayes House offers sgl & dbl en-suite rooms with AC, fridge, TV & tea-making equipment. There's a communal lounge & small shared veranda. Wi-Fi. **£**

**Clarence House** (20 rooms) A hostel in feel, if not in name, Clarence House has small but perfectly adequate rooms with 2 or 3 beds sharing plenty of toilets & showers, & a communal lounge. **£**

**Paradise Beach Bungalow** This self-catering 2-bedroom bungalow has a large enclosed patio & great views overlooking the Pierhead & Clarence Bay. *15 days min, £1,162.50*

## ✕ WHERE TO EAT AND DRINK, AND NIGHTLIFE *Map, opposite*

If accommodation is better value on Ascension than on St Helena, restaurant prices are generally higher, and there's little choice, especially in the evening.

Most of the island's entertainment is supplied by the clubs, including those at Two Boats Village (page 145) and the American and RAF bases (page 149). Between the four of them, they take turns to host discos on Friday and Saturday nights. All are open to non-members.

**✕ Anchor Inn & Restaurant** Obsidian Hotel; ☎6246; restaurant ⊕ 07.30–09.00, 12.30–13.30 & 19.00–20.30 daily; bar ⊕ 18.30–23.30. The Obsidian's open-sided à la carte restaurant is relaxed & relatively informal, with surprisingly good food. Dinner menus change daily, always with 2 choices – meat or fish – & a vegetarian option on request. Reservations essential. Lunch **£–££**, dinner **££££–£££££**

**✕ The Fishtrap** ☎6522; ⊕ b/fast, lunch & dinner Mon–Sat. In 2015, fishing entrepreneur Colin Chester was opening a South African-inspired surf 'n' turf restaurant on the site of the old Tasty Tucker. Diners will congregate in a marine-inspired, semi open-air setting for BBQ steaks, seafood platters, sushimi & bunny chow – a South African speciality of crusty bread stuffed with curry & salad. Tea, coffee, cakes & light lunches are also anticipated, as is an on-site outlet for sportswear, fishing & diving kit, chandlery & iPads, etc. **££££**

**♀ Saints Club** ☎6344; food ⊕ 10.00–noon Mon–Wed, 10.00–14.00 Thu–Fri; bar ⊕ 16.00–23.30 Mon–Wed, noon–23.30 Thu–Sat, noon–22.00 Sun. During the day, the Saints Club is quiet & low key, a pleasant enough spot for a drink or simple bite to eat, take-away style, at outdoor tables to a backdrop of cheerful music. In the evening it morphs into a lively club, with various gaming machines, darts, pool & snooker tables & a disco every other week on Fri or Sat night. **£**

**SHOPPING** See also pages 146 and 149.
### Food and supplies
**Solomon's** ☎6320; e solomon-trading@atlantis.co.ac; ⊕ 09.00–18.00 Mon–Fri, 09.00–14.30 Sat. The island's main grocery store stocks most of the basics, including a range of frozen food, but there may well be shortages of certain items, especially fresh produce. They also sell toys, gifts, electrical goods, cards, stationery & fishing tackle.

**Clothes, books and souvenirs** In addition to the following, both the tourist office/conservation centre (page 141) and the museum (page 145) have excellent little gift shops with a range of books, postcards and T-shirts, etc. For sports kit, see The Fishtrap restaurant (above).

**Glamour**  Exiles Bldg; ⏲ 10.00–13.00 Sat. Fashion & beauty products.

**Obsidian Hotel Gift Shop**  ⏲ 08.00–17.00 Mon–Fri, 10.00–noon Sat. The largest selection of Ascension Island gifts & souvenirs on the island, as well as a selection of books.

**Rock Shop**  Behind Solomon's; ⏲ 17.00–18.30

Wed, 10.30–13.00 Sat. Men's, women's & children's clothes & shoes, as well as gifts & G-Unique jewellery (page 102).

**Sue Ryder Boutique**  Exiles Bldg; ⏲ 17.00–18.00 Fri, 10.30–11.30 Sat. Familiar to visitors from the UK, this charity shop sells very good used clothing.

**OTHER PRACTICALITIES**  Ascension Island's only post office and bank (page 136) are located in Georgetown, as is the police station.

## WHAT TO SEE AND DO

### A walking tour of Georgetown  With its vantage point overlooking Clarence Bay, Georgetown is very small, very quiet, and very easy to explore on foot. Starting at the Obsidian Hotel, turn right and head down towards **Long Beach**. It's a beautiful beach at any time, but during turtle-nesting season (pages 139–40) is particularly special at first light, when the last of the nesting females make their way slowly back to the sea. It's a magical sight, definitely not to be missed if you have the faintest interest in the natural world.

From here, wander west along the coast, passing at the end of the beach the **Turtle Ponds** (below), where live turtles were held during the 19th century ready for loading on to passing ships. Then for an overview of the beach, climb up on to **Fort Thornton**, behind the fire station. Built by the Royal Marines as part of the island defences during Napoleon's exile on St Helena, it once stood alongside the earlier Fort Cockburn, though little is visible of that nowadays. Fort Thornton itself is none too well preserved, but it's very accessible and open all the time. From the western side of the fort, you'll be looking down on the Pierhead, where ships' passengers come ashore. Unless there's a vessel in harbour, when the Pierhead is closed to the general public, this is the perfect place for a spot of **fishing**.

You'll need to retrace your steps a little before heading inland. Standing on its own is the pretty little church of **St Mary** (page 145), picturesque in the sunshine against the deep-red backdrop of Cross Hill. Close by is the colonial-looking **Exiles Building**, complete with colonnaded terrace and clocktower. Built as a barracks for the Royal Marines in 1830, and extended in 1848, it was later home to the Ascension Club. Today it feels rather redundant, with just a few rooms on the ground floor used by local shops.

Turning slightly back on yourself and off to the left, you'll pass Fort Hayes and the coach house before reaching the **museum** (page 145), which has responsibility for both. If they're open, do take the time to look round; it's well worth it. Then continue on down this road to the **cemetery** at Dead Man's Beach, which contains the graves of those who died in the 19th and 20th centuries. You'll need to retrace your steps to get back to the hotel, but to round off your walk, consider popping in to the Saints Club or the Anchor Inn (page 143) for a cool drink.

### Turtle Ponds  Built in 1829 on the site of the island's first harbour, overlooking Long Beach, then enlarged in 1845, the Turtle Ponds were crucial to the ships that stopped at Ascension for provisions. Live turtles would be kept in the shallow water, ready to be taken on board to provide fresh meat for the sailors (and, on occasion, turtle soup for the Lords of the Admiralty and even the king). The ponds fell into disuse sometime around the 1920s, and – like the turtles themselves – are now protected. Restoration was in hand in 2015.

**St Mary's Church** The Anglican Church of St Mary falls within the Diocese of St Helena and is the only property on Ascension that is privately owned. The low, immaculately whitewashed building was built between 1843 and 1847, but was not consecrated until 1861. It is also the only church on Ascension with regular services (*10.30 Sun, 19.00 Wed*), and as such it serves the whole island community, regardless of denomination. Inside, the wooden ceiling and pews, and simple stained-glass windows, invite quiet reflection, and the church is open 24 hours a day for private prayer (although the door may be closed to prevent sheep or donkeys from entering).

**Museum** (✆ 6655; e *ascensionheritagesociety@gmail.com*; ⊕ *17.00–19.00 Mon, 10.00–noon Sat; £2*) Run by an enthusiastic and knowledgeable group of volunteers, this great little museum was fully restructured and modernised in 2015. Down-to-earth displays take in the history of the island, from its volcanic origins through telegraphy, maps and some wonderful pictures, to its role in 21st-century telecommunications. It's all very well laid out, with straightforward text and some hands-on exhibits which definitely have child appeal.

The main gallery is housed in an unremarkable building dating to the 1960s, but within the museum's remit are a magazine, which features exhibits on social history, the coach house, where a World War II Jeep has pride of place, and the adjacent **Fort Hayes**. This last, built around 1860 on the site of an earlier battery, is home to the museum's military artefacts, and affords superb views over Clarence Bay.

To round it off, there's a good little shop, a book swap overflowing with books, and the island's archives, where letters and books trace its history from the 1840s.

**Swimming pool** Tucked away opposite the fire station is Georgetown's saltwater swimming pool (⊕ *daily exc Thu; free*). It's relatively small – about 15m long – but crystal clear and with good shower facilities. The pool is open more or less all the time, but there's no lifeguard.

## BEYOND GEORGETOWN

While Georgetown feels relatively sedate, the 44 volcanic craters, caves, lava tunnels, old forts, cannons and cemeteries that dot the landscape of Ascension Island are anything but. It's not always a pretty environment, but there's no disputing the underlying drama. Add to this the natural beauty of Green Mountain, some stunning beaches and the ornithological phenomenon of the Wideawake Fairs, and there's plenty to see and explore.

**TWO BOATS VILLAGE** Primarily a residential area, and the site of the island's only school, Two Boats Village lies about three miles (5km) inland from Georgetown, at an altitude of 600ft (190m). It was constructed for communications workers in the 1960s, two-thirds of the way along the route between Georgetown and the old water-collection sight on Green Mountain. In the 19th century, to mark the route, a single longboat (now One Boat) was upended about a third of the way from the town, then a further two longboats at the two-thirds point were made into a shady place to rest for those collecting water. Though the boats themselves have been replaced a number of times since the 1826 originals, the name – Two Boats – has stuck.

## ✖ Where to eat and drink, and nightlife

🍷 **Two Boats Club** ✆ 4439, 4610; lunch ⊕ noon–14.00 Mon–Fri; bar ⊕ noon–16.30 & 19.30–midnight Mon–Thu, noon–00.30 Fri, noon–01.00 Sat, 13.00–23.00 Sun. With a great

**LIZARD STONE**

If you're driving between Georgetown and Two Boats, you'll pass at the side of the road a painted pile of rocks that has the look of something between a rather gaudy snowman and an ornamental candle.

Known as the Lizard Stone, the rocks are said to be topped with the shape of a lizard, though under all that paint he's hard to make out. Tradition has it that people leaving Ascension, never to return, should secretly paint the lizard before they leave. Among the many stories that circulate about the rock, one holds that anyone who painted the lizard then returned to the island would die. In the early days you actually painted the lizard. Nowadays, though, most people just pour a can of paint over it.

You'll find the rock between the junction at Cross Hill that leads to the US main base and the junction leading to English Bay.

location at the foot of Sisters Peak & overlooking Clarence Bay, Two Boats is open to all members of the public. As well as a bar & restaurant, the club has a snooker room, darts, gaming machines, skittles alley & tennis court. It is also one of the clubs that rotates a regular disco on Fri or Sat nights, sometimes with live music. Lunchtime snacks such as toasties & burgers are available most days but there's no food in the evenings. £

## Shopping

**JAMS** Ocean View; ⏱ 11.30–13.30 & 15.30–18.30 Mon–Fri, 11.00–14.30 Sat. You'll find the basics here – drinks, groceries & frozen food – but little in the way of fresh produce.

**Amenities** Adjacent to Two Boats Club is a large, very inviting triangular **swimming pool** (⏱ *10.00–19.00 daily; free*) with a diving board, and a multi-sport outdoor court.

**SISTERS PEAK** Close to the centre of the island, Sisters Peak has the neat triangular appearance of a quintessential volcano. Technically a young ash cone, it rises up behind Two Boats Village, its apparently smooth sides a rich, deep red.

The site of one of the letterbox walks (*approx 2hrs*), Sisters Peak is easily accessed from Two Boats Club. The path to the top is steep with quite a lot of loose scree and no shade, so is best walked early or late in the day.

**GREEN MOUNTAIN NATIONAL PARK** The only national park on Ascension Island, Green Mountain covers an area quite unlike any other on Ascension. Home to much of the island's wildlife, including land crabs and six of Ascension's seven endemic plants, its upper reaches are frequently shrouded in mist. Yet this cloudforest, which supports an extraordinary range of dense vegetation, is effectively manmade, the result of an audacious experiment conducted in the 19th century (see box, opposite).

The mountain itself rises to 2,817ft (859m). Along with the introduction of trees and shrubs came the establishment of a farm up here. It was only in the early 21st century that work ceased, the farm fell into disrepair, and the island became almost totally dependent on imported fresh produce.

The park is also home to the administrator's residence, known simply as The Residency. High up on the slopes of the mountain, it was once a yellow fever hospital. It is not open to visitors, but you can take a look at Monkey Rock Cemetery on the slopes below, where some of the victims of yellow fever are buried.

When the first military personnel were garrisoned on Ascension Island in 1815, theirs was not a happy lot. Very little grew on the dry, volcanic terrain, bar a few ferns and tufts of foliage at the top of the mountain on the eastern side of the island. Rain ran off the bare hillsides and soon evaporated. For the marines based in the only settlement, now Georgetown, the trek towards the hills in search of water was long and arduous. For the authorities, this problem of water was a real barrier to expansion.

The story of what is now known as Green Mountain goes back to 1836, when naturalist Charles Darwin, on board HMS *Beagle*, called at the island for three days on his voyage between St Helena and England. On his return to England, Darwin wrote at length of the barren landscape of Ascension, and its potential for transformation into a green oasis, and a copy of the proofs was sent to fellow naturalist and explorer Sir Joseph Hooker.

It was to be seven years before Hooker himself made it to these shores, as assistant surgeon on HMS *Erebus*, part of Captain James Ross's expedition to the Antarctic. Hooker, a botanist by inclination who had taken up medicine only to fund his real passion, was intrigued by the lack of vegetation and the possibility of improving the land. Following discussions with the British Admiralty, he put forward a plan that he believed would increase rainfall, prevent erosion, and provide food for the garrison.

There followed a frenzy of activity so intense that it's only with hindsight that the audacity of the project can truly be appreciated. Between 1847 and 1850, 330 carefully selected trees and shrubs were despatched to Ascension from Kew Gardens, where Hooker's father was the director. Success was almost immediate, 'affording shelter and protection where none could have been obtained before'. In the ensuing two decades, thousands more plants were shipped over, and by 1865 the mountain was populated with exotic trees and shrubs from all over the world. Today, the narrow road that winds up the mountain is lined with dense stands of eucalyptus, banana, wild ginger, Norfolk Island pine and more, while at the very top walkers to the Dew Pond will find themselves dwarfed by a towering forest of bamboo. Whether or not Hooker succeeded in creating rain, there can be no doubt that he succeeded in the greening of the mountain.

**Getting there and away** From the entrance to the national park, there's a single-track road that switchbacks up the mountain, the vegetation and the gradient increasing as you climb higher. Unless you're heading to the Monkey Rock Cemetery, in which case follow the first turning to the left to the Residency, ignore any turnings until you come to a sign indicating that no vehicles should go beyond that point. If you're told to drive to the Red Lion, or the barracks, or Garden Cottage, this is where you stop! There's very little parking space, but from here you'll have to walk.

 **Where to stay** *Map, pages 122–3*

**Garden Cottage** (3 rooms) Contact the Obsidian Hotel (page 142). Set high up on Green Mountain, this is the oldest domestic building on Ascension, dating back to the 1820s. The rooms are old-fashioned, very basic & damp for much of the year, & access is challenging to say the least, but on a clear day the views from the garden are fantastic, & it's right at the start of several good walks. *From £245/7 nights*

The 17th-century explorer and privateer, William Dampier, had a chequered career navigating the world's oceans, and nearly met his end in 1701. As captain of the ill-fated HMS *Roebuck*, he was returning to England from western Australia when his ship sprang a leak. The crew managed to nurse the vessel from St Helena to Ascension, but there, in the harbour, attempts to plug the hole failed and the vessel went down.

Marooned on the island, Dampier and his men set off in search of water. Their quest brought them to a 'fine spring on the southeast side of the high mountain' where, despite 'the continual fogs' and 'unwholesome' atmosphere near the water, they lived in a cave for six weeks until they were rescued.

Almost exactly 300 years after the *Roebuck* was sunk, in April 2001, its wreck was discovered off Long Beach, Clarence Bay, by Australian marine archaeologists, led by Dr Mike McCarthy. Three of the artefacts retrieved from the site – a ceramic lid, a ship's bell and a huge shell – are considered to be from the wreck and are on display in the museum.

## What to see and do

***Dampier's Drip*** Just 500 yards (457m) or so uphill from the entrance to the national park, or a round-trip walk of about 1½ hours from Two Boats, this is said to be the spot where Captain William Dampier and his crew discovered a much-needed spring (see box, above). There was indeed a spring here, and much later, in the 1820s, about 50 men, women and children lived in the caves around the drip, collecting water in casks for transport to Georgetown by donkey. But the drip is on the northeast side of the mountain, and it is far more likely that Dampier and his crew were higher up the mountain, near the catchment area in Breakneck Valley. According to island legend, the men supposedly buried treasure there, though it is yet to be found. And aside from a none-too-clear 'Dampier's Drip' sign at this site, there's little to be seen here, either, though the view is pretty good.

***The Red Lion and the farm*** A short walk uphill from the end of the road brings you to the Red Lion. Something of a misnomer, it's neither a pub, nor a hotel, but an old marine barracks, complete with Italianate clocktower. It was built in 1863 for farm workers from the Royal Marines, who were charged with providing fresh produce for the garrison. The farm itself has fallen into disrepair, but the manager used to live at Garden Cottage, which is now available to rent (page 147). This is also the sight of the endemic plant centre; if you'd like to be shown round, ask at the Conservation Centre in Georgetown. There are picnic tables in the garden, and in case of emergency, there's a phone at the Red Lion.

Continuing uphill, you'll come to the start of the Dew Pond walk (page 149), which leads in turn to the 19th-century **water catchment** in Breakneck Valley. Constructed by the marines without any machinery, it was an extraordinary achievement, bringing fresh water to the troops stationed in Georgetown.

***Letterbox walks*** (Page 139) The starting point for many of the walks on Green Mountain is Garden Cottage, next to the Red Lion, or the Red Lion itself. Several of the trails date back to the 19th century when they were forged by the military, in those days across bare rock with some precipitous drop offs. One of the best is **Elliot's Pass**, a two-hour circular walk just below the summit with some wonderful views. For a longer walk, it combines well with **Bishop's** (*1hr 20mins*), to the west of the barracks. A torch would be useful for the tunnels, and waterproof shoes are a must.

Also popular is the **Dew Pond walk** (*1hr 30mins*) to the mountain summit, though despite the height, this is not one to take for the views. The start of the path is reached along the track from the Red Lion, and is signposted at the top of the track. You'll pass the water-catchment area, before rising steeply up through a forest of towering bamboos to the Dew Pond. The summit itself is marked by a chain a little further on, but that's it; the view is obscured by dense vegetation. Muddy and damp in places, the path can be slippery, especially through the bamboos at the end, but wooden walkways have been installed at the most challenging spots. If you've huffed and puffed your way to the top, it's slightly galling to know that the record for the annual Dew Pond Run, which starts at the Turtle Ponds in Georgetown, is a mere 48 minutes.

Two other linear walks, **Rupert's** and **Cronk's**, start within the garden of Garden Cottage. For each, allow about two hours' round trip. From the cottage garden there's also a 300-yard-long **tunnel**, originally constructed to carry water from one side of the mountain to the other, which acts as a short cut. This, though, has been deemed unsafe by the authorities, and in 2015 was not open to the public.

**TRAVELLER'S HILL** Built in 1983, Traveller's Hill is home to the RAF and their contract workers on Ascension. From a visitor perspective, it has a small shop which is particularly useful if you're in need of cash, a snack bar and a nightclub, and a 27-yard (25m) lifeguarded **swimming pool** that is open to the public (🕐 *17.00–19.00 Tue & Thu, 13.00–17.00 Sat & Sun; £2*).

## ✖ Where to eat and drink, and nightlife
🍷 **Mountain View Club** ☎3270, 3351; snack bar 🕐 09.00–11.00 Mon–Fri, 10.00–15.00 Sat/Sun, 19.00–22.15 daily; bar 🕐 19.00–23.00 Mon–Thu, 19.00–midnight Fri, noon–15.00 & 19.00–23.00/ midnight Sat/Sun. Another in the series of 4 clubs that rotates a disco on Fri/Sat nights, the RAF's club is more of a social place than an eating venue.

## Shopping
**NAAFI** 🕐 09.00–21.00 Mon–Sat, 10.00–17.00 Sun. The RAF's small shop next to the club sells basic groceries, drinks, hot pies & fresh bread – though you'll need to get there early for the bread. If you're short of cash, you can get cashback against a debit or credit card here.

**CAT HILL** The US base area at Cat Hill is scarcely two miles south of Georgetown, and incorporates Wideawake Airfield (known locally as the Airhead). Along the main road to the east, you'll pass the tiny open-sided Chapel of our Lady of Ascension, or Grotto. There's no longer a priest here, but it makes an unexpected spot for tranquil prayer or reflection.

The US base has a new **swimming pool** which is also open to the public (*adults only; £2*) when there is a lifeguard, usually at weekends and late afternoon during the week.

## ✖ Where to eat and drink, and nightlife
✖ **Volcano Club** American Base; snack bar ☎2429; 🕐 17.00–22.00 Tue–Fri, 16.00–21.00 Sat; bar ☎2269; 🕐 16.30 to around 22.00 daily, closing late Fri/Sat. With burgers, steaks & salads, the snack bar at the Volcano Club on the edge of the American base has the style & ambience of a 'real' American bar. Along with weekly entertainment (discos, country dancing, karaoke, etc), there are several pool tables. The club accepts US dollars, St Helena pounds & British pounds, but change is always given in US currency. £–££

**COMMAND HILL CAVE** If you've ever wondered what it's like to be inside a volcano, here's your chance to find out. About a mile (1.6km) east of Cat Hill, turn towards the airstrip, and on the seventh telegraph pole you'll see a sign to Command Hill Cave. Follow the path from here just a hundred yards or so, then look up, and you'll see what looks like a cave. It's not! The real cave is slightly to the right, marked by a cairn, and easily accessed up the rugged path. It's a bit of a scramble down inside, and it's not at all picturesque, but you'll find yourself inside a lava tube. These are created when the surface of a lava flow solidifies, but the molten interior continues to flow, leaving a cavern such as this. Bring a torch.

**NASA SITE** The starting point for many of the island's letterbox walks, the erstwhile NASA site offers magnificent views of the coastline out to the Letterbox Peninsula, against the backdrop of Green Mountain. The winding approach road from Cat Hill takes you through a wilder, more natural environment than much of Ascension, clothed with greenery and largely free from the blight of communications paraphernalia. There are rumours of the site being reopened, but don't let that stop you; the drive alone is worthwhile.

## AROUND THE COAST
**Comfortless Cove** This small, picturesque cove about 1½ miles (2.5km) north of Georgetown is one of the few beaches on the island where it is usually safe to swim. Popular at weekends with families, it's also a good spot for snorkelling.

Originally called Sydney, then Comfort Cove, the inlet became notorious in the mid 19th century when it was used as a quarantine spot for sailors with yellow fever, contracted while working on ships off the west coast of Africa. Members of the garrison in Georgetown would leave food for the victims between Long Beach and the cove, but conditions were miserable and many died: hence Comfortless Cove. Several victims of the epidemic, including those from the HMS *Bonetta*, were buried in the small Bonetta Cemetery, behind the beach, though not particularly easy to find. Nearby is Trident Cemetery and the HMS *Archer* memorial. Note the way that many of the graves were marked, with a plank or piece of driftwood instead of a stone.

**English Bay** The only beach of any size that's both easily accessible and reasonably safe for swimming, English Bay is beautiful, its soft golden sands lapped by clear turquoise waters. A roped-off area demarcates the swimming zone and the snorkelling's good, too, especially close to the rocks which shelter the likes of spotted moray eels and spiny lobster. Smartly striped sergeant-major fish nibble the algae along the rope and below you'll see triggerfish by the hundred. A blue-and-white buoy off Powerhouse Beach, to the east, marks the wreck of the *Derby*, which on a calm day can be reached by strong, confident swimmers, ideally with fins.

Look behind you, though, and you could be forgiven for thinking you were on an entirely different planet, the dark volcanic rocks liberally planted with pylons and dishes of all shapes and sizes. Once the site of an unsuccessful guano-collecting undertaking, remains of which can still be seen, English Bay is now dominated by the BBC Atlantic Relay Station, as well as the power station that supplies much of the island with electricity and water.

**Hannay's Beach** Nestled at the bottom of the cliffs, Hannay's Beach is notable for one large and powerful blowhole along with many smaller ones. A short but fairly tricky walk southeast along the cliffs from here brings you to Hummock Point, from where there's a clear view towards Boatswain Bird Island. While it's not close enough to see the birds on the island itself, there are plenty of seabirds to reward even the most casual observer, from brown noddies to the Ascension frigatebirds that may hover overhead as if calculating your next move.

You can park above the beach near the rather ramshackle building – which perhaps unexpectedly is the Ariane tracking station belonging to the European Space Agency.

## Wideawake Fairs

Up to 200,000 pairs of sooty terns, or 'wideawakes' congregate to breed on the rocky flats south of the airport known as the Wideawake Fairs. The birds nest every ten months, so the size of the colony waxes and wanes, but at its height it's a noisy, smelly place, the call of the birds rising to a frenzy when frigatebirds in search of young chicks glide overhead.

Walking through the colony brings you very, very close to the terns, but they are ground nesters, so do be careful. Each female lays her single egg in a shallow scrape in the sand, so it's very important to stick to the paths.

***Getting there and away*** Access to the Wideawake Fairs is across the airport, so you'll need to request permission at the American military base. In reality, this just means popping into the office on your way there, where you'll be signed into a book; just don't forget to sign out when you pass back that way later in the day. You'll be given directions from the office, including a suggested place to park – up high, before the track deteriorates. From here, it's an easy walk down to the colony, and on to the rocky beach at Mars Bay.

## Boatswain Bird Island

Just off the east coast of Ascension, the sheer, flat-topped rock is 400 yards (365m) long and 300ft (91m) high. Yet statistics tell nothing of the importance of this small rock as a bird sanctuary. Over the years, as feral cats increased their predatory hold on the main island, seabirds were increasingly forced offshore for protection. Although some have now returned to the mainland to nest, the island remains crucial to the survival of the seabird colonies, and a superb spot for keen birdwatchers.

***Getting there and away*** Boatswain Bird Island is strictly off-limits for landing, but with at least two weeks' notice, you can organise a boat with a guide through the tourist office (*approx £400, max 25 passengers*), or with Colin Chester of Seven South (*from £35pp, depending on numbers; page 141*). The round trip from Georgetown takes about four–five hours, depending on sea conditions. Sadly the island is not usually seen from the RMS *St Helena*, which usually heads due south from Georgetown.

From land, the island can be seen from Hummock Point, but for a closer view you'll need to tackle one of the more challenging letterbox walks that cover the southeast of the island: Weather Post, Louie's Ledge, Letterbox and White Horse or – hardest of all – Boatswain Bird View. Note, though, that for all these you'll need a head for heights.

# Part Three

TRISTAN DA CUNHA

## TRISTAN DA CUNHA AT A GLANCE

**Location** South Atlantic Ocean, 1,743 miles (2,805km) west of Cape Town and 1,509 miles (2,429km) southwest of St Helena
**Size** 38 square miles (98km$^2$)
**Highest point** 6,760ft (2,062m)
**Status** British Overseas Territory, with St Helena and Ascension
**Capital** Edinburgh of the Seven Seas
**Currency** Pound sterling
**Population** 267 (2015)
**Language** English
**Religion** Christian
**Time** GMT
**Electricity** 240V, 50Hz; standard electrical socket 15-amp round pin.
**International dialling code** +44 (0)20 3014 (via London at London local rates)
**Motto** 'Our faith is our strength'
**Flag** Blue with flag of UK in upper left quadrant and Tristan da Cunha shield centred on outer half of flag. The shield features four albatrosses flanked by a pair of Tristan crawfish, and topped by a crown beneath a Tristan longboat.
**Public holidays** 1 January, Good Friday, Easter Monday, Whit Monday (day after Whitsuntide), 2nd Saturday in June, 14 August, last Monday in August, 25–26 December
**Website** www.tristandc.com

# 8

# Background Information

Widely billed as the most remote inhabited island in the world, Tristan da Cunha has something of the air of a Scottish island in the middle of the South Atlantic. Viewed from the sea, it is dominated by the mountain, while its only settlement presents an attractive picture of freshly painted, colourful houses.

Within the Tristan archipelago are the neighbouring islands of Inaccessible and Nightingale, and the small Stoltenhoff and Middle or Alex islands, all of which are uninhabited, whereas the more distant island of Gough, some 218 miles (350km) away, has an inhabited weather station. The islands have a very distinctive flora and fauna, and are an important breeding ground for seabirds.

## GEOGRAPHY

Tristan da Cunha lies in the South Atlantic at ✪ 37°4'S, 12°19'W, roughly midway between Buenos Aires and Cape Town. Almost 1,500 miles (2,414km) south of St Helena and 250 miles (400km) east of the Mid-Atlantic Ridge, it covers an area of just 38 square miles (98km²), a little over three-quarters the size of St Helena. From sea level, the centre of the island soars a vertiginous 6,760ft (2,062m) to the top of the island, Queen Mary's Peak.

The island is almost circular – some 6–7.5 miles (10–12km) in diameter and 24 miles (38km) around the coast.

**THE VOLCANO** The Tristan volcano first erupted just three million years ago from the ocean floor, 11,483ft (3,500m) below. Over the years, successive ash and lava eruptions have built a cone 30 miles (48km) wide and 18,045ft (5,500m) high, culminating in Queen Mary's Peak, which overlooks a heart-shaped crater lake.

On the flanks of the main volcano, parasitic cones each represent a separate eruption. One of these, Stony Hill, erupted in the mid 18th century, producing an extensive black lava field on the southern part of the island. A second, in 1961, threatened the settlement of Edinburgh on the northwestern plain and resulted in the evacuation of the entire population to the UK. Little more than 40 years later, in 2004, the island was again shaken by tremors, but this time from an undersea eruption. Fortunately the only visible effects were the blocks of pumice that floated to the surface from an epicentre close to the ocean floor.

**THE MOUNTAIN** Radiating steeply from the central peak, ash and lava slopes are dissected by streams that flow only in heavy rain. Lower down, at around 1,640–2,380ft (500–1,000m), convex slopes level off to a plateau known as the Base, which is covered in thick peat soils derived from decayed vegetation. Intermittent streams cut deep ravines, or gulches, on the Base, which are always dangerous to cross, and impossible after heavy rain, when they tumble as waterfalls and cataracts over the cliffs. These cliffs form a barrier between the mountain and the coastal plains below, and range

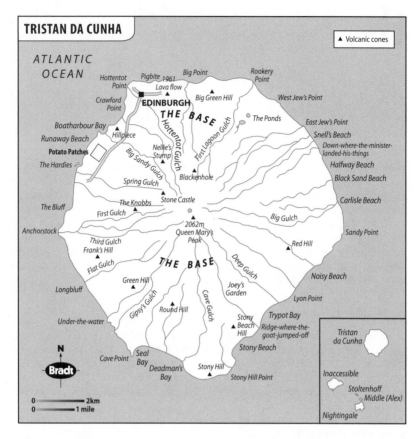

▲ Volcanic cones

ATLANTIC
OCEAN

Hottentot Point
Pigbite 1961
Big Point
Rookery Point
Lava flow
Crawford Point
EDINBURGH
Big Green Hill
West Jew's Point
THE BASE
Boatharbour Bay
Hillpiece
The Ponds
East Jew's Point
Runaway Beach
Snell's Beach
Potato Patches
Nellie's Stump
Down-where-the-minister-landed-his-things
The Hardies
Big Sandy Gulch
Halfway Beach
Hottentot Gulch
First Lagoon Gulch
Blackenhole
Black Sand Beach
Spring Gulch
Stone Castle
Carlisle Beach
The Knobbs
The Bluff
First Gulch
Big Gulch
Anchorstock
2062m
Queen Mary's Peak
Sandy Point
Third Gulch
Frank's Hill
Red Hill
Flat Gulch
THE BASE
Deep Gulch
Green Hill
Noisy Beach
Longbluff
Joey's Garden
Lyon Point
Gipsy's Gulch
Round Hill
Cave Gulch
Under-the-water
Stony Beach Hill
Trypot Bay
Ridge-where-the-goat-jumped-off
Cave Point
Seal Bay
Stony Beach
N
Deadman's Bay
Stony Hill
Bradt
Stony Hill Point

Tristan da Cunha

Inaccessible
Stoltenhoff
Middle (Alex)
Nightingale

0    2km
0    1 mile

from over 3,280ft (1,000m) in the northwest to 985ft (300m) in the more sheltered southeast. Highly unstable, they consist of alternate layers of basaltic lava, ash and cinder, covered with a loose peat soil and the tenuous hold of ferns, trees and lichens.

**COASTAL LOWLANDS** Most of the island's coast consists of narrow boulder beaches or rocky promontories, with sheer sea cliffs rising behind. The Settlement Plain forms the only extensive lowland area, and is home to Edinburgh of the Seven Seas. East of Edinburgh, the landscape is dominated by the 1961 volcano and lava flow, and the stony outwash plain known as Pigbite. To the west, where the plain narrows behind the dramatic parasitic cone of Hillpiece, is the island's largest plain, a cultivated grass-covered area known as the Potato Patches.

In the south of the island, Cave Point forms a distinctive rocky peninsula backed by a small grassy plateau, accessible by beach to the larger Stony Hill Plain and 18th-century lava flow. The west of the island has a small area of rocky lowland named Anchorstock, formed by three gulches disgorging their loads to form a delta; while in the east, Sandy Point is a sloping plateau above a black sand beach. In the rain shadow of the prevailing winds, this is the warmest and driest area on Tristan, where islanders planted pine trees and informal fruit orchards.

**CLIMATE** Tristan has a cool temperate oceanic climate, with high rainfall year-round and – perhaps unexpectedly – high levels of humidity. In summer

(December–February), daytime temperatures average around 20°C, and rarely exceed 24°C, while winter temperatures, although typically topping 14°C in July and August, can plummet to 4°C. The island is buffeted by frequent storms, whose gale-force winds bring persistent cloud and regular rainfall. Even at sea level this amounts to more than 1,500mm a year, but higher up the mountain precipitation increases to 3,000mm a year, often falling as snow in the winter months.

## NATURAL HISTORY AND CONSERVATION

**NATURAL VEGETATION** The tall, dense and abrasive tussock grass (*Spartina arundinacea*) dominates lowland areas of all the outer islands, but on Tristan da Cunha was eradicated by land clearance for agriculture, and by rodents. This vegetation decays to a rich peat soil and provides the environment for many burrowing, nesting seabirds and favoured sites for penguin rookeries. Higher up there is a fern bush zone, dominated by bog fern (*Blechnum palmiforme*) and the only native tree (*Phylica arborea*), known as the 'island tree', which was previously cut extensively for firewood in the north and west of the island. On the Base, between 750m and 900m, vegetation is dominated by *Rumex* and *Holcus* grasses and mats of ground-hugging ferns (*Blechnum penna-marina*).

The mountain summit is more sparsely vegetated, having large areas of bare rock and loose ash, with mats of the dwarf shrub island or peak berry (*Empetrum rubrum*) and byophytes.

### BIRDS
**Seabirds** Often best seen from ships travelling to and circumnavigating the islands, seabirds can provide one of the highlights of a visit. Armed with a good bird guidebook and a pair of binoculars, people never before interested in ornithology can become enthusiastic birdwatchers overnight at the majestic sight of a soaring Tristan albatross or the activity of storm petrels at sea. On land, the breeding seabird colonies on the wilderness of Nightingale Island offer a dramatic wildlife experience to visitors.

*Albatross* The Tristan da Cunha group and Gough Island are extremely important for three separate species of breeding albatross, two of them classified as endangered (particularly in relation to long-line fishing activity), and the third – the Tristan albatross – as critically endangered.

The endemic **Tristan albatross**, or gony (*Diomedea dabbenena*), has a wingspan of up to 118in (300cm) and can weigh 15lb (7kg). It is very graceful in strong winds, often following ships and resting on the ocean at night. Ashore, however, it is fairly clumsy, requiring large open areas to land and take off (always into the wind for uplift), and thus breeds on windswept uplands. They are biennial breeders, with eggs laid in January and chicks hatched in March and fledged by December. Successful breeders then take a year off to moult and recover body condition. Despite the name, the birds were extinct on Tristan itself by 1907 due to hunting (which also almost eliminated the Inaccessible population). Up to 1,700 pairs breed annually on Gough Island and the occasional pair on Inaccessible, figures that represent a decline of some 96% in the last 60 years.

The **Atlantic yellow-nosed albatross** or molly (*Thalassarche chlororhynchos; wingspan up to 83in/210cm; weight up to 6lb/2.8kg*) is one of the smallest albatrosses. Adults have a distinctive golden stripe along the top of their bill and are fairly agile ashore, nesting in a variety of upland habitats and eating mainly fish and squid.

Eggs are laid in September, with chicks hatching by December and fledging by April. Pairs often breed every year, remain faithful, and may live for at least 30 years. Total breeding pairs across the Tristan group are estimated at around 13,900, a considerable decline on the 20,000 pairs of the 1970s.

Only a little larger, the **sooty albatross** or peeoo (*Phoebetria fusca; wingspan up to 83in/210cm; weight 7lb/3.2kg*) has a distinctive sooty-brown appearance with a white eye ring. The birds nest on ledges on exposed cliffs and ridges from which they can launch into the air. Eggs are laid in October, with chicks hatching by December and fledging by May. Most pairs breed every other year. As well as squid and fish, they also eat larger prey, including seabirds and even penguins. Populations are declining, with estimates indicating some 3,157 pairs on the Tristan group, and around 5,000 on Gough.

**Penguins** The small **northern rockhopper penguin**, or pinnamin (*Eudyptes moseleyi; height up to 25in/65cm*) normally weighs up to 5lb (2.2kg) – but this increases up to 8lb (4kg) immediately before their land-based 'starvation' moult. Adapted for underwater pursuit, they dive to a depth of 230ft (70m) at up to 5mph (8km/h) for crustaceans, small fish and squid. Adults have luxuriant golden-yellow head plumes and red eyes. They are fairly agile ashore, hopping over rocks and boulders to their land-based colonies, often among dense tussock grass but also on rocky shores and gulches. Two whitish eggs are laid in September, but usually only one chick survives when the eggs hatch by early November, and it is fledged by January. Almost entirely endemic to the Tristan group, there were estimated to be 6,700 pairs on Tristan, 25,000 pairs at Nightingale, up to 83,000 pairs at Middle Island, 54,000 pairs at Inaccessible, and 64,700 at Gough, based on 2006 and 2009 figures.

**Petrels** The Tristan islands form breeding sites for 12 main petrel species. The largest is the **southern giant petrel**, nellie or stinker (*Macronectes giganteus; wingspan up to 83in/210cm; weight 12lb 2oz (5.5kg)*). A huge, lumbering grey-brown petrel with a massive bill, it gathers in groups of 50–100 to scavenge at food sources such as fishing boats and dead whales. An estimated 2,300 pairs breed on Gough; but on Tristan they were extinct by 1900.

The **spectacled petrel** or ringeye (*Procellaria conspicillata; wingspan up to 57in/144cm; weight up to 3lb/1.3kg*), with its distinctive white spectacle, is a burrowing seabird. It is endemic to Inaccessible Island where the current 20,000 pairs has been growing steadily since the 1930s, following earlier near-extinction from predation by feral pigs.

The **great shearwater** or petrel (*Ardenna gravis; wingspan 46in/118cm; weight up to 2lb 6oz/1.1kg*) breeds in burrows up to 5ft (1.5m) long and dug into peat. It is strongly seasonal, returning to colonies from late August to lay single eggs in November which hatch in January; the chicks fledge by May. Near-endemic to the Tristan islands, great shearwaters migrate to the North Atlantic in winter, most travelling to waters off Newfoundland and Greenland for June and July and returning along a more easterly route. The species is not threatened, with an estimated five million pairs within the Tristan group, and up to three million on Gough.

The **broad-billed prion** or nightbird (*Pachyptila vittata; wingspan up to 26in/66cm; weight up to 8oz/230g*) is the most common prion in Tristan waters, occurring in large groups at sea, and feeding mainly on crustaceans by surface seizing, hydroplaning and diving to 65ft (20m). They return to their nest burrows after dark and can be attracted by the lights of vessels anchored offshore. It is estimated that there are two million pairs on Gough, 100,000 on Nightingale and Inaccessible, and up to 5,000 on Tristan.

Other petrels include the summer-breeding **Kerguelen petrel** or blue nighthawk (*Lugensa brevirostris*), the **soft-plumaged petrel** or whistler (*Pterodroma mollis*), the **common diving petrel** or flying pinnamin (*Pelecanoides urinatrix*), the **white-faced storm petrel** or skipjack (*Pelagodroma marina*), and the **white-bellied storm petrel** or storm pigeon (*Fregetta grallaria*). Winter breeders are the **great-winged petrel** or black haglet (*Pterodroma macroptera*) and the endangered **Atlantic petrel** (*Pterodroma incerta*), which is endemic to Tristan.

***Other seabirds*** The endemic **Tristan skua** or seahen (*Catharacta antarctica hamiltoni; wingspan up to 63in/160cm; weight up to 4lb/1.8kg*) is a large, brown gull-like bird which defends its territory fiercely and is not considered threatened. It feeds mainly on seabirds (prions, great shearwaters, penguin chicks and eggs), but also eats offal, rats, landbirds, and young lambs and hens.

The **Antarctic tern** or kingbird (*Sterna vittata*) is an attractive, small, grey-and-white tern with a full black cap, long outer-tail streamers and striking red bill and legs. It breeds on coastal cliff ledges and stacks. A sub species (*Sterna vittata tristanensis*) is endemic to Tristan, where it is frequently seen around the Settlement beaches.

Although normally a tropical bird, the **brown noddy** or wood pigeon (*Anous stolidus; page 44*) also breeds in small numbers on Tristan and the outer islands.

**Landbirds** Tristan's endemic landbirds are all considered to be rare and threatened with extinction. They provide remarkable case studies of evolution, especially with regard to the **Inaccessible Island rail** (*Atlantisia rogersi*), the smallest flightless bird in the world. An estimated 8,400 live at high density amongst the tussock grass there, but very few have been seen or studied.

The **Gough moorhen** or island cock (*Gallinula comeri*) is found in tussock grassland and fern bush on Gough Island and is now relatively widespread on Tristan da Cunha. The **Tristan thrush** or starchy (*Nesocichla eremita*) also has sub species that are recognised on Nightingale and Inaccessible. Omnivorous birds, they eat seeds, small crustaceans and scavenging carrion. They approach people readily on the outer islands, but are restricted mainly to the south and east of Tristan.

Although extinct on the main island, the **Tristan bunting** or canary (*Rowettia acunhae*) has distinct subspecies on Nightingale and Inaccessible, commonly found amongst tussock grass where they feed mainly on seeds (Nightingale) and insects (Inaccessible). The **Gough Island bunting** (*Rowettia goughensis*) is very tame and eats small seeds, fruits and insects.

One of the rarest birds in the world, **Wilkins'** or **Tristan large-billed bunting** or big canary (*Nesospiza wilkinsi*) is restricted to fewer than 120 birds that survive in woodland on Nightingale Island, where its main diet of *Phylica* nuts is found.

**MARINE LIFE** The seas around the Tristan group of islands are rich in marine life. The food web is based on an abundance of phytoplankton (which thrives in the nutrient-rich waters) grazed by shoals of zooplankton like krill. These shrimp-like creatures are the sole food for the **southern right whale** (*Eubalaena australis*), which breeds around the main island, but was over-hunted, especially by 19th-century American whalers for whom it was the 'right' one to catch.

Extensive **kelp** (*Macrocystis pyrifera*) surrounds all the islands, rooting to a depth of about 65ft (20m) offshore and providing shelter for numerous organisms. The **crawfish** (*Jasus tristani*) is found inshore to depths of 1,312ft (400m) around all the islands. Other common local fish include the **false jacopever** or **soldier fish**

(*Sebastes capensis*), **Tristan wrasse** or **concha** (*Nelabrichthys ornatus*), **fivefinger** (*Acantholatris monodactylus*) and **bluefish** (*Hyperpoglyphe antartica*).

Top predators include the **common broad-nosed seven-gilled** or **rock shark** (*Notorynchus cepedianus*) and **Shepherd's beaked whale** (*Tasmacetus shepheri*), which has been identified from strandings on Tristan beaches. **Subantarctic fur seals** (*Arctocephalus tropicalis*), whose mature males sport a 'mohican' tuft on their head, haul up to breed and moult on all the islands during the summer months. Extinct on Tristan a century ago, they are now represented by a growing colony at Cave Point, as well as on Nightingale and Inaccessible. Gough Island hosts about three-quarters of the world's population. The large **southern elephant seal** (*Mirounga leonina*) breeds only on Gough Island (just a few pups a year) but immature adults haul up on Tristan and Inaccessible beaches.

**CONSERVATION** Conservation and study of the flora and fauna are important elements of modern Tristan da Cunha, which values its unique ecosystem, depends on a sustainable craw-fishing industry for its income and recognises that specialist ecotourism will become more important in the 21st century. Following a Conservation Ordinance enacted in 2006, Tristan da Cunha was included in the international agreement on the conservation of albatrosses and petrels.

Central to this ordinance is the recognition of Gough and Inaccessible islands (both with World Heritage Site status) as nature reserves, making them effectively off-limits to tourists. The ordinance also gives protection to wildlife on the main island, where all the northern rockhopper penguin rookeries have been designated as nature reserves.

Tristan has an active Agriculture and Natural Resources Department, with a full-time conservation officer. Regular wildlife monitoring is carried out in a range of habitats, including dives in marine areas offshore and fieldwork on all the outer islands using modern inshore patrol boats for Tristan, Nightingale and Inaccessible, and the concession-owner's fishing vessel to visit Gough Island.

## HISTORY

**DISCOVERY AND SETTLEMENT** Admiral Tristão da Cunha, commanding an ill-fated Portuguese fleet between Lisbon and India, first discovered and named the island after himself in October 1506. The island then became well known to navigators after the Dutch East India Company instructed its commanders to use the longer but quicker route from Europe to the Cape of Good Hope (via West Indies–Brazil coast–Tristan) to take advantage of prevailing winds and currents. Several expeditions carried out surveys and landed to take on water, exploit the abundant seal populations and land an occasional goat. American Jonathon Lambert arrived in 1810 to make the first serious settlement attempt with ambitious plans to turn Tristan into a trading station named the 'Islands of Refreshment', but was subsequently lost at sea with two companions during a fishing trip.

In 1816, the British government seized Tristan da Cunha on behalf of King George III, acting on dual fears that American ships might continue to land on the island for supplies after the 1812–14 Anglo-American War, and that Tristan could be used as a staging post for an improbable attempt to rescue Napoleon, who by then was held on St Helena. A small force arrived from Cape Town on 14 August (now celebrated as Anniversary Day) and built a settlement of stone buildings known as Fort Malcolm. A decision was soon taken to withdraw this expensive and unnecessary garrison, but William Glass (a senior NCO of the Royal Artillery) persuaded the authorities to grant him permission to remain on the island with his wife and two children. They were joined by two Devonian stonemasons and began a most remarkable colony.

Initially trading seal oil and bartering with passing ships, the colony grew and thrived. It attracted several other men, including 52-year-old bachelor Thomas Swain in 1826 who had led a colourful life and claimed to have held the dying Lord Nelson on the deck of HMS *Victory*. After Swain's arrival there were five bachelors and a growing Glass family, but the long-term viability of the community was in doubt without more women. The solution was as neat as it was bizarre. The bachelors persuaded regular visitor Captain Amm to try to persuade five willing ladies to accompany him on his next voyage from St Helena on what may be the world's first 'blind date'. On his return call in 1827 he indeed brought five women. One couple became six, and a viable community on Tristan da Cunha became a real possibility.

William and Maria Glass had 16 children and the Christian society they led (with common rights to farm and trade) was attractive to other male settlers who found ready brides. They included Pieter Groen from Holland, who escaped the wreck of his ship *Emily* in 1836 (changing his name to Peter Green), and American whalers Thomas Rogers (1836) and Captain Andrew Hagan (1849), who both married daughters of William Glass.

**INCREASING ISOLATION** From the mid 19th century, a series of events transformed Tristan da Cunha from a thriving trading station to an impoverished subsistence economy. After the death of William Glass from cancer in 1853, the entire Glass clan emigrated to Massachusetts – though his son and a grandson, Joshua Rogers, returned ten years later. Then, in 1857, the island's first resident priest, Rev William Taylor, led a further exodus of 45 to South Africa. Fortunately, the remaining tiny community of 11 households gained status when Prince Alfred (the first Duke of Edinburgh and second son of Queen Victoria) visited the island in 1867, after which the village was named 'Edinburgh of the Seven Seas' in his honour.

Meanwhile, the American Civil War of 1861–65 caused American whaling around the islands to cease, then the opening of the Suez Canal in 1869 and the replacement of sail by steam combined to ensure that the days of taking the long southern route (from Europe to the Far East) were numbered. In 1864, at a time when no proof of British ownership could be offered, the commander of a US confederate ship proceeded to land 40 Union prisoners on the island. As a result, Tristan was formally declared a dependency of the British Empire in 1875.

Worse was to follow with an environmental disaster in 1882, when the US ship *Henry A Paul* was deliberately wrecked at Sandy Point and a few black rats escaped to populate the island. Their descendants quickly decimated small seabird populations and threatened harvests of potatoes and wheat – a crop which, as a result, was permanently abandoned. Islanders became desperate to obtain flour, sugar, clothes and other items to supplement local produce, so whenever there was a passing ship, each family sent a representative to share in the bartering. On 28 November 1885, 15 men set out in a recently donated lifeboat to attempt to trade with the sailing vessel *West Riding*. They were never seen again, presumed drowned. The community was reduced to 92 inhabitants with only four married men, all over 45. Although complete evacuation was proposed, a core population of 50 remained. Then, in early 1892, another ship, the *Italia*, foundered at Stony Beach, effectively delivering to the island two much-needed male immigrants: Italians Gaetano Lavarello and Andrea Repetto.

8

Tristan then entered its most isolated phase when British warship visits were curtailed by both the Boer War and World War I, and islanders underwent a period of ten years with no incoming mail or supplies. Although they faced hardship through lack of provisions, poor harvests and loss of stock during harsh winters, they never starved and their diet was supplemented by regular hunting trips to Inaccessible and Nightingale islands to harvest seabirds and their eggs as well as fish.

**PROGRESS AND PROSPERITY** The 1920s saw the construction of St Mary's Church and the establishment of an Island Council under the direction of Rev Henry Rogers. Cruise-ship visits were heralded in 1927 with the arrival of the liner *Asturias*, which gave the islanders a new opportunity to barter souvenirs, including penguin-skin tassel mats, knitted socks and model longboats. The Norwegian Expedition of 1937–38 put Tristan literally on the map when a first detailed land survey was produced and the visiting scientists investigated many aspects of the island. In particular the expedition publicised the unique good health of the isolated islanders, especially their fine teeth and the fact that most deaths were caused by accidents and old age. Before the expedition departed Tristan officially became a dependency of St Helena.

World War II ended Tristan's complete reliance on bartering, and saw the introduction of currency, when a top-secret Royal Naval Station arrived in 1942 to monitor German U-boat movements by radio. The station, officially 'Job 9' and then Atlantic Isle, provided paid employment to islanders in the construction and maintenance of wooden buildings for accommodation, offices, a school, a hospital and a store (known as the canteen), where locals could for the first time spend money on their island.

A wartime padre, Rev Lawrence, returned in 1948 to head an expedition leading to the establishment of the Tristan da Cunha Development Company. This went on to build a crawfish-canning factory above Big Beach, maintaining and extending the employment opportunities through fishing and processing jobs for islanders. The first civilian administrator, Hugh Elliot, arrived in 1950, taking over from previous Anglican priests and wartime commanders in a leadership role. By 1953, the company had become profitable and in 1957 Tristan welcomed Prince Philip, Duke of Edinburgh, who arrived aboard the Royal Yacht *Britannia*, and laid the foundation stone for a new community centre, to be known as the Prince Philip Hall.

**VOLCANIC INTERLUDE** Tristan was shaken by a series of earth tremors from August 1961, culminating in a massive earthquake which produced a rock fall from a cliff directly behind the Settlement on 8 October. Houses on the eastern side of the village suffered cracks and jammed doors and windows so their inhabitants moved in with their western neighbours overnight. The following day the cracks had closed and life went on as normal, until a fissure opened almost halfway between the fishing factory and the first house, pushing upwards into a bank, then into a dome some 10m above the surrounding land. An emergency meeting was convened and the 264 islanders and 26 resident expatriates were evacuated overnight to huts at the Potato Patches, and thence the next day via longboats and the fishing vessels *Frances Repetto* and *Tristania* to nearby Nightingale Island.

Meanwhile the growing dome erupted, plumes of sulphurous gas blew in the air and lava bombs were blown out, precursors of an imminent lava flow that later ignited fuel in factory storage tanks, destroyed the factory itself, and extended the coastline by burying the island's two best landing beaches. Having both fishing vessels available was lucky, but the arrival on 11 October of the liner *Tjisadande*, with spare berths for all the evacuees, was a miracle. On 16 October, the ship sailed into Cape Town where, for a hectic few days, reluctant islanders (most travelling abroad for the first time) found themselves in the international media spotlight, before travelling on the *Stirling Castle* to Southampton and what was assumed to be a permanent home in England.

The evacuated islanders were first housed in Surrey and then moved into 50 houses in a renamed Tristan Close in Calshot, Hampshire, where they began to integrate into local society, attending schools, taking up a variety of employment and enjoying at least some advantages of the 'Swinging Sixties'. But the community never settled. A Royal Society expedition to Tristan in early 1962, with two islanders as guides, established that the volcano had ceased erupting and that village homes at least had their walls still standing. Islanders campaigned to return home, and by November 1962, the British government, which had initially been relieved that the islanders were all safe and well provided for in England, reluctantly announced that they would fund resettlement to the active volcanic island. During 1963, two groups journeyed south and by 10 November most of the population had returned to their remote home.

**REBUILDING THE TRISTAN COMMUNITY** Early priorities were to build a new harbour and a replacement crawfish-freezing factory, which were both in use by 1966. Foreign income from fishing royalties and the sale of postage stamps provided the income to rebuild a modern village, with a new Administration Building, island store, hospital and school all complete by 1975. Islanders who benefited from improved local education and overseas training began to take over posts of responsibility. Albert Glass became the first island policeman and Basil Lavarello factory manager. Later, islanders took over responsibility from expatriate contract officers for the agriculture, public works, treasury, post office and finally education departments.

Yet there have been many setbacks to progress. In 1975, demand for crawfish plummeted during a global economic recession and no royalties were paid. In 1983, an experimental and expensive wind generator blew down, leaving the community entirely dependent ever since on electricity produced by a factory-based diesel generator. Environmental challenges remain, too: fatal accidents have occurred on the mountain, along the coast and while fishing. A hurricane in May 2001 devastated the village, especially the new buildings unprotected by flax hedges and by the massive rock-hewn gable ends of the traditional Tristan cottages. By 2006, when the Tristan da Cunha Association organised a cruise to celebrate 500 years of human history, almost all the 115 passengers were able to spend several days ashore. Since then, there has been environmental devastation in 2011, when a ship was wrecked off Nightingale, and triumph in 2012 with the opening of a new museum.

## GOVERNMENT AND ADMINISTRATION

Tristan da Cunha is part of the UK Overseas Territory of St Helena, Ascension and Tristan da Cunha, whose governor is based on St Helena. Regular visits by the governor to Tristan have been curtailed since 2004, when the annual stopover at Tristan by the RMS *St Helena* was discontinued (but see page 55 for her final voyage south). There is, however, a resident island administrator, appointed by the British government and advised by the Island Council.

Elections are held every three years for the post of chief islander, who leads the Island Council, and for the eight elected council members (including at least one woman). A further three members are appointed. The Administration Building, which houses the administrator's office, the treasury and the internet café, is worth a look inside to view the council chamber.

Tristan has its own legislation, supplemented by the laws or 'ordinances' of St Helena and UK law, provided that these don't conflict with local laws or circumstances. There is one full-time police officer and two special constables. The administrator is the magistrate, but crime is practically non-existent.

Departments include the treasury, police, post office and telecommunications, agriculture and natural resources, education, health, island store, and public works (mechanical, carpentry, electrical and transport). All government heads of departments except for the medical officer are islanders. Aside from these two permanent overseas workers, the fishing company also employs an expatriate factory manager, and the Anglican Church a priest, and there are regular visiting workers, for example dentist, optician and technical support.

## ECONOMY

Tristan da Cunha's economy is largely based on traditional subsistence farming and fishing; the only regular employment outside this is within government-run organisations and for the fish factory.

The island's most valuable commodity is Tristan rock lobster (crawfish), but additional revenue comes from the sale of fishing licences, stamps and commemorative coins, and tourism. However, the economy remains weak, with 21st-century income lower than that of a couple of decades ago.

**FISHING** Crawfish (*Jasus tristani*), the local name for crayfish and marketed as Tristan rock lobster, is found in abundance around the Tristan islands and has been exploited commercially since 1949. The modern processing factory, incorporating freezing technology, is set above Calshot Harbour and is the mainstay of the island's economy. In addition to a small permanent workforce, it offers seasonal work for many more islanders.

The industry is operated by 12 power boats, each with a crew of two, who drop baited traps to the sea floor. There is a strict size and tonnage quota for Tristan, which is fished by islanders, and for each of the outlying islands (Nightingale, Inaccessible and Gough), where fishing is the domain of the concession holder, currently the South African company Ovenstone Agencies.

Technically, the fishing season starts on 1 July and extends until February/March, although every effort is made to catch the quota by Christmas in time to reach the markets in the USA (for lobster tails) and Japan (for whole lobster). That said, the weather plays a significant role. In 2014–15, only 17 fishing days were possible in the first five months – and only four in the peak month of November. On a more positive note, this was the first year to see exports of Tristan lobster to the EU, a major breakthrough for the economy.

**AGRICULTURE** Subsistence farming is at the heart of Tristan life. The land is communally owned, with fencing maintained by the government, which also controls the numbers of stock animals to prevent overgrazing, and organises the import of livestock. Nevertheless, families own their own livestock, tend their gardens and cultivate crops – especially potatoes – in tiny walled fields known as the Potato Patches, each enclosed by loose volcanic stone walls for protection from the prevailing northwest winds.

Huge time commitment goes in to the cultivation of the crop using only hand tools, with an elaborate range of fertilisers (including wool, crawfish offal, kelp and penguin guano) employed to maintain good yields, despite monoculture for nearly 200 years.

Cattle are limited to two cows per family or one for a single householder. The milking herd rotates around Settlement fields (known as 'fences'): one being the Settlement itself, and another doubling as the school playing field. There are small breeding herds at Stony Beach and Cave Point, and also some steers at Sandy Point. Small yields of milk are taken each morning by hand, but butter- and cheese-making has discontinued, and cattle are kept mainly for their meat.

Sheep numbers, too, are limited – to seven ewes per household, or three for a single householder – although they are far more efficient grazers than cattle as they are sure-footed and able to nibble short grass. Around 1,000 sheep graze the Settlement Plain, while more are kept on the mountain, led up the sheer cliffs by teams or 'gangs' of islanders to the lush pastures of the Base. Here they remain virtually untended except for marking and shearing – and are the source of the best-flavoured meat for the traditional stuffed roast mutton at Christmas or Easter.

Other animals kept around the Settlement include poultry, ducks and a few donkeys (the last being remnants of a herd used until the 1980s for transport, together with teams of bullocks tethered in pairs to wooden carts).

**TOURISM** Income from tourists staying on the island is minimal as visitor numbers are currently limited by a lack of berths on the shipping services to the island. Even with cruise-ship visitors, annual visitors numbers are no more than 400–1,000 a year. Cruise ships, however, now call more frequently than in the past and provide useful income through the purchase of stamps, coins and souvenirs, including local crafts.

## PEOPLE

The community's continued existence owes more to the resourcefulness of its people than to economic or environmental benefits. Most are farmers, but often combine their own farming with government-paid work, part-time work for the fish factory, and hunting and gathering trips to Nightingale Island. They co-operate with friends and family in building projects, and in teams, for example in keeping flocks of mountain sheep, or maintaining boats. They also have a full social programme which still recognises Sunday as a day to dress up, go to church and not to work or fish. On fine Saturdays the Settlement can seem like a ghost town as most people will be out at the Potato Patches, often going out in their pick-up trucks or 'bakkies' on Friday afternoons and staying at the family 'camping hut'.

Tristan's population has remained stable in recent years, in part the result of a restrictive immigration policy in place because of limited resources. Visitors are welcome, but permanent residency is confined to those born on the island, or born to a parent who was, and their respective spouses and dependants. For over a century, Tristan residents shared just seven surnames, all dating back to the original male settlers: Glass, Swain, Green, Rogers, Hagan and, later, Repetto and Lavarello, but recently these have been augmented by a further two: Collins and Squibb. Although several island women have married men with other surnames, none currently live permanently on the island.

Visitors to Tristan usually find the people to be friendly but reserved, but remember that this is a working community – not a tourist attraction. Islanders are understandably wary of those who appear not to respect their right to privacy, though longer-term visitors who stay as guests are warmly welcomed.

## LANGUAGE

The English spoken on Tristan da Cunha is a distinct local dialect, with vocabulary derived from the cultures of the original settlers: Scottish, English, St Helenian, South African, American, Dutch, Italian and Irish. That said, visitors often find it clearer than some regional British accents!

## EDUCATION

Tristan's children all attend **St Mary's School**, which caters for ages three to 16. The school has five classrooms, a hall, a computer suite, a cookery room, and a craft/science room, with a separate library housed in the attached resource centre. On leaving school, youngsters are offered the opportunity to work in a number of departments through a Youth Employment Scheme. For those wishing to pursue further education and training, however, the only option is to go overseas.

## TRAVELLING POSITIVELY

If you are keen to give something back to the community, making direct contact with the island, perhaps to help one of the churches or the school, would be hugely beneficial.

**Tristan da Cunha Association**  e secretary@ tristandc.com; www.tristandc.com. Before or after their visit, many visitors join this association, a UK-based organisation that exists to serve the people of Tristan, to foster good relations with them & to promote interest in the archipelago. Tristan islanders are automatically members & the association has a strong & growing international membership (UK £25/yr; overseas members £30/yr).

The association maintains close links with the island community, & publishes 2 illustrated newsletters a year, sent free to members. There is also an annual gathering, normally held in Southampton over the weekend after Easter. In addition, they run the Tristan da Cunha Education Trust, a UK-registered charity to provide support for islanders' training & further education.

**UPDATES WEBSITE**

You can post your comments and recommendations, and read the latest feedback and updates from other readers, online at www.bradtupdates.com/sthelena.

# 9

# Visiting Tristan da Cunha

## WHEN TO GO AND HIGHLIGHTS

Remote, difficult to access and with unpredictable weather, Tristan wouldn't appear to top the list of holiday destinations. Yet would-be visitors have many different reasons to make the long journey. For some, the whole point of visiting Tristan is simply because it is so remote. Others come for the natural history: the birdlife, the volcano; the sheer wilderness. And for others, it's an opportunity to experience, even for a short while, the life of the Tristan islanders. Whatever your motivation, consider carefully the best time of year for your trip.

### HIGHLIGHTS
**Wildlife** For wildlife viewing, the seasons are all-important: you will not see rockhopper penguins ashore in July, or Atlantic yellow-nosed albatross chicks until January. To help identify key months, see pages 157–60.

**Hiking and boat trips** Getting out and about is going to be a far more attractive option during the austral spring and summer months, around October to March. You can still expect plenty of wind and rain, but snow should be off the agenda, and temperatures milder. See also *Climate*, pages 156–7.

**PUBLIC HOLIDAYS AND FESTIVALS** In addition to the standard British public holidays held on St Helena (page 52), Tristan has several of its own festivals. **Queen's Day**, in February or March, celebrates the island's links with the UK, with traditional sports, fishing and a produce show, while **Anniversary Day**, on 14 August, commemorates the date on which the islands were claimed for the British Crown. **Sheep-shearing Day**, usually just before the Christmas holiday, is a further opportunity for the community to come together. And then there's **Ratting Day**, in early May, when the island's menfolk, together with the children, form competitive gangs to hunt rats, while the women produce a sumptuous midday feast to keep everyone going.

## RED TAPE

No visas are required for Tristan, but all visitors planning to staying on the island must have a a valid passport, together with confirmed and fully paid return passage, comprehensive medical insurance (see below), sufficient funds for the duration of their stay and a **permit** from the Island Council. To apply for a permit, contact the administrator's office (e *enquiriestdc1@gmail.com*) at the time of booking your passage (see below).

For **consular assistance** in Tristan you'll need to contact the police (\+44 (0)20 3014 2010), but lost passports are handled by the administrator's office (\+44 (0)20 3014 2001).

**TRAVEL INSURANCE AND WAIVER** All visitors are required to sign a passenger indemnity declaration (accident waiver) form before coming ashore, and must have adequate travel insurance to cover the costs of any medical treatment including, if required, the cost of medical evacuation to Cape Town.

**LANDING FEES** Anyone wishing to land on Tristan, even if they are not staying on the island, is required to have a landing stamp. Current charges for visitors are:

| | |
|---|---|
| **Tristan** | £30 (yacht passengers £15) |
| **Nightingale** | £20 |
| **Inaccessible/Gough** | £20 (but landing restricted; pages 180 and 182) |

Landing stamps may also be issued to passengers and crew of cruise ships who are not intending to go ashore, but who wish their passports to be endorsed as a souvenir of their visit.

## GETTING THERE AND AWAY (For details on getting to Cape Town, see page 183)

There is no airstrip on the island and all journeys are made by sea, usually between Cape Town and Tristan.

If you want just a glimpse of the island, then you'll probably join one of the majority of visitors who arrive on cruise ships. Typically these offer a one- or one-and-a-half-day stopover at Tristan, when passengers will spend their time on the Settlement Plain, in and around the village of Edinburgh of the Seven Seas. To stay on the island itself, you'll need to arrive on a scheduled ship, which will afford one, three or more weeks: time to explore further afield, climb up to the Base, make excursions to Nightingale Island, or simply enter into village life as part of the community.

Whatever your plans, note that 2016 marks the bicentenary of the first settlers on Tristan, an occasion that is bound to add to the number of visitors wishing to visit.

**SCHEDULED SHIPPING** Ideally, start planning at least a year in advance; provisional berths can be booked as soon as sailing schedules are published on the government website (*www.tristandc.com*). Once you have an idea of your plans, contact the secretary to the administrator (✆ +44 (0)20 3014 2001; e *enquiriestdc1@gmail.com*) or specialist tour operator Island Holidays (page 53) to outline the purpose of your visit, proposed sailing dates, and type of accommodation sought.

The Tristan government controls passages on all ships providing scheduled services, and operates a priority booking system. Thus, for example, a Tristan resident with a medical emergency, or someone on official business, will take priority over a tourist. This means that even if a booking is secured, sailings cannot be guaranteed, although passage on the *Agulhas II* is considered the most reliable option.

Accommodation should be booked in advance, but all trips and excursions will depend on the weather so can only be arranged after arrival.

**Fishing vessels** Under the terms of the crawfish licensing agreement, the concession holder, currently Ovenstone Agencies, provides eight or nine cargo/passenger services a year between Cape Town and Tristan, with sailings linked to the fishing operations. In 2015, departures were in January, April, May, June, August, September and November, though all sailing dates are provisional and subject to change at short notice. This relates to departures in either direction, so while most trips provide for a stay of up to five days on Tristan (a few are longer), visitors already ashore may have to leave early if their ship needs to depart ahead of schedule. For this reason, connecting flights to and from Cape Town, and any transit accommodation bookings there, should be booked on a flexible basis so that they can be changed without incurring financial penalties.

The service is operated by two ships, the MV *Edinburgh* and the MV *Baltic Trader*, with the journey from Cape Town taking a minimum of six days. Although up to 12 passenger berths are available on each sailing, most of these are booked in advance for use by the islanders. In 2015, the **fare** for tourists with no family connection to Tristan was US$500 (approx £333) each way, with children aged two to 15 half price, and those under two free.

**SA *Agulhas II*** The South African research vessel SA *Agulhas II* calls at the island in September/October each year on its annual voyage from Cape Town to service the staffed weather base on Gough Island. Some of the 40 passenger berths are reserved for visiting dentists or opticians, or for those on official visits such as training, research, or conservation projects. The remainder are allocated to islanders, relatives and friends, and other visitors on a first-come, first-served basis, with latecomers placed on a waiting list. This is the most reliable way of booking a trip, but it's advisable to reserve your passage at least a year in advance.

Tourist **fares** for the *Agulhas II* are quoted in South African rand. In 2015, the adult price for tourists with no family connection with Tristan was R4,475 (approx £263 at 2015 rate of exchange) each way, with children aged six to15 half price and, unusually, children under six travelling free of charge.

The voyage takes a minimum of five days, depending on sea and weather conditions, and passengers are usually ferried ashore by helicopter. Visitors can stay on Tristan for up to three weeks before the return sailing.

**CRUISE SHIPS** The islands have grown in popularity as a call for South Atlantic cruise ships, despite the vagaries in local weather and sea conditions that can prevent passengers landing at the Settlement. (In such a case, and if circumstances permit, an official party of islanders will board the ship to sell stamps and souvenirs and to endorse passports with a record of the visit.)

Some cruises include in their itineraries a circumnavigation of Gough Island, and also a trip to Inaccessible and Nightingale islands (up to an hour's sailing from Tristan itself). Landings are not normally permitted on Gough or Inaccessible, which are protected as World Heritage Sites, but local guides – conditions permitting – may take small groups ashore on Nightingale.

The main cruise-ship season is from November to April, with vessels calling at Tristan either southbound from Brazil, St Helena or Cape Town, or northbound from Argentina, Chile, South Georgia or the Falkland Islands. Details of proposed sailings are posted on the Tristan website (*www.tristandc.com*). Cruise operators and specialist tours include the following:

**Birdquest** See page 58.
**Oceanwide Expeditions** See page 58.
**Silversea Cruises** Level 3, Asticus Bldg, 21 Palmer St, London SW1H 0AH; \0844 251 0837;

www.silversea.com. 22-day Ushuaia–Cape Town cruise in Mar, via Gough & Tristan. On-board specialists include birders & marine biologists. £7,350pp exc flights.

**ARRIVAL AND DEPARTURE** Landing on Tristan is by no means straightforward. The island's small harbour is shallow, offers little protection against heavy seas, and

**RADIO CONTACT** Tristan Radio (VHF 14/16; HFSSB 4149/6230/8282MHz) acts as coastal radio station and port control. Prior to arrival, visiting yachts should contact the communications officer, Andy Repetto, at Tristan Radio ZOE (e *tristanradio@tdc-gov.com*), and before departure should advise their estimated departure time and proposed destination.

**CLEARANCE** Advance arrangements should be made with the visits liaison officer at the Police Department (📞 *+44 (0)20 3014 2010;* e *tristandcpolice@ gmail.com*). Yachts without such arrangements must obtain clearance from the harbourmaster, medical officer and immigration officer before anchoring or disembarking and completing the relevant formalities.

**ANCHORAGE** All visiting yachts should seek advice from the harbourmaster on a safe anchorage position (✠ *37°03.75'S, 12°18.56'W*), where the depth is around 50m on a rocky bottom. Anchoring overnight off Nightingale, Inaccessible or Gough islands is not permitted.

**DISEMBARKATION** Calshot Harbour (✠ *37°03.847'S, 12°18.798'W;* 🕙 *closed to visiting vessels 1 Oct–31 Mar 19.00 GMT, 1 Apr–30 Sep 17.00 GMT*) is too shallow for most boats, with a maximum depth to the top of the landing steps at low tide of 4ft 3in (1.3m).

Visiting yachts should use their own boats for ship-to-shore transfers if suitable for use in the shallow harbour. Alternatively, a RIB can be hired (£100/day, including crew).

**REPAIRS** The islanders may be able to help with limited repairs, as may the government workshop, but a yacht in serious trouble would have to await the arrival of a vessel with towing or lift capabilities to be shipped out.

is accessible for only some 60–70 days a year. All ships have to anchor offshore, with most passengers ferried ashore by smaller boats (although those on the SA *Aguilhas II* may be transported by helicopter). In bad weather, not only can this transfer be hazardous, but it can also prevent anyone going ashore at all. Similarly, those already on land may have to return to their ship early if bad weather is forecast.

## HEALTH AND SAFETY

Although Tristan is part of a British Overseas Territory, medical treatment is not free and medical insurance is compulsory. Major treatment can be very expensive, especially if repatriation to Cape Town is needed. On the island, a straightforward consultation with a doctor will set you back £21.

Pharmaceutical supplies are limited so make sure you take with you sufficient stock of any regular prescription medication.

The small Camogli Hospital, named after the home town of Italian settlers Andrea Repetto and Gaetano Lavarello, sits on an exposed site at the west end of the Settlement. It is staffed by local nurses and a resident doctor, but for anything complex, patients are usually referred to Cape Town – though the infrequency of ships calling at the island can result in significant delays. For other health matters, see pages 59–61.

## WHAT TO TAKE

Although rainfall is frequent on Tristan, it can be warm in summer, with high humidity, so take clothing suitable for similar seasons in the northern hemisphere, along with good-quality waterproofs. Walking boots and hiking poles would be good too. For other items, see pages 62–3.

## MONEY AND BANKING

The local currency is the UK pound sterling. Euros, US dollars and South African rand may be exchanged at the Treasury in the Administration Building during office hours at current rates of exchange, as may travellers' cheques. Credit cards and personal cheques are not accepted anywhere on the island, although payments may now be made by PayPal. Payment of fees for shipping or accommodation may be made via the Finance Department (e *tristandcfinance@gmail.com or finance@tdc-gov.com*).

## MEDIA AND COMMUNICATIONS

**TV AND RADIO** BFBS TV and radio is beamed to the island by satellite, but BBC Atlantic FM is no longer broadcast. A regular newsletter is produced by the Tristan da Cunha Association (page 166), but plans to set up a weekly newspaper are still in the pipeline.

**TELEPHONE AND INTERNET** International phone calls are routed via London (dialling code ✎ +44 (0)20 3014) and are at UK rates: approximately 10p per minute. There's an internet café in the Administration Building, opened at the time of the quincentenary. Internet access costs 10p per minute for day visitors, or £10 a month for those staying on the island.

**POST OFFICE AND MAIL** The post office (⊕ *during office hours – see below – & at additional times during cruise-ship visits*) sells a range of stamps, postcards and philatelic collectors' items – including date-stamped first-day covers on attractively designed envelopes. Staff will sometimes board visiting ships to sell stamps and souvenirs to those who are unable to come ashore.

---

### STAMPS AND COINS

Inspired by the island's unique history and rich environment, Tristan da Cunha postage stamps are sought after by philatelists. Often featuring stunning designs, they are produced through a partnership with Pobjoy Mint (*www.pobjoystamps.com*) and Creative Direction in the UK. There is also great interest in stamp history, especially when the rare, locally produced first stamps (sold in 1946 for four potatoes or 1 penny, and correctly known as 'potato stamp stickers') come up for sale. Tristan's post office handles a worldwide mail-order service, increasingly through the internet.

Over the years, several Tristan da Cunha Crown coins have been minted and sold to collectors, their value appreciating with time. More recently, other officially approved commemorative coins have been minted by the Commonwealth Mint & Philatelic Bureau (*www.thecommonwealthmint. co.uk*). These are marketed to collectors and provide welcome royalties to the island, where they are also legal tender.

Mail posted to or from Tristan can take months to arrive, but the cost of stamps is surprisingly reasonable: 35p for an airmail letter to the UK or US – always accepting, of course, that the letter's initial journey is by sea!

## OPENING HOURS

Government departments, including the post office and the Island Store, are open five days a week (⊕ *summer 08.00–14.30 Mon–Thu, 08.00–13.00 Fri; winter 08.30–15.00 Mon–Thu, 08.30–14.30 Fri*).

## GETTING AROUND

Tristan has only one navigable road, between the Settlement and the Potato Patches – a distance of about 1½ miles (2.4km). A regular **bus** along this road runs between Monday and Saturday, leaving the Settlement at 07.30, 08.30, 11.15 and 13.40.

Alternatively, you can hire a **vehicle with driver** for £5 per person, but note that there is no insurance, so passengers travel at their own risk. Self-driving is not an option. See also *Hiking* (below) and *Boat trips* (page 173).

A **map** of the island is available from the Tourism Department (page 175).

## ACTIVITIES

**HIKING** Visitors are permitted to walk alone between the Settlement and the Potato Patches, a half-hour walk along a tarmac road, but elsewhere hikers must be accompanied by at least one local guide. Most hikes need to be organised in advance through the **tourism co-ordinator**, Dawn Repetto (☏ *+44 (0)20 3014 2037*), and are subject to suitable weather conditions. Be aware, too, that if a 'fishing day' is declared, the guides may be otherwise occupied and even pre-organised excursions could be cancelled.

**1961 volcano** (*30mins; moderate; £32 per guide*) Hiking to the summit of the 1961 volcano, at about 400ft (120m), is relatively straightforward, though you'll need to beware of loose, uneven rocks. Park 61, at the foot of the volcano, provides a pleasant spot for a picnic before or after the trek.

**The Base** (*At least 2hrs; challenging; £60 per guide*) Tackling the Base, where the cliffs level off at around 2,000ft (610m) before climbing to the summit, is altogether more demanding. The islanders have made narrow paths (known as 'roads') which they use to guide visitors up here in suitable weather, but landslides are common. A good level of fitness and strong walking shoes or boots are essential. One visitor reports, 'We had a fantastic walk up, but we were fit and used to walking/climbing. It rather over-faced quite a number of our party.'

**Queen Mary's Peak** (*Allow 5–10hrs, depending on fitness; challenging; £200 for 2 guides*) A minimum of two guides are essential to climb the Peak, which at 6,760ft (2,062m) high is a serious undertaking.

**GOLF** Visitors are welcome to play at the island's nine-hole golf course. To organise a game, contact the tourism department (☏ +44 (0)20 3014 2037) during office hours. The cost is £20, which includes hire of clubs, scorecard, certificate and hat.

**SWIMMING** There's a 20m outdoor freshwater swimming pool ($\oplus$ *summer only, Nov–Apr; free*) in front of the Prince Philip Hall complex. It is dangerous to swim in the harbour or on open beaches due to strong currents and the presence of sharks.

**BOAT TRIPS AND FISHING** Weather permitting, fishing trips can be organised in Tristan waters for up to eight passengers through the tourism department (☏ *+44 (0)20 3014 2037; boat hire approx £50; guide £32*). Alternatively, you can arrange to go fishing with one of the locals, and perhaps set a few lobster pots. Fishing for crawfish is strictly prohibited.

To organise an excursion to Nightingale or Inaccessible, you need to contact the Conservation and Police departments (☏ *+44 (0)20 3014 5016 & 2010*). Numbers are limited to five or six, and for both safety and wildlife conservation reasons, visitors must be accompanied by a local guide, whether or not they are planning to land. For visiting ships, guides must be taken on board at Tristan, and returned before nightfall.

## EDINBURGH OF THE SEVEN SEAS

Despite the grand name, Tristan's 'capital' is little more than a small village, nestled at the foot of the mountain. Widely known as the Settlement, it sits on an undulating slope some 500m wide and above low sea cliffs. The Settlement is home to some 70 families – almost the entire population – and a number of domestic animals. Most of their sturdy modern bungalows are long single-storey buildings of white-washed block or with wood cladding, roofed with zinc-coated corrugated iron and sometimes surrounded by low stone walls. Typically they're equipped with piped spring water, gas cookers and water heaters, fitted kitchens, bathrooms and toilets, and a sewage system. Electricity is supplied by the fish factory.

**WHERE TO STAY** *Map, page 174*
For visitors to Tristan, accommodation options range from guesthouses providing full board or self-catering facilities to homestays that include fantastic home-cooked meals, as well as simple camping huts and one rather quirky option: a night at the Thatched House Museum (page 176).

With the exception of the museum, visitors are usually allocated a guesthouse or homestay by the government, rather than choosing their own. To make a reservation, contact the secretary to the administrator (e *enquiriestdc1@gmail.com*) once your passage has been booked.

Unless otherwise stated, **rates** are per person per night and are the same for all establishments:

**Full board** Adults £50; children under 12 £25; children under two £5.
**Self-catering** Adults £25; children under 12 £12.50; children under two £2.50; gas, electricity, TV and phone rental extra.

**Camping huts** The island equivalent of holiday homes, these are rudimentary huts of concrete or zinc construction where families may escape for a weekend to tend their crops or just to chill out. A few huts are available for rent on Tristan (at the Potato Patches, The Caves, Stony Beach and Sandy Point) and on Nightingale Island, with prices on application. Other than this, camping is not permitted.

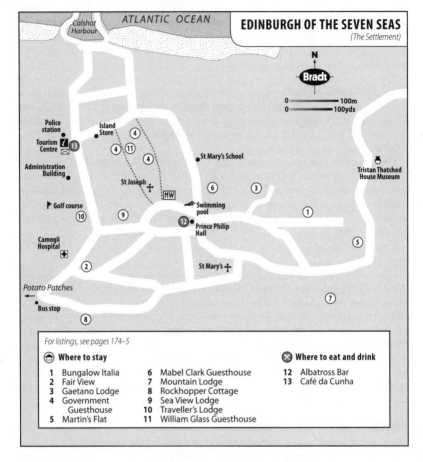

ATLANTIC OCEAN

Calshot Harbour

**EDINBURGH OF THE SEVEN SEAS**
(The Settlement)

N

Bradt

0 ———— 100m
0 ———— 100yds

Police station

Island Store

④

Tourism Centre ✉ ⑬

④ ⑪

Administration Building

④

St Mary's School

St Joseph ✝

MW

Tristan Thatched House Museum

Golf course

⑩

⑨

Swimming pool

⑥

③

①

⑫ Prince Philip Hall

Camogli Hospital ✚

⑤

②

St Mary's ✝

Potato Patches

Bus stop

⑦

⑧

For listings, see pages 174–5

🏠 **Where to stay**

| | | | |
|---|---|---|---|
| 1 | Bungalow Italia | 6 | Mabel Clark Guesthouse |
| 2 | Fair View | 7 | Mountain Lodge |
| 3 | Gaetano Lodge | 8 | Rockhopper Cottage |
| 4 | Government | 9 | Sea View Lodge |
| | Guesthouse | 10 | Traveller's Lodge |
| 5 | Martin's Flat | 11 | William Glass Guesthouse |

🍴 **Where to eat and drink**

| | |
|---|---|
| 12 | Albatross Bar |
| 13 | Café da Cunha |

## Guesthouses

🏠 **Bungalow Italia** (2 bedrooms) Pretty white-washed building with bright soft furnishings in dbl & twin rooms. Bathroom with shower & bath; open-plan kitchen/living area.

🏠 **Fair View** (1 bedroom) Mountain & sea views, an enclosed garden with BBQ, & a dbl or twin bedroom with shower room & open-plan kitchen.

🏠 **Gaetano Lodge** (3 bedrooms) All dbl bedrooms, plus lounge, kitchen & dining room.

🏠 **Government Guesthouse** (2 bedrooms) 3 separate bungalows, each with 2 bedrooms, lounge, dining room & kitchen.

🏠 **Mabel Clark Guesthouse** (5 bedrooms) Larger than most, with 3 dbl & 2 sgl rooms (1 en suite). Bathroom, kitchen & living room.

🏠 **Martin's Flat** (1 bedroom) East of the village, with sea views. Dbl en-suite room, open-plan kitchen & covered veranda.

🏠 **Mountain Lodge** (2 bedrooms) Neatly built home overlooking village from the east. Dbl & sgl rooms, bathroom with shower & bath, & open-plan kitchen/living area.

🏠 **Rockhopper Cottage** (3 bedrooms) A smart red roof atop white walls with mountains rising behind.

🏠 **Sea View Lodge** (2 bedrooms) A dbl & a sgl room with lounge & open-plan kitchen/ dining room.

🏠 **Traveller's Lodge** (2 bedrooms) Shower, open-plan lounge & kitchen.

🏠 **William Glass Guesthouse** (4 bedrooms) Central, wood-clad house with 2 sgl & 2 dbl rooms, bathroom with bath & shower, lounge, kitchen & laundry, plus enclosed garden with BBQ area.

## ✕ WHERE TO EAT AND DRINK  *Map, page 174*

The social hub of Tristan da Cunha is Prince Philip Hall, at the centre of the village, which plays host to the dance, receptions and parties that are important features of community life, and also has a bar.

🖳 **Café da Cunha**  Post & Tourism Dept; ⏱ 08.30–14.30 Mon–Thu, 08.30–13.00 Fri. As well as hot & cold drinks, cakes, etc, the café serves light lunches, such as soup or pasta, every Wed, with other meals on request. **£–££££**
🍷 **Albatross Bar**  Prince Philip Hall; ⏱ Oct–Mar

18.30–21.30 Mon–Sat, noon–15.00 Sun; Apr–Sep 18.00–21.00 Mon–Sat, 13.00–16.00 Sun. With a comfortable lounge area, & a separate games room for pool & darts, the Albatross has a pub-like feel, with alcoholic & soft drinks, & light refreshments such as sandwiches, burgers & cake. **£**

**SHOPPING**  The self-service **Island Store** stocks a range of groceries, clothing and household goods. Tristan rock lobster, either raw or cooked, is available only from the factory (📞 *+44 (0)20 3014 5008*).

**Crafts**  Top among the island crafts are beautiful hand-knitted jerseys, marketed under the brand name 37 Degrees South. Most are made from island wool in natural shades of cream, grey and brown that the women have carded and spun by hand. There are hats and socks, too, and if you fancy knitting your own, you can also buy the wool. Knitted items apart, model wooden longboats are much sought after, alongside more prosaic items from keyrings and notebooks to tea towels and shopping bags.

Two excellent sources of crafts in the Settlement are the **Handicrafts and Souvenir Shop** (*Post & Tourism Dept;* ⏱ *08.30–15.00 Mon–Thu, 08.30–14.30 Fri; additional times during cruise-ship visits or by prior arrangement; mail order www. tristandc.com/handorderform.php*), and the **Rockhopper Gift Shop** (*Station La;* e *rockhoppergiftshop@gmail.com*). Crafts may also be bought at the Island Store, and in some local homes.

**TOILETS**  Public toilets are located adjacent to the café, in Prince Philip Hall, and on the ground floor below the council chamber in the Administration Building.

## WHAT TO SEE AND DO

**Churches**  Tristan's two churches are long, low, white-painted buildings, similar in construction to many an island home. The Anglican church, **St Mary's** (*services 08.00 Sun; 10.00 Wed*), was built in the 1920s. Inside are several inter-denominational features and a number of brass memorial tablets, alongside items such as wood and a bell drawn from shipwrecks – and a large portrait of Queen Victoria on the wall. The Catholic church of **St Joseph** (*services 09.00 Sun, occasional mass 17.00 Wed*) has a beautifully serene stained-glass window depicting a Tristan longboat that is well worth a visit in its own right.

Three **cemeteries** chart the social history of the islands. In the first you'll find the grave of William Glass, founder of the Settlement, who died in 1853; the second is the resting place of Agnes Rogers, a Roman Catholic South African of Irish extraction who founded St Joseph's Church. And in all you'll find a succession of the seven original island family names: Glass, Green, Hagan, Lavarello, Repetto, Rogers and Swain.

**Administration Building**  Housing the administrator's office, the treasury and the council chamber, this is the only two-storey building on the island. In the council chamber you'll find photographs of past councillors, as well as some of the island archives.

**Museum** (*Post Office & Tourism Dept;* ⊕ *08.30–14.30 Mon–Thu, 08.30–13.00 Fri; free*) Displays at this small museum range from the discovery and settlement of the island, through island families and their home life over the intervening years, to shipwrecks, sealing and whaling.

**Traditional Thatched House Museum** (⊕ *hours flexible; £3*) Set on a lush hillside just above the Settlement, the new museum – opened in 2012 – is a replica of the traditional home on Tristan. It was built entirely by community workers, from the thick stone walls and wooden floor to the shaggy thatched roof, all within a compound bounded by sturdy dry-stone walls. Inside, rustic furniture, a simple table setting and an open hearth beneath a portrait of HM Queen Elizabeth II are set up as remembered from their childhood by older members of the team.

To enter fully into the spirit of the place, two people can book to stay at the museum overnight (*£100/night*) – though it's a far cry from the blockbuster movie, *Night at the Museum*! Here, with sleeping bags, candles and a traditional Tristan cooked meal, it's all quite simple, and the optimum way to get a feel for the 'old' Tristan ways.

## THE OUTER ISLANDS *with Julian Fitter*

**NIGHTINGALE ISLAND** Although considerably smaller than the neighbouring Inaccessible Island, Nightingale is the most frequently visited of the outer islands. It was first named Gebroocken (Broken) Island by the Dutch Nachtglas expedition in 1656, and renamed Nightingale Island in 1760 by the English Captain Gamaliel.

Nightingale has a very steep rocky coast with no beaches, so traditionally Tristan islanders approached the island in light-framed longboats, which could be hauled to safety onto the rocks above the waterline. In the past they have visited to collect spare penguin eggs, guano, and the eggs and mature chicks of the great shearwater, rendering the seabirds down to produce a distinctive cooking fat. Today's hunters make the journey in more modern craft, and confine their hunt to selected young shearwaters, rather than their eggs. Over the years, a number of small huts were built on Nightingale for shelter and storage, but many were destroyed by the 2001 hurricane and have not been totally replaced.

**Geography** At 18 million years, Nightingale is by far the oldest and the most heavily eroded island of the Tristan group, resulting in the most varied topography. Lying some 24 miles (38km) to the southwest of Tristan, it is just 1½ miles (2.5km) long and just under a mile (1.5km) wide, with a high point of 1,197ft (365m) above sea level. The coast is rugged and consists largely of cliffs. There are two smaller offshore islands: Stoltenhoff and Middle.

### Natural history
**Vegetation** Nightingale is largely covered with a tall, coarse, tussock grass (*Spartina arundinacea*), which grows up to 10ft (3m) in height, and makes excellent cover for the large colonies of seabirds found on the island. The only other significant vegetation is the island tree (*Phylica arborea*). There are a number of groves or woods of this low, often spreading tree, on the island. The clearance of alien species such as New Zealand flax (*Phormium tenax*) both here and on Inaccessible Island, is ongoing.

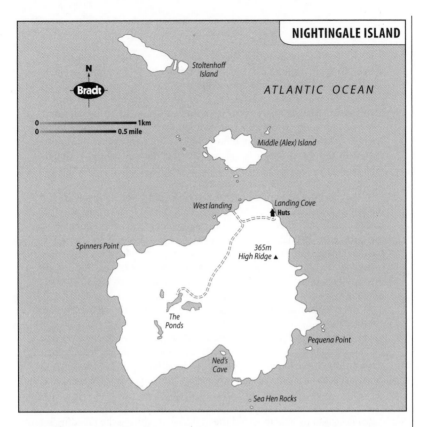

ATLANTIC OCEAN

Stoltenhoff Island

0 — 1km
0 — 0.5 mile

Middle (Alex) Island

West landing    Landing Cove
                Huts

Spinners Point

365m
High Ridge ▲

The Ponds

Pequena Point

Ned's Cave

Sea Hen Rocks

**Seabirds** In the centre of the island, reached by a broad path cut through the tussock, are four ponds. *Phylica* woods line the path and around the ponds are colonies of **Atlantic yellow-nosed albatross** (*Thalassarche chlororhynchus*). You will also find nesting **Tristan skuas** (*Catharacta antarctica hamiltoni*) on the path, each nest surrounded by carcases of **broad-billed prions** (*Pachyptila vittata*), which nest there in their thousands. Its bill is similar to that of a duck; inside are bits like velcro that help it to strain plankton.

Other seabirds that breed on Nightingale include the **northern rockhopper penguin** (*Eudyptes moseleyi*), which has colonies close to the landing area and whose antics are a constant source of pleasure and amazement; the **great shearwater** (*Puffinus gravis*), the **Atlantic petrel** (*Pteradroma incerta*), which is a winter breeder, and the diminutive **common diving petrel** (*Pelecanoides urinatrix*), a bird that prefers to be under the water and which seems to have real trouble becoming airborne, so short are its wings. At least two **storm petrels** also nest there. Virtually all petrels and shearwaters come to the nest burrows at night and can often be seen congregating offshore towards dusk.

On the cliffs around the island, you will find small colonies of **Antarctic tern** (*Sterna vittata*) and **sooty albatross** (*Phoebetria fusca*). The latter is also found on some inland cliffs.

Once ashore, look for the grooves cut into the rocks by the toes of the rockhopper penguins. Further inland, on many of the isolated rocks, you will see similar grooves cut into the rock over millennia by the toes of countless great shearwaters. If you are

Visiting Tristan da Cunha    THE OUTER ISLANDS    9

Environmental disaster hit Nightingale Island early on the morning of 16 March 2011, when the 75,300-tonne bulk carrier MS *Oliva*, *en route* between São Paulo and Singapore, ran aground at the rocky promontory of Spinners Point. As the ship began to break up, 1,500 tonnes of fuel oil leaked from its hold, spreading a deadly film of oil over a radius of some eight miles out to sea.

It was not long before the first northern rockhopper penguins to be affected became a black tide of misery, as wave upon wave of birds became coated in the thick, tarry mess. March falls at the end of the penguins' breeding cycle, so most were already underweight and ill-prepared for any further stress. The impact was devastating.

Within days the authorities had the first of the distressed penguins aboard the fishing vessel MV *Edinburgh*, destined for hastily assembled rehabilitation facilities on Tristan. Here, staffed by Tristan islanders and environmentalists, the birds were cleaned, hand fed on strips of raw fish and transferred to the swimming pool to preen themselves. Only when their plumage was considered to be waterproof again were they ready for release. Yet despite the very best efforts of all concerned, only about 10% of the 3,718 birds brought to the centre were returned to the sea.

As if this weren't enough, the impact on Tristan's fisheries was equally dire. Already affected by oil pollution, they also had to contend with the *Oliva*'s cargo: 65,000 tonnes of soya beans. Soya beans that caught on the lobster traps, and spread across the seabed, their rotting mass a potential for havoc within the food chain. As a result, the Nightingale fishery was closed for the 2011–12 season, and quotas reduced for Inaccessible, but normal practice resumed the following year.

fortunate enough to be able to spend the night ashore during the breeding season, be prepared for the constant cacophony of tens of thousands of breeding seabirds, and get up early to watch them depart.

**Landbirds** There are only three species of landbirds on Nightingale: the **Tristan thrush** or starchy (*Nesocichla eremita*), which appears to live in family groups and is very curious, often congregating around visitors in a manner reminiscent of mockingbirds in the Galápagos; the **Tristan bunting** (*Nesopiza acunhae*); and **Wilkins' bunting** (*Nesopiza wilkinsi*). Both are endemic sub-species and may, in fact, be distinct species. The Tristan bunting has a small bill and is a generalist feeder whilst the Wilkins' bunting has a larger beak and is a specialist, feeding on fruits of the island tree.

**Getting there and away** Access to Nightingale is sometimes possible from Tristan, and some cruise ships stop here, but as with everything in this region it is strictly 'weather permitting'. A landing has been made and a trail has been cut up to the Ponds to enable visitors to access the interior of this amazing bird island.

All ships wishing to land passengers at Nightingale Island, or to conduct Zodiac trips around Nightingale or Inaccessible, must first call at Tristan to obtain clearance and to pick up at least one local guide (page 173).

**INACCESSIBLE ISLAND** Inaccessible was named by a certain Captain d'Etchevery, who having landed on Tristan and Nightingale aboard the French royal corvette *Etoile du Matin* in 1778, failed to land on this third island.

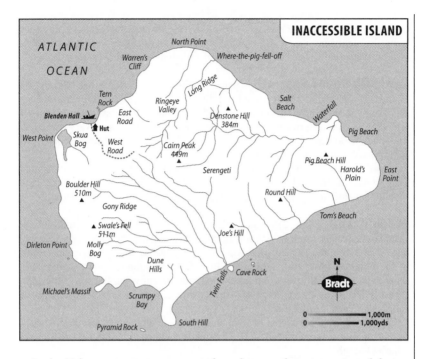

In the 19th century, goats were put ashore, but were later exterminated during an attempt to settle on the island by the German Stoltenhoff brothers in 1871–73. (The brothers left their mark on one of Nightingale's satellite islands, now known as Stoltenhoff Island.) Over 60 years later, a plan to establish a farm colony at Salt Beach on the west coast in 1937–8 failed after poor potato yields. And while the island was frequently visited by Tristan islanders in the early 20th century to hunt seabirds and gather eggs, the very tricky access up fringing cliffs, dense with tussock grass, made movement difficult as the island lived up to its name!

**Geography** Inaccessible Island is an extinct shield volcano, some six million years old, lying 28 miles (45km) to the west of Tristan. Measuring about three miles (5km) from east to west and a maximum of 2.5 miles (4km) north to south, it's the third-largest island in the Tristan archipelago, and rises to the summit, Swales Fell, at 1,677ft (511m) above sea level. (The summit was named after Michael Swales, leader of the Denstone Expedition to Inaccessible in 1982–83 and now life-president and chairman of the Tristan da Cunha Association.)

**Natural history** The island is a high plateau surrounded by steep cliffs up to 300m high. Vegetation on the plateau is largely *Phylica* woodland to the east and dwarf tree fern (*Blechnum palmiforme*) heath in the west.

Inaccessible is home to the world's smallest flightless bird, the **Inaccessible rail** (*Altantisia rogersi*), as well as one of the world's largest flying birds, the **Tristan albatross** (*Diomedea dabbenena*), although only up to two or three pairs nest there. Other bird species of interest are the **Atlantic yellow-nosed albatross** (*Thalassarche chlororhynchus*) and the **sooty albatross** (*Phoebetria fusca*). Inaccessible is also home to thousands of other petrels, especially great shearwater (*Puffinus gravis*), and the endemic and clearly identifiable **spectacled petrel** or **ringeye** (*Procellaria* *conspicillata*). Around the coasts, there are colonies of **northern rockhopper penguin** (*Eudyptes moseleyi*), especially along the northwest coast, as well as **southern fur seal** (*Arctocephalus tropicalis*) and **elephant seal** (*Mirounga leonine*).

**Getting there and away** Although marginally closer to Tristan than Nightingale Island, Inaccessible was aptly named. Landing is always tricky and often impossible, and access to the plateau is difficult. In addition, Inaccessible has been designated a UNESCO World Heritage Site and a nature reserve, and visits are very restricted. Those few who are granted permission to visit by the Conservation Department must be accompanied by a guide.

Expedition groups with such permission may be allowed to use the hut at Blenden Hall, which was erected by the Denstone Expedition and has since been refurbished. The hut lies close to the only road to provide safe access to the interior plateau.

**GOUGH ISLAND** Some 218 miles (350km) south-southeast of Tristan, Gough Island defies categorisation. A World Heritage Site, in partnership with Inaccessible Island, it is remote, rugged, wet, windswept and yet at the same latitude south of the Equator as Madrid, Sardinia or Philadelphia in the northern hemisphere. Its climate is mild and very humid, and yet truly warm when the sun comes out. As with Tristan, it creates its own weather, with clear days on the highest point, Edinburgh Peak, being rare.

Gough was first discovered in 1505 and was originally named Gonzalo Alvarez by Portuguese seamen, but in 1731 its name was changed by the British Captain Charles Gough.

Following a Cambridge University expedition to Gough Island in 1955–56, the South African authorities established a permanent meteorological station here, paving the way for a mutually beneficial relationship whereby, in return for the leased land, the South African government provides subsidised passenger berths and cargo space on the annual SA *Agulhas II* relief voyage from Cape Town to Gough via Tristan da Cunha.

**Geography** The second-largest island in the Tristan group, Gough is an extinct volcanic island some six million years old. From north to south it extends to just eight miles (13km); from east to west a mere three miles (5km) at most; and from sea level to its summit, Edinburgh Peak, is 2,985ft (910m). Gough is the wettest, coldest and most rugged island of the Tristan group, with many areas remaining only partly explored.

Running along the spine of the island, from South Peak in the southeast to Triple Peak in the north, is a high and very windy ridge. To the east of this the land falls away sharply in a series of dramatic valleys, the Glens. To the west the land is more gentle with the wide boggy plains of Gony Dale and Albatross Plain. Virtually the whole of the coastline is formed by often abrupt cliffs except where the Glens cut through them. These cliffs are noted for their striking and varied waterfalls; one of them near Gaggins Point on the west coast emerges from halfway down the cliff.

The most dramatic features of the Gough landscape are the volcanic dykes and trachyte plugs. The former often run for several kilometres in variable states of erosion, some like gigantic dry-stone walls. The largest and most impressive of the trachyte plugs is the Hag's Tooth, which rises to just under 2,300ft (700m) above the Glens.

### Natural history
*Flora* The vegetation is dominated by grasses, mosses and ferns. Much of the island is covered in coarse tussock grass with several extensive bogs and mires.

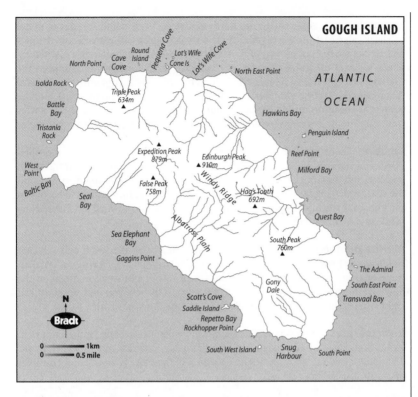

GOUGH ISLAND

Isolda Rock
North Point
Cave
Cove
Round
Island
Cove
Peguena Cove
Lot's Wife
Cone Is
Lot's Wife Cove
North East Point
ATLANTIC
OCEAN
Battle
Bay
Tristania
Rock
Triple Peak
634m ▲
Hawkins Bay
Penguin Island
West
Point
Baltic Bay
Expedition Peak
879m ▲
Edinburgh Peak
▲ 910m
Windy Ridge
Reef Point
Milford Bay
False Peak
758m ▲
Hag's Tooth
692m ▲
Seal
Bay
Albatross Plain
Quest Bay
Sea Elephant
Bay
Gaggins Point
South Peak
760m ▲
The Admiral
South East Point
Scott's Cove
Saddle Island
Repetto Bay
Rockhopper Point
Gony
Dale
Transvaal Bay
N
Bradt
South West Island
Snug
Harbour
South Point
0 ▬▬▬ 1km
0 ▬▬▬ 0.5 mile

Above 600m the vegetation changes to fellfield, or wind desert, dominated by mosses, the **dwarf shrub** (*Empetrum rubrum*) and sedges. In the more sheltered lower areas in the Glens and in the south, the vegetation is a combination of the **island tree** (*Phylica arborea*), the **dwarf tree fern** (*Blechnum palmiforme*) and the tussock grass (*Parodiochloa flabellate*). Around the coast the dominant vegetation is the **tall tussock grass** (*Spartina arundinacea*).The only other tree is a small stand of **kowhai**, pronounced 'cofae' (*Sophora microphylla*), in Sophora Glen, a plant otherwise found only in New Zealand and southern Chile.

**Birds** Gough is one of the most important seabird islands in the world. The dominant fauna are seabirds, with 19 breeding species, against just two landbirds. Most prominent are three species of **albatross:** the huge Tristan albatross (*Diomedea dabbenena*), the smaller Atlantic yellow-nosed (*Thalassarche chlororhynchus*) and the graceful sooty albatross (*Phoebetria fusca*). Virtually the entire population of the Tristan albatross breeds on Gough, preferring the open windswept grasslands of the west, while the Atlantic yellow-nosed breeds in more sheltered areas, particularly among the *Phylica* and *Blechnum* 'forests' in the south. The sooty nests on cliffs and ledges, both coastal and inland. During the breeding season the air is rich with their haunting 'Peeeoooo' call, from which they derive their local name of peoo, and with the sight of their graceful aerial courtship.

**Other seabirds** These include the **southern giant petrel** (*Macronectes giganteus*), which breeds in two colonies in the west, its most northerly breeding location. The **northern rockhopper penguin** (*Eudyptes moseleyi*) is found in colonies all around the coast, especially to the north and west. Twelve other species of petrel or shearwater nest on the islands. Their burrows make walking difficult at times and attract a large population of **Tristan skuas** (*Catharacta antarctica hamiltoni*). Huge flocks of the **great shearwater** (*Puffinus gravis*) congregate offshore in the evening – a sight not to be missed. Two members of the tern family, the graceful **Antarctic tern** (*Sterna vittata tristanensis*), which breeds around the coast, and the **brown** or **common noddy** (*Anous stolidus*), which nests in the island tree and is more commonly associated with tropical climes, complete the seabird cornucopia.

**Landbirds** There are only two landbirds, both endemic: the Gough moorhen (*Gallinula comeri*), which is widespread in the more vegetated areas in the south and east, and the Gough bunting (*Rowettia goughensis*), which is found only around the coast and at higher altitudes. The bunting's restricted range is most likely due to the impact of the introduced house mouse (*Mus musculus*), which has become the most serious conservation issue on Gough.

***Marine mammals*** Around the coasts, particularly on the south and east, are significant colonies of **subantarctic fur seal** (*Arctocephalus tropicalis*) – more than three-quarters of the world's population (page 160) – and small numbers of the huge **southern elephant seal** (*Mirounga leonina*). Offshore you may see **southern right whales** (*Eubalaena glacialis australis*) or **orca** (*Orcinus orca*).

***Invertebrates*** Being very isolated and windy, the invertebrate fauna is not rich, and is dominated by insects, including a flightless moth and a flightless crane fly. They provide, along with species on Tristan and the other islands, good examples of adaptive radiation.

**Conservation** The chief threat to the wildlife of Gough is from introduced species, hence the severe restriction on landing there. The house mouse, which is larger here than anywhere else, has developed the habit of attacking and eating alive the chicks of the Tristan albatross and Atlantic petrel. The mice are thought to pose a significant threat to the albatross, which is already classified as endangered due to its small numbers and very limited breeding range. The chicks appear to have no defence mechanism against the mice, which gang up and chew on their legs and wings. Assessment by the RSPB to clear the island of mice has been in hand for several years. While the problems involved in such a campaign are considerable, mice have successfully been eradicated from Australia's Macquarie Island, which is a similar scale, so there is a precedent.

Other conservation projects on Gough include clearance of the procumbent pearlwort (*Sagina procumbens*).

**Getting there and away** Like Inaccessible, Gough Island is off-limits to most visitors, unless they have permission from the Conservation Department, in which case they must be accompanied by a local guide.

# 10

# 24 Hours in Cape Town

*Telephone code +27 (0)21*

Towering above the bay, Table Mountain is seen at its best from the sea – which is good news for passengers on the RMS *St Helena* and for Tristan da Cunha, who are strongly recommended to stay at least one night in Cape Town at the end of their trip. Given the five nights at sea, it could feel like just another delaying tactic, but for one thing – Cape Town consistently tops the lists of the best cities in the world to visit.

But take note – it's a big, buzzing city with loads of options. This just skims the surface, so make sure your first port of call is **Cape Town Tourism** (*The Pinnacle Bldg, cnr Burg & Castle sts;* m *086 132 2223;* e *info@capetown.travel; www. capetown.travel*), who can help with pretty much anything city-related, including accommodation, restaurants, transport and tours.

## GETTING THERE AND AWAY

**BY AIR** The only direct flights to Cape Town from the UK are with **British Airways** (*www.britishairways.com*), who have one overnight flight a day, with a second on Thursdays and Saturdays. Most of the major airlines, including **South African Airways** (*www.flysaa.com*) and **Virgin** (*www.virgin-atlantic.com*) have long-haul connections with Johannesburg, from where there are regular internal flights to Cape Town, including with BA and SAA.

**Airport transfers** For Cape Town International Airport, about 13 miles (20km) from the city centre, a taxi will set you back around R250 (£15) – do agree the fare up front. Alternatively, take a taxi to the Civic Centre in the Central Business District (CBD), where you can link up with the MyCiTi airport shuttle (*http:// myciti.org.za;* ⊕ *every 20mins 05.10–22.00; R69/£4*).

**FROM THE PORT** (*For information on the RMS* St Helena *& ships to Tristan da Cunha, see pages 55–7 & 168–70*) Most hotels on the Victoria & Alfred Waterfront will meet their guests off the ships and transfer them to the hotel for a small fee; for the others, you'll need to get a taxi. From the harbour, a taxi to the Mount Nelson Hotel/Kloof Street should cost about R70 (£4). To pre-book a transfer, contact the tourist office or try Julian and Charmaine Swain (⟨ *531 2907;* e *swain@iafrica.com*).

## GETTING AROUND

How do you do justice to the city that seems to be everybody's favourite in just 24 hours? Well the good news is that you can – with a little help.

If budget's no option, then a **private guide** (available through the tourist board) could be the answer. Alternatively, swallow any prejudices you may have and take the **tourist bus**. City Sightseeing Red Bus (*www.citysightseeing.co.za/capeTown.*

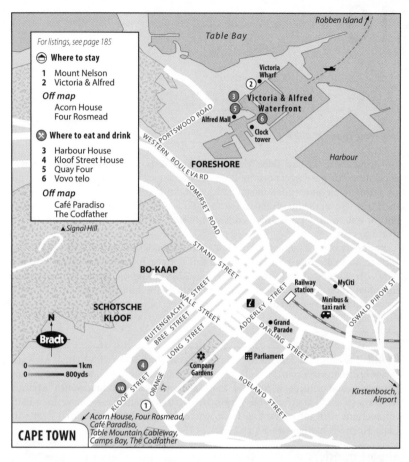

For listings, see page 185

🛏 **Where to stay**

1  Mount Nelson
2  Victoria & Alfred

*Off map*
   Acorn House
   Four Rosmead

✖ **Where to eat and drink**

3  Harbour House
4  Kloof Street House
5  Quay Four
6  Vovo telo

*Off map*
   Café Paradiso
   The Codfather

▲ *Signal Hill*

Robben Island
*Table Bay*
Victoria Wharf
**Victoria & Alfred Waterfront**
Alfred Mall
Clock tower
**FORESHORE**
*Harbour*
WESTERN BOULEVARD
WESTPORTSWOOD ROAD
SOMERSET ROAD
STRAND STREET
**BO-KAAP**
**SCHOTSCHE KLOOF**

N
0 ——— 1km
0 ——— 800yds
BUITENGRACHT STREET
WALE STREET
BREE STREET
LONG STREET
ADDERLEY STREET
DARLING STREET
Railway station
MyCiti
Minibus & taxi rank
OSWALD PIROW ST
Grand Parade
Parliament
KLOOF STREET
ORANGE ST
Company Gardens
ROELAND STREET
Kirstenbosch, Airport
✈ *Acorn House, Four Rosmead, Café Paradiso, Table Mountain Cableway, Camps Bay, The Codfather*
**CAPE TOWN**

*php*) operates two hop-on, hop-off bus routes between 09.00 and 17.00 daily. The red route (*every 15mins, tour about 2hrs inc downtown extension; R150pp*), takes in the V&A Waterfront (also the Robben Island ferry terminus), Table Mountain cableway station and downtown Cape Town. The longer blue route (*every 20mins, tour about 3hrs inc wine tour; R150pp*) also covers the V&A, plus Kirstenbosch Gardens, Constantia Nek, Hout Bay and Camps Bay. You can also buy a two-day ticket taking in these and other add-ons for R270 per person.

For greater flexibility, summon a **taxi** (R9/km; Waterfront to Table Mountain about R125) – they're clearly marked on the streets – or take the **MyCiTi bus**. For this, you'll need a MyConnect bus card (R35), preloaded with the fare (as a guide, the 15-minute ride from the V&A Waterfront to Kloof Street/the Mount Nelson is about R6.50 one way). For details, contact the tourist office.

🏠 WHERE TO STAY *Map, above*

Cape Town has literally hundreds of hotels, but to set you in the right direction, the following will take you from top-drawer luxury to a simple but personal B&B; from the buzz of the V&A Waterfront to relatively quiet residential streets or the sanctuary of a private estate.

🏠 **Mount Nelson** (133 rooms, 65 suites) 76 Orange St; 📞 483 1000; www.belmond.com/mount-nelson-hotel-cape-town. A winning combination of luxury, space & excellent service, in tranquil grounds with heated outdoor pool. **£££££**

🏠 **Victoria & Alfred Hotel** (68 rooms, 26 'lofts') V&A Waterfront; 📞 UK 020 3564 2773; http://victoria-and-alfred.hotel-rv.com. Smart & stylish hotel with an unbeatable waterfront location & stunning views to Table Mountain. **££££–£££££**

🏠 **Four Rosmead** (8 rooms) 4 Rosmead Av; 📞 480 3810; www.fourrosmead.com. Contemporary style blends into traditional surroundings at this intimate boutique hotel, where all the artwork is for sale. **££–£££**

🏠 **Acorn House** (9 rooms, 1 cottage) 1 Montrose Av; 📞 461 1782; www.acornhouse.co.za. Personal & friendly guesthouse dating back to 1904, close to Table Mountain. **£**

## ✖ WHERE TO EAT AND DRINK *Map, opposite*

Most of Cape Town's hotels have good restaurants, but for something more personal, here are a few hints. At lunchtime, consider fish and chips with a view at Camps Bay, or – more expensive – the V&A Waterfront. The Mount Nelson (above) is to afternoon tea what Raffles is to the Singapore sling: a must! In the evenings, if you can tear yourself away from the water, join the edgy set for street food in Bree Street, or make for the slightly classier Kloof Street, where eateries come in all shapes and sizes, and the atmosphere is buzzing. Reservations are recommended, especially at weekends. Credit cards are accepted pretty well everywhere, and there are plenty of ATMs in strategic locations such as Kloof Street and at the Waterfront.

✖ **The Codfather** Camps Bay; 📞 438 0782/3; www.codfather.co.za. Not cheap (prices geared to weight of fish) but a great seafood experience. **£££–£££££**

✖ **Harbour House** V&A Waterfront; 📞 418 4744; www.harbourhouse.co.za. Classy spot with serious food: both traditional & from a sushi bar. **££–£££££**

✖ **Kloof Street House** 30 Kloof St; 📞 423 4413; www.kloofstreethouse.co.za. A little gem with a varied, hearty menu & great atmosphere.

**££–££££**

✖ **Café Paradiso** 110 Kloof St; 📞 423 8653; www.cafeparadiso.co.za. Well-priced & good food. **££–£££**

✖ **Quay Four** V&A Waterfront; www.quay4.co.za. An easy-going spot to watch the world go by. Come for sundowners, then tuck into seafood, steak or burgers. Occasional live music. **£–£££**

✖ **Vovo telo** V&A Waterfront & 60A Kloof St; www.vovotelo.co.za. Platters & artisan paninis in shabby-chic surroundings. Wi-Fi. **£–££**

## WHAT TO SEE AND DO IN 24 HOURS

**V&A WATERFRONT** The throbbing heart of Cape Town combines a colourful marina with brightly lit shopping malls and an apparently 24-hour restaurant scene. By all means stay somewhere more tranquil, but do make time to stroll along the quays and take in the atmosphere.

**ROBBEN ISLAND MUSEUM** (*www.robben-island.org.za; tours from V&A Waterfront ⏰ 09.00–15.00 daily (weather permitting); R280/150 adult/child; booking essential; allow at least 3½hrs*) Nelson Mandela's prison for 27 years makes a compelling and sometimes chilling half-day excursion that belies the holiday atmosphere on the ferry. The 45-minute bus tour of the island takes in its history as a leper colony, mental institution and World War II defence outpost as well as its infamy as a political prison. Your guide around the prison itself will be an ex-prisoner, who

**10**

makes the facts feel all too real. Sightings of terns, seals and African penguins from the boat are an uplifting bonus.

**TABLE MOUNTAIN CABLEWAY** (*www.tablemountain.net*; ◷ *08.00 daily, last car 18.00–20.30, but closed in high winds; R225/110 return adult/child; book ahead to avoid the queues*) The slowly rotating cable cars up Table Mountain whisk you to the top in minutes, to a cooler, windswept plateau at 3,573ft (1,089m) with spectacular coastal views through the clouds. There are free guided walks on the hour during the day, or watch with drink in hand as the sun goes down.

**CAMPS BAY** The beautiful crescent of pure white sand at Camps Bay is certainly inviting, but only the intrepid brave seas that rarely top 60°F (15°C). Come instead for the backdrop of the 12 Apostles, the view, and a relaxing lunch. This is a place to see and be seen!

**KIRSTENBOSCH NATIONAL BOTANICAL GARDENS** (*www.sanbi.org/gardens/ kirstenbosch*; ◷ *Sep–Mar 08.00–19.00 daily, Apr–Aug 08.00–18.00 daily; R50/ R10 adult/child; specialist guide from www.meetusinafrica.co.za*) The setting alone justifies the journey to Kirstenbosch, nestled against the slopes of Table Mountain with an undulating series of gardens that take in proteas, ericas, fynbos and much more. See the yellow *Strelitzia* bred in honour of Nelson Mandela, or a baobab in a glasshouse, and don't miss the Boomslang canopy walkway. Unstructured nature trails make the gardens fun for children, and in summer, regular sunset concerts add an extra dimension.

## FOLLOW BRADT

For the latest news, special offers and competitions, subscribe to the Bradt newsletter via the website www.bradtguides.com and follow Bradt on:

f www.facebook.com/BradtTravelGuides
🐦 @BradtGuides
📷 @bradtguides
📌 www.pinterest.com/bradtguides

# Appendix 1

Many of the following titles can be supplied by Ian Mathieson (*Miles Apart, Callender Hse, 90 Callender Lane, Ramsbottom, Lancs BL0 9DU, UK;* ✆ *01706 826467;* e *imathieson2000@yahoo. co.uk; www.sthelena.se/miles*), who has a wide selection of books on St Helena, Ascension and Tristan da Cunha.

## ST HELENA
## Books

***General history*** The first full history of the island was published in 1808 by the then government secretary, Thomas Brooke, as *A History of the Island of St Helena From Its Discovery By The Portuguese to the Year 1806*. A second edition, published in 1824, extended the coverage to 1823 and included the period of Napoleon's captivity. This work remained the standard reference for the next 100 years although some notable additions were produced during the period.

The island-born Governor Hudson Janisch appreciated the value of the government archives and published his *Extracts from the St Helena Records and Chronicles of Cape Commanders* in 1885. A revised second edition was published in 1908 and this was subsequently reprinted by W A Thorpe and Sons in 1981. Melliss's *St Helena* (page 189) also included a good historical section.

E L Jackson's *St Helena* appeared in 1903 and is described by Alan Day as 'one of the corner stones of St Helena historiography ... although its seven chronological and thematic chapters sometimes lack cohesion'. Its lack of index diminishes its value as a reference but it is an interesting and well-illustrated read.

It took another government secretary, G C Kitching, to lay the foundations for an updated history of St Helena in the 1930s. Although his *Handbook and Gazetteer of the Island of St Helena Including a Short History of the Island Under the Crown 1834–1902* was never published, Kitching effectively documented the remainder of the 19th century following on from Brooke, and provided inspiration and guidance for what remains the standard reference in English, Philip Gosse's *St Helena 1502–1938* (see below).

Brandreth H R and Walpole E *A Precarious Livelihood. St Helena 1834: East Indian Company Outpost to Crown Colony: The Commissioners of Inquiry Report* Society of the Friends of St Helena, 2014. Transcribed and edited by Colin Fox and Edward Baldwin.

Cannan, Edward *Churches of the South Atlantic 1502–1991*, 1992

Chevallier, Bernard, Dancoisne-Martineau, Michel and Lentz, Thierry *Sainte-Hélène: Île de Mémoire* Fayard, Paris, 2005. Published in French, this huge, comprehensive and magnificently illustrated book is by far the most significant publication on St Helena's history in recent years. Mainly concerned with the captivity of Napoleon, it also covers other aspects of the island's history.

Evans, Dorothy *Schooling in the South Atlantic 1661–1992*, 1994

Field, Margaret *The History of Plantation House – St Helena* Patten Press, Penzance, 1998. A good account of one of the island's main buildings.

Fox, Colin *The Bennett Letters: a 19th-century Family in St Helena, England and the Cape* Choir Press, UK, 2006. An interesting account of life on the island in the mid 19th century.

Gosse, Philip *St Helena 1502–1938* Cassell, 1938, republished Anthony Nelson, 1990. The standard historical reference on St Helena to be published in English, now with a new introduction by island historian Trevor Hearl.

Hearl, Trevor W, ed Alexander Schulenburg *St Helena Britannica: studies in South Atlantic Island history* Friends of St Helena, 2013. The most important historical book to appear in recent years covers 30 of Trevor Hearl's essays, covering a time span between the 17th and mid 20th centuries, with the greatest emphasis on the 19th century. Topics range from horse racing, the early telegraph system, the photography of John Isaac Lilley and Baptism to penal reform, East Indiamen and insects.

Pearson, A, Jeffs B, Witkin, A, and MacQuarrie, H *Infernal Traffic: Excavation of a Liberated African Graveyard in Rupert's Valley, St Helena* 2011. Well illustrated academic account

Royle, Stephen *The Company's Island: St Helena, Company Colonies and the Colonial Endeavour* I B Tauris, 2007. This important publication covers the East India Company's attempts to create a society on an uninhabited island. Far from settling in 'love and amity', a repressive and turbulent regime ensued. The civilian population rebelled, the garrison mutinied, and a slave rebellion was savagely punished.

Smallman, David *Quincentenary*, 2003. Written by an ex-governor of St Helena, this includes chapters on the island under the East India Company and on the current political and managerial system.

Teale, Percy and Gill, Robin *St Helena 500: A Chronological History of the Island*, 1999.

Wild, Antony *Coffee: A Dark History* Norton & Co, USA, 2013. The story behind St Helena's coffee industry.

**Napoleon**  There are some fascinating insights into Napoleon's exile in St Helena in the Hudson Lowe Papers (*Add MSS 20115–20229*) in the British Library in London. These documents, some in French, are written in original hand, and cover an enormous field of interest including intelligence reports, and letters from many of Napoleon's contemporaries on St Helena and in Europe.

On a purely domestic note, there are lists of provisions for Longwood House (including a very extensive wine list); a list of the ships that visited St Helena (with names of passengers); and catalogues of the furniture in Longwood House at the time of Napoleon's death and of the 1,847 books in his library.

The literature examining Napoleon's captivity on St Helena is vast, though anyone seriously interested in Napoleon should take a look at *Sainte-Hélène: Île de Mémoire* by Chevallier, Dancoisne-Martineau and Lentz (see *History* above). Although many of the published works contain good incidental descriptions and illustrations of the island, the majority are derived from principal works written by eyewitnesses. Of the contemporary accounts, Barry O'Meara's *Napoleon in Exile,* published in various editions between 1822 and 1880, is probably the most enjoyable.

Benhamou, Albert *Inside Longwood: Barry O'Meara's Clandestine Letters* Albert Benhamou Publishing, 2012. Casts a new light on O'Meara's role as Napoleon's doctor and seeks to restore his much-maligned reputation.

Blackburn, Julia *The Emperor's Last Island: A journey to St Helena* Random House, UK, 1993. Based on a visit made by the author in the 1980s, this well-written and entertaining account of Napoleon's six years on St Helena describes the island's strange history, and recounts the stories, myths, and absurdities that surround him.

Brookes, Mabel *St Helena Story* Heinemann, 1960. A very readable account.

Chaplin, Arnold *St Helena Who's Who* London, 1918. Describes both major and minor players in the Napoleonic drama.

Desmond, Gregory *Napoleon's Jailer, Lt Gen Sir Hudson Lowe: A Life* Associated University Presses, London, 1996.

Forshufvud, S *Who Killed Napoleon?* 1962, and Forshufvud, S and Weider, B *Assassination at St Helena Revisited,* 1995. These two books are central to understanding the view that Napoleon was poisoned by a combination of arsenic and chamomile.

Giles, Frank *Napoleon Bonaparte, England's Prisoner: The Emperor in Exile 1816–1821* Constable & Robinson, London, 2001

Howard, Martin *Napoleon's Poisoned Chalice: the Emperor and his doctors on St Helena* History Press, 2009. A balanced account of Napoleon's medics on St Helena.

Kaufmann, John-Paul *The Black Room at Longwood: Napoleon's Exile on St Helena,* 1999. This account by a former Lebanese hostage provides an interesting perspective on the mind of a captive.

Levy, Martin *Napoleon in Exile: The Houses and Furniture Supplied by the British Government for the Emperor and his Entourage on St Helena* The Furniture History Society, Leeds, 1998.

Martineau, Gilbert *Napoleon's St Helena* 1968, and *Napoleon's Last Journey* 1976. Both provide good introductions to the facts, if a somewhat out-of-date interpretation.

O'Connor, Hubert *The Emperor and the Irishman* A & A Farmar, 2008. Perspectives on Dr O'Meara from his Irish roots.

Richardson, Robert *The Apocalypse of Napoleon Bonaparte: His Last Years from Waterloo to St Helena: A Medical Biography* Quiller Press, 2009. Medical text promoting the idea that Napoleon's death was caused not by cancer but by a gastric ulcer, unknown to medical science in 1821.

Unwin, Brian *Terrible Exile* I B Tauris, 2010. A good and very readable account of Napoleon's captivity, from start to finish, an approach which few other authors have attempted.

**Natural history** The first descriptions of St Helena's flora were provided by the early navigators such as Linschoten and Cavendish, and their accounts are available in reprinted form as part of much larger works.

During the 19th century, the awareness of St Helena's unique flora and fauna gradually increased. Early writings included observations by Joseph Banks, the naturalist on Cook's first voyage; William Burchell; and Alexander Beatson's *Tracts Relative to the Island of St Helena* (1816), which alongside an account of new agricultural methods introduced to the island covered much about the natural history, including William Roxburgh's listing of plants.

In 1875, John Charles Melliss published *St Helena a Physical, Historical and Topographical Description of the Island,* covering the island's unique flora and fauna in great detail, with a dazzling array of colour prints. The book remained a standard reference work for over 100 years until it was superseded in 2000 by Ashmole and Cronk's landmark publications (see below).

Aptroot, A and Darlow, Andrew *Lichens of St Helena* Pisces Publications, UK, 2013. Includes all 225 known species, including at least nine endemics, most with full-colour illustrations.

Ashmole, Philip and Myrtle *St Helena and Ascension Island: A Natural History* Anthony Nelson, Oswestry, 2000

Baker, Ian *St Helena: One Man's Island* 2004. A thoughtful, personal and exceptionally well-written account of the island from a geological perspective.

Baker, Ian *The Saint Helena Volcanoes: A Guide to the Geology for Visitors and Walkers* Southern Cross Publishers, Cape Town, 2010. Ian Baker has the gift of making a difficult subject extremely accessible; esssential reading for those with any interest in the island's geology.

A1

Brown, Judith *Marine Life of St Helena* NatureBureau, 2015. Full-colour field guide, in the same series as Lamdon and Darlow's guide to the plants.

Cronk, Quentin C B *The Endemic Flora of St Helena* Anthony Nelson, Oswestry, 2000.

Edwards, Alasdair *Fish and Fisheries of Saint Helena Island,* 1990

Grove, Richard *Green Imperialism: Colonial Expansion, Tropical Island Edens & The Origins of Environmentalism 1600–1860,* 1995. A scholarly overview of the influence of St Helena's experience on the development of environmental thinking.

Lamdon, Phil and Darlow, Andrew *Flowering Plants & Ferns of St Helena* Pisces Publications, UK, 2013. The must-have guide for anyone with a genuine interest in the island's flora, though it's by no means a handy tome. Covers around 600 species with some 1,600 colour photographs.

McCulloch, Neil *A Guide to the Birds of St Helena and Ascension Island* Sandy, UK, RSPB, 2004. A very readable introduction with good, clear illustrations.

Rowlands, Beau W et al *The Birds of St Helena: An Annotated Checklist* British Ornithologists' Union, Tring, 1998

Weaver, Barry *Guide to the Geology of St Helena,* 1990. A good account of the latest thinking about the formation of St Helena.

Wigginton, Martin J *Mosses & Liverworts of St Helena* Pisces Publications, UK, 2013. Of the 100 species included in this guide, 60 have been newly identified by the author and other specialists since 2005.

**Philately and coins** The first publication on St Helena's stamps was a booklet produced by Fred Melville in 1912. This is still sought after by collectors but the definitive work is by Edward Hibbert.

Hibbert, Edward *St Helena Postal History and Stamps,* 1979

Mabbett, Bernard *St Helena, the Philately of the Camps for the Boer Prisoners of War 1900–1902* 1985

*St Helena & Dependencies: Commonwealth Two Reign Stamp Catalogue* Stanley Gibbons, 1988

Vice, David *The Coinage of British West Africa and St Helena 1684–1958* 1983. The only publication dealing with coins.

### Photographic and illustrative books

Andrews, Chris and Johnston, Peter *St Helena – A Little Souvenir* Chris Andrews Publications, St Helena, 2013. A photographic guide to the island.

Castell, Robin *St Helena,* Robin Castell, 1979. Written and published by the owner of Prince's Lodge and its vast collection of papers and photographs, this features illustrations of many island homes.

Castell, Robin *St Helena: a Photographic Treasury 1856–1947* Robin Castell, 2008. In his latest book, Castell reproduces more than 750 early photos of the island, including the work of John Lilley, Melliss and many others.

Castell, Robin *St Helena Illustrated* Robin Castell, 1998. St Helena has a particularly rich inheritance of 19th-century prints which has yet to be formally studied; this provides a glimpse of what has been produced.

Crallan, Hugh *Island of St Helena: Listing and Preservation of Buildings of Architectural and Historic Interest,* 1997. Offers a more authoritative and well-illustrated account of the island's architecture than Castell, albeit in report format.

St Helena Historical Society and Hansen, Mariam *St Helena: Images of America* Arcadia, 2010

Schulenburg, H and A *St Helena South Atlantic Ocean,* 1997. A large range of black-and-white photographs of mainly architecture and natural heritage.

Tonks, Jon *Empire* 2nd edition, Dewi Lewis, 2014. A photographic appreciation of the British

Overseas Territories of the South Atlantic: St Helena, Ascension, Tristan da Cunha and the Falkland Islands.

Wooltorton, S *Doctor's Thoughts on St Helena* 1988. A long-term and inexpensive favourite, which provides good colour photos with a medical text.

**Guidebooks** The earliest general descriptions of St Helena date from the early 19th century and include *A Description of the Island of St Helena; Containing Observations on its Singular Structure and Formation; An Account of its Climate, Natural History and Inhabitants,* published anonymously in 1805, *A Geographical and Historical Account of the Island of St Helena,* also published anonymously in 1812, and *A Tour Through the Island of St Helena* by Captain John Barnes (1817; reprinted 2007 with a new introduction by Robin Castell).

Napoleon's captivity caused a minor publishing boom for about ten years from 1815. Virtually all works produced during this period were aquatint prints, often by earlier visitors to the island attempting to cash in on the great national interest that was suddenly aroused; the best known are by Bellasis and Pocock (both 1815) and Wathen in 1824. Throughout the 19th century, numerous travellers, mainly on their way back from the East, called at St Helena and provided a descriptive chapter on the island supported by a print or two in works otherwise concerned with India and the Orient. One of the earliest and best of these accounts was in *Viscount George Valentia's Voyages and Travels to India, Ceylon and the Red Sea, Abyssinia and Egypt in 1802–1806,* reprinted in 1994.

The first tourist guide was Benjamin Grant's *A Few Notes on St Helena and Descriptive Guide to which is Added Some Remarks on the Island as a Health Resort* published in 1883. This was followed in about 1900 by a *Souvenir of St Helena* by E L Jackson. This guide was taken up, modified and issued in a variety of forms over the next 40 years by E J Warren. A good description of the island was produced in Findlay's *A Sailing Directory for the Ethiopic or South Atlantic Ocean* in 1874 and this maritime descriptive process has been continued to the present in the *Admiralty Pilot for the South Atlantic.*

More detailed but informal accounts of the island were produced by Oswald Blakeston in *The Isle of St Helena* in 1957 and by Margaret Stewart Taylor in *Ocean Roadhouse* in 1969.

Carter, Laurence and Mathieson, Ian *Exploring St Helena a Walker's Guide,* 1992. The first detailed guide to the island for walkers, now of greatest interest for what can be seen along the way.

Cross, Tony *St Helena Including Ascension and Tristan da Cunha* David and Charles, 1980. The first proper descriptive book of the islands.

Hillman, Sheila and Darlow, Andrew (eds) *A description of the Post Box walks on St Helena* NatureBureau, 2014. The one book that everyone tackling the postbox walks should take with them.

**Scientific expeditions** St Helena has been visited by numerous scientific expeditions, the majority of which have recorded descriptions and illustrations of the island in works principally devoted to other subjects. Halley, Maskelyne, Cook (and Forster), Bligh, J C Ross, Darwin and Hooker are probably the big names with publications generally still in print in some form or other. Two 20th-century Antarctic expeditions include quite detailed accounts of St Helena – the Scottish National Antarctic Expedition and the Quest Expedition, which visited after its leader, Shackleton, had died on South Georgia.

More detailed accounts are provided by some of the less well-known expeditions, such as Prior's *Voyage Along the Eastern Coast of Africa to Mocambique, Johanna and Quiloa to St Helena... 1819,* and Webster's *Narrative of a Voyage to the South Atlantic Ocean in the Years 1828, 29, 30 performed in HM Sloop* Chanticleer, which was reprinted in 1970.

**Sailing and travel literature** As 19th-century sailing-boat travellers gave way to 20th-century yachtsmen, a number of yachting books were spawned with a chapter or two on St Helena. The genre was started by Joshua Slocum, whose *Sailing Alone Around the World* was published in 1900 and included details of a talk given by him on the island. Others travellers passing through who have covered St Helena in their writings have included:

Bain, Kenneth *St Helena The Island, Her People and Their Ship* 1993. An informal travel account.

Green, Lawrence *Islands Time Forgot*, 1962. A collection of the best of this South African writer's prolific island works, into almost all of which he managed to weave references to St Helena or Tristan.

Wilson, Robert *RMS St Helena and the South Atlantic Islands* Whittles, 2006, reprinted by the author, 2014. The original account of the two RMS's serving the island since 1989 has been expanded with additional photographs, and published alongside a companion volume covering the role of the RMS in the Falklands conflict.

Winchester, Simon *Outposts*, 1985

Young, Gavin *Slow Boats Home*, 1985

## Culture

Creative Saint Helena Writing Group (ed) *Speaking Saint: Yarns from the island* 2015. A collection of 23 tales, mainly by island authors.

Dancoisne-Martineau, Michel *St Helena Then and Now as Seen Through the Eyes of Our Children* 2007. Photographs of change on St Helena taken by pupils from Prince Andrew School.

Ladies' Craft Group *What's Cooking on St Helena* 2010. Recipes from around the island.

Schreier, D *St Helenian English: Origins, Evolution and Variations* John Benjamins, 2009. An academic study of the island language.

Yon, Emma-Jane *For The Love of The Music: Capturing the Enthusiasm and Passion of the Saints* 2007. A history of the island's music.

**Fiction** St Helena has hardly featured in fiction at all. What exists is mainly concerned with the period of Napoleon's captivity.

Gallo, Max *The Immortal of St Helena: No 4* Pan, 2005. Translated from the French, the fourth in this popular series of novels about Napoleon deals with his final exile on St Helena.

Hoole, Louise *Black Rock* Barranca Press, 2014. Whodunnit with a ghostly twist set in Napoleonic times. The author is the daughter of a former governor.

Pynchon, Thomas *Mason & Dixon* Vintage Classics, UK, 1998. A rather curious doorstop of a novel in which St Helena plays a prominent part.

Robertson, Bobby *The Stowaways and Other Stories from St Helena* 1996

Stamp, Geoffrey *Seasoned Tales* Baobab Publishing, 1993. Short stories from Ascension Island and St Helena.

## Children's books

Brighton, Catherine *My Napoleon*, Francis Lincoln, UK, 1998. A colourful and well-illustrated children's book focusing on Napoleon's life on St Helena.

George, Basil *The Pepper Tree* Lupa Design Creative Studio, St Helena, 2014. The first in a series of charming 'Tree' stories, introducing English dialogue as spoken on St Helena, and illustrated by different St Helenian artists. A second, *The Banyan Tree*, is also available.

Hofmeyr, Dianne and Daly, Jude *Faraway Island* Frances Lincoln, 2008. Children's book loosely based on the Lopes story.

Watt, Duncan *Skulduggery in the South Atlantic* Tynron Press, UK, 1995. The first in Watt's series of Wallace Boys adventures is set on St Helena. Out of print but available as an e-book.

## Journals and magazines

*The St Helena Connection* Published twice yearly by the Friends of St Helena. Contains news, articles, reviews and general matters of interest to 'St Helena watchers'.

*Wirebird* Annual publication of the Friends of St Helena, featuring historical articles.

## Websites

**www.saint.fm/independent** The website of *The St Helena Independent*, published weekly online and in print.

**www.sainthelena.gov.sh** The official website of the St Helena government.

**www.sams.sh/L2_sentinel.html** St Helena's other weekly newspaper, *The Sentinel*, is also available online.

**www.sthelena.se** Established by a couple of Swedes who have visited St Helena several times, the site has information about flora and fauna, and a section on stamps, and links to some helpful sites. Those wishing to discuss St Helena with like-minded individuals can join their mailing list.

**www.sthelenatourism.com** The official website of St Helena Tourism is clear, well laid out and with a large amount of practical information.

**www.solomons-sthelena.com** The website of Solomon's, the main trading company on St Helena, with details of their individual shops and other outlets.

**www.sure.co.sh** The official website of the island's internet service provider, Sure, includes an online telephone and email search facility.

**www.thorpes.sh** Thorpes imports and sells groceries and hardware to both retail and wholesale customers, and features a list of products on their website. The site also includes details of self-catering accommodation at several locations.

## UK-based organisations
A number of organisations based in the United Kingdom help to retain contact between those overseas with aspects of life in St Helena.

**Friends of St Helena** e subscriptions@sthelena. uk.net; http://sthelena.uk.net. Founded in 1988, the Friends is a registered charity that aims to promote public education about the island of St Helena, including its history, culture & environment, & to support practical projects of benefit to the islanders. In the past, these have included substantial fundraising for conversion of the building that now houses the St Helena Museum.

Twice a year the society publishes its own magazine, *The St Helena Connection*; with a second publication, *The Wirebird*, published annually. Both are distributed free to members.

The society also holds 2 meetings a year, in summer & autumn, each with specialist speakers, & has recently started publishing books about the island under the Wirebird imprint.

**St Helena, Ascension and Tristan da Cunha Philatelic Society** www.shatps.org. USA-based philatelic society which publishes both a quarterly magazine & other publications. Mainly philatelic but branches into historical areas as well.

**St Helena Association** www.sthelenaassociation.

org.uk. The St Helena Association brings together many St Helenians who now live in the UK, but who keep strong links with their relatives & friends on the island. Non-St Helenians are welcome to attend their activities, which include an annual dance in north London, & the Reading Sports, a big gathering of Saints held at Reading Abbey Rugby Club on the last Sun of Aug each year. Over the years, the association has given considerable help, financial & otherwise, to both individuals & specific causes on the island.

**The St Helena Institute** e admin@st-helena.org; www.archeion.talktalk.net/sthelena. Founded in 1997, this aims to provide a focal point for research into the islands of St Helena, Ascension & Tristan da Cunha, & to foster a greater public awareness of these islands. One of its main services is the maintenance of research registers & the provision of resources for St Helena family history.

**UK Overseas Territories Conservation Forum** www. ukotcf.org. Dedicated to conservation in all of the UK's overseas territories, the UKOTCF publishes *Forum News* 4 times a year, as well as an annual report, & holds regular conferences on environmental topics.

A1

## ASCENSION
## Books
### History
Bartlett, L S *Ascension Island, 1960s.* The author was the resident magistrate on Ascension Island from 1934 to 1936.

Keilor, John *Memories of Ascension 1929–1931* Miles Apart, 1997. Written by a Cable and Wireless telegraph officer who spent two years on Ascension.

McQueen, Capt Bob *Island Base: Ascension Island In The Falklands War* Whittles Publishing, Scotland, 2005. As the commander of the British forces support unit, McQueen was well placed to tell the inside story of Ascension's role in the Falklands conflict.

Ritsema, Alex *A Dutch Castaway on Ascension Island in 1725* lulu.com, 2010. Sorts out fact from fiction of the story of Dutch sailor Leendert Hasenbosch, who was set ashore by his captain in May 1725.

### Natural history
Ashmole, Philip and Myrtle *St Helena and Ascension: A Natural History* Nelson, 2000. Compares the development of flora and fauna on the two islands. Great detail with photos, maps, diagrams and line drawings.

Bingeman, John and Jane, *Ascension Island: Inshore Sea Life* Coach House Publications, 2005. A detailed look at the marine life that's likely to be seen by divers and snorkellers.

Fairhurst, Wendy *Flowering Plants of Ascension Island*, 2004. A detailed, colourful field guide, written by the wife of a former administrator.

Huxley, R C *Ascension Island and Turtles: A Monograph* Ascension Heritage Society, 1997. Contains new material from government archives.

Morris, John H *Ascension Island: An Introduction to its Physical Structure and History* 2012. Prepared for a field excursion by a research associate in earth sciences at the University of Bristol.

Packer, J E and L *Contributions Towards A Flora of Ascension Island*, 1997. Contains plant history and description with checklist.

### Philately and coins
Attwood, J H *Ascension: The Stamps and Postal History* Christie's-Robson Lowe, 1981

### Photographic books
Schafer, Kevin *Ascension Island: Atlantic Outpost* Coach House Publications, Isle of Wight, 2004. A well-illustrated overview of Ascension.

### Guidebooks and travel literature
Colley, Paul *Diving and Snorkelling Ascension Island: Guide to a marine life paradise* Dived Up, 2014. Essential reading for divers and even snorkellers, this well-presented manual identifies 21 dive sites, including seven wrecks, all graded by difficulty.

Hart-Davis, Duff *Ascension: The Story of a South Atlantic Island* Constable, 1972.

MacFall, Neil *Ascension Island Walks* Ascension Island Heritage Society, 1998. Essential reading for anyone tackling one or more of the Ascension Island letterbox walks. Every walk is ranked according to difficulty, with directions and a map for the full route.

### Fiction
Pelembe, Tara *Mary the Masked Booby* 2007. Children's story set on Ascension with photos by Anselmo Pelembe.

Stamp, Geoffrey *Seasoned Tales* Baobab Publishing, 1993. Short stories from Ascension Island and St Helena.

# Websites

**www.ascension-island.gov.ac** The all-inclusive government website covers almost every aspect of life on Ascension, from tips and information for visitors, to conservation issues, to details about the administrator, the savings bank, police station and the post office (including Ascension Island postage stamps).

**www.heritage.org.ac** The website of the Ascension Island Heritage Society gives superb historical information broken down into several categories.

**www.seaturtle.org/mtrg** The home page of the Marine Turtle Research Group (MTRG), dedicated to undertaking fundamental and applied research on marine turtles worldwide. On Ascension, their aims include assessing the current size of the green turtle population, the reproductive output of individual turtles and the sex ratio of hatchlings, and identification of the feeding grounds of the turtles through the use of satellite transmitters.

**www.the-islander.org.ac** Online edition of the weekly Ascension newspaper, *The Islander*.

**www.wunderground.com/global/stations/61902** As well as detailing the current weather conditions at Wideawake Airfield, this website has a well-presented ten-day forecast.

## TRISTAN DA CUNHA
## Books
### History

Crawford, Allan *Tristan da Cunha – Wartime Invasion* George Mann, UK, 2004. Eyewitness account of Tristan da Cunha during World War II.

Mackay, Margaret *Angry Island: The Story of Tristan da Cunha (1506–1963)* Barker, 1963

### Natural history

Hänel, C, Chown, S L and Gaston, K J *Gough Island: a Natural History* Sun Press, 2005. The first book to provide an overall account of the island and its natural history.

Ryan, Peter (ed) *Field Guide to the Animals and Plants of Tristan da Cunha and Gough Island* Pisces, Newbury, 2007. A detailed and lavishly illustrated guide to the distinctive wildlife of the Tristan islands; a must for visitors.

Van Ryssen, W *The Birds of the Tristan da Cunha Group and Gough Island* Cape Town University, 1976

### Philately

Crabb, George *The History and Postal History of Tristan da Cunha*, 1980. Vast detail.

### Guidebooks

Glass, J and Green, A *A Short Guide to Tristan da Cunha*, 2003. A 12pp colour booklet produced by islanders.

Schreier, Daniel and Lavarello-Schreier, Karen *Tristan da Cunha and the Tristanians* Battlebridge, London, 2011. Developed from the authors' first book, *Tristan da Cunha: History, People, Language*, this new publication takes a more in-depth look at the island, the Tristan community, and their dialect.

### Biography and travel literature

Barrow, K M *Three Years in Tristan da Cunha* 1910, reprinted Echo Library, 2005. The diary of a minister's wife, dating to 1905.

Booy, D M *Rock of Exile – A Narrative of Tristan da Cunha* Dent, London, 1957. Regarded by many as the most sensitive account of the island community.

Carmichael, Capt D *Description of the Island of Tristan da Cunha*, 1817

Crawford, Allan *Memoirs: North, South, East and West* George Mann, UK, 2006. An illustrated autobiography that includes Crawford's involvement with Tristan da Cunha.

Crawford, Allan *Penguins, Potatoes and Postage Stamps* Anthony Nelson, 2000. A personal chronicle of a lifetime's involvement with the stamps, history and people of Tristan da Cunha.

Crawford, Allan *Tristan da Cunha and the Roaring Forties* Skilton, Edinburgh, 1982. The standard account by the doyen of Tristan writers.

*Denstone Expedition to Tristan da Cunha* Denstone College, 1993. Account of the 1993 expedition.

Falk-Ronne, Arne *Back to Tristan*, Allen and Unwin, UK, 1967. The story of the resettlement of the island after the volcanic eruption of 1961.

Flint, Jim *Mid Atlantic Village*, Best Dog, 2011. An account of life on Tristan following the 1961 evacuation by the schoolteacher who went back with the islanders.

Glass, A, Grundy, R, Hentley, M and Swales M *Commemorative Publication to celebrate the 500th Anniversary of Tristan da Cunha* Tristan da Cunha Association, 2006. Illustrated history with sections on modern island life and aspirations.

Glass, Conrad *Rockhopper Copper* Orphans Press, 2005. Island life through the eyes of their policeman.

Helyer, Patrick and Swales, Michael *Bibliography of Tristan da Cunha* Nelson, 1998. Entries on every available topic, sourcing over 1,500 books, articles, films, etc.

Kornet-van Duyvenboden, Sandra *The Quest for Peter Green, A Dutchman on Tristan da Cunha* George Mann, UK, 2007. A Dutch lady from Peter Green's home town retraces his steps and discovers his legacy.

Lajolo, Anna and Lombardi, Guido *Tristan da Cunha, the legendary island/L'isola leggendaria* Genoa, 1999, with parallel text in Italian and English. Outstandingly illustrated.

Munch, Peter *Crisis in Utopia*, Prentice Hall, 1971. Effects of the evacuation on the community.

Munch, Peter *Glimpsing Utopia: Tristan da Cunha 1937–38* George Mann, UK, 2008. Diary of the author's time spent on Tristan with a Norwegian scientific expedition.

Perry, Roger *Island Days* Stacey International, 2004. Experiences on the Galápagos, Christmas Island and as administrator on Tristan.

### Fiction

Harris, Zinnie *Further than the Furthest Thing* Faber, 2000. A play about the 1961 eruption performed in London during 2000.

### Children's books

Watt, Duncan *Trouble in Tristan* Tynron Press, UK, 1991. The third in Watt's Wallace Boys series sees the boys' yacht hijacked and forced to sail to Tristan da Cunha. Available only as an e-book.

# Websites

www.tristandc.com The official joint website of the Tristan da Cunha government and the UK-based Tristan da Cunha Association combines a comprehensive visitor's guide to the islands with regularly updated news, the latest on philately, details of island handicrafts, including a mail-order option, and information on history, wildlife and conservation, economy and government. The Tristan Association pages provide news of forthcoming events and an order form to purchase publications and membership. Links to other relevant sites are a further bonus.

www.tristantimes.com The 'online newspaper of Tristan da Cunha' is far from up to date, but it could make interesting background reading.

www.sthelena.se/tristan The Tristan section of a site on St Helena, run from Sweden, with a particularly interesting selection of old photographs.

# Index

## INDEX OF ADVERTISERS